SOUND DECISIONS

Welcome to the *Sound Decisions Self-Care Guide*! This reference book provides you with the information and guidance to become a more active partner in your health care and to make informed decisions about your health concerns. You will also have the opportunity to learn about preventive care recommendations for you and your family.

As you read through the guide, you'll frequently see a phone symbol. That's your cue to call the *Sound Decisions Health Line* at 1-800-859-1730 for more information or support. You can call the Health Line whenever you have questions about the material in this book or any other health-related issue. Your call will be answered 24 hours a day by a professionally trained nurse who also has a copy of this guide.

As with all aspects of the Vital Measures program, all of your discussions with the nurse are *strictly confidential*.

We look forward to being a "sound" source of health and wellness information for you and your family!

Sound Decisions Health Line
1-800-859-1730

VITAL MEASURES
A BOEING-SPONSORED PROGRAM FOR HEALTH AND WELL-BEING

A Practical Guide to
Everyday Health Decisions

SOUND
DECISIONS

With 104 illustrations and 34 color photographs

Mosby Consumer Health

ACCESS NETWORK℠

Sound Decisions features FirstHelp algorithm-based assessment.

FirstHelp is a trademark and Access Network is a service mark of Access Health, Inc.
U.S. Patent 5, 471, 382

The material in this publication is for general information only and is not intended to provide specific advice or recommendations for any individual. Your medical provider or other health professional must be consulted for advice with regard to your individual situation.

Editor in Chief: Mary Kane, R.N.
Medical Editor: Barry Wolcott, M.D.
Medical Reviewers: David Johnson, Ph.D.; Anya Kirvan-Jones, R.N.;
David Jones, M.D.; Marci Thiel, M.D.
Manuscript Editor: Stephanie Slon
Illustrations: Joan Orme, Nancy Olson
Design and Layout: Seventh Generation Design

Mosby Consumer Health
263 Summer Street
Boston, MA 02210
(800) 729-5285

Access Health, Inc.
310 Interlocken Parkway, Suite A
Broomfield, CO 80021
(303) 443-4600

International Standard Book Number ISBN 1-56066-720-6

97 98 99 00 01 / 9 8 7 6 5 4 3 2 1

INTRODUCTION

Whether or not you are aware of it, you probably make decisions about what level of care you need every time you are sick or injured. When this happens, you usually ask yourself a series of questions such as:

- Do I need to call 911? If not,

- Do I need to be treated immediately in the hospital emergency department? If not,

- Do I need to see a medical provider as soon as possible?

Take the case of George.

It's Tuesday morning. George is just getting out of bed, on his way to another busy day at the office. But this morning there is a problem. George has a very sore ankle—an injury he got while playing basketball with his friends the night before. He knows his ankle isn't broken, but it's a little swollen and tender. He's able to walk, but with a limp. As the morning wears on, his ankle seems to feel worse rather than better. He asks co-workers for their advice and gets many different opinions on treatment.

After moving through the immediate questions about the care you need, you may determine that you don't need emergency treatment. Then, you probably move on to another set of questions such as the ones that follow to figure out the level of care you do need.

- Should I see my medical provider sometime in the next few weeks? If not,

- Should I speak to my medical provider on the phone? If not,

- Are there steps I can take at home that will help my problem?

Let's go back to George and see how he's handling his situation.

George wishes he could discuss his symptoms with a medical expert over the phone, but he knows he will have to make an appointment for an office visit to get the advice he needs. By lunchtime George has decided to make an appointment. He is not happy about the inconvenience of having to leave work early just to face a long wait in the medical provider's waiting room while they try to "squeeze him into the schedule."

In the past, it hasn't been easy to get the information you need to answer questions about the level of care you need. While most people know to call 911 in an emergency, many, like George, may not know when they need to see a medical provider if the situation is less serious.

Here's what happened at George's visit with the provider.

After examining his ankle, George's medical provider tells him to do several things: rest the ankle; apply ice to it; wrap it in an elastic bandage; and elevate it. The medical provider also tells George to take some anti-

inflammatory medication. George has finally gotten the advice he needs, but at a price—3 hours of missed work and the cost of an expensive office visit.

Unlike George, you no longer need to call your medical provider, the hospital emergency department, or 911 to get information on everyday health problems. You have a tremendous service available to you in the form of this self-care book and the telephone nurse advice service. These tools can help you determine when you need to get medical care and when you can try self-care.

First, you have been provided with this book. The advice in this self-care book is based on information gathered from many sources. Informed Access Systems, a nationally recognized leader in telephone advice services and telephone triage, developed the Decision Guides that form the core of this book. The Decision Guides summarize the best current information about how, when, and why to treat a particular medical problem. Research conducted by Informed Access Systems suggests that the common medical problems presented here are among the top 60 conditions for which their nurse advice lines across the country receive calls. Other experts have also coordinated efforts to bring you the most up-to-date clinical and medical information available. Nationally published medical references were also used. The book contains specific information and treatments just like the recommendations George received from his medical provider.

In addition, you have telephone access to a registered nurse who can help you decide what to do when you are faced with medical symptoms or injuries. Simply call the phone number of your advice nurse and you will get help in determining the appropriate course of care. This service is available 24 hours a day so you can call any time of the day or night. If this service had been available to George, he could have easily made the call as soon as he injured his ankle. He would have described his symptoms to a registered nurse and received recommendations for treatment—all right over the phone—and probably avoided a visit to the medical provider's office.

Why are you being offered these services? Because a large part of providing good medical care is making sure you get the type of care you need when you need it. Together, the self-care book and the nurse advice line provide you with a comprehensive, integrated information and resource service that you can take advantage of whenever you need it. The result will be the kind of care you want—responsive, consistent, and convenient.

To make the most of these tools, we suggest that you review this book thoroughly before you are faced with a medical problem. That way you will know whether to dial 911, call the advice nurse, or try self-care when the time comes.

TABLE OF CONTENTS

TABLE OF CONTENTS

SECTION ONE
HOW TO USE YOUR
HEALTH CARE SYSTEM

To get the most out of your health care, it is important to learn to use the system effectively. This section will discuss how and when to use the different options that have been made available to you. Choices—ranging from the advice nurse service and this self-care book to urgent care and after hours centers to the hospital emergency department—are all discussed. These pages will also offer guidelines for identifying situations that may require a call to 911. Finally, the section will cover steps you can take in emergencies while waiting for help to arrive.

USING THIS SELF-CARE BOOK

This book is organized into three major sections. **Section One: How to Use Your Health Care System** describes how to use the various medical services available to you—this book, the advice nurse system, the hospital emergency department, and the emergency ambulance service (911). It also gives you information about how to respond to some common medical emergencies and what you can do in these situations before professional help arrives.

Section Two: Self-Care for Common Medical Symptoms provides general information and Self-Care Steps for some of the most common health problems. The discussion of each topic includes an easy-to-use Decision Guide to help you determine when to use self-care, when to call the advice nurse, and when, in rare cases, you need to seek medical help immediately.

Section Three: Useful Medical Information includes information and education on many health issues of common concern and addresses frequently asked medical questions. In addition to information on topics such as behavioral issues, medical screening practices, newborn care, and immunization schedules, this section includes a Health Information Resource Guide listing the toll-free phone numbers for organizations that can supply additional information.

This book also includes 34 color photos illustrating many common skin problems and a comprehensive index which can quickly point you to any topic covered in the book.

This self-care book cannot replace care from your medical provider, but it can help you decide how to respond safely when you are sick or injured. You must always consider your own health history and medical condition when reading the advice in this book. If you are not sure that the book's recommendations apply to you, call the advice nurse. The nurse will discuss your problem with you and help determine the best action to take.

Remember, too, this book and the advice nurse phone service are not designed to replace emergency medical services. In the event of a life-threatening condition that you think requires care on site or in the ambulance on the way to the hospital, immediately call 911 or your local emergency service number.

USING THE ADVICE NURSE SERVICE

The advice nurse service is available 24 hours a day, 7 days a week. The nurses are specially trained to help you determine the next best steps for the evaluation and treatment of your illness or injury based on the signs and symptoms you report. All the nurses have at least 5 years nursing experience in areas of medicine ranging from pediatrics, obstetrics/gynecology, and adult medicine to behavioral health and geriatric care. After listening to you describe your problem, the nurse will ask you some specific questions in order to evaluate your illness or injury. Based on your initial description and your answers to the questions, the nurse will make a recommendation for your care.

The advice nurse will also make sure you have the information necessary to follow the recommendation. This may include giving you the phone number of your medical provider's office, providing directions to the nearest urgent care facility or emergency department, or discussing self-care steps you can use at home.

In some instances, the advice nurse may arrange a follow-up call to see how you are feeling. If at any time you are unsure about the instructions the nurse has given, you may call back and speak to the nurse again.

KEY PARTS OF SELF-CARE INFORMATION

When the advice nurse offers self-care steps over the phone, the information generally will have four parts:

- general information about your symptoms

- steps to relieve the symptoms

- changes in the symptoms that would require another call to the advice nurse

- any arrangements for the nurse to call you back

HOW TO USE THE DECISION GUIDES

The **Decision Guides** found throughout this book can help you make decisions about the best course of treatment when you are ill or injured. If you still have doubts after using the guides, call the advice nurse.

Decision Guides Are Not for Newborns
The Decision Guides do not apply to infants **under 3 months old**. Call the advice nurse if your infant is sick or injured.

The Decision Guide Symbols
The symbols offer a general guide to how and when to seek care:

Emergency, call 911 Symptoms in this category can be life threatening and require immediate medical treatment by an emergency medical technician.

Seek help now Symptoms in this category are serious and should usually be evaluated within 2 hours.

Call the advice nurse Symptoms may be treated at home or they may require a visit to your medical provider. Usually, you and the advice nurse need to share additional information about your condition to decide what is best for you.

Use self-care Symptoms can usually be treated at home. If symptoms persist or you are uncertain about the self-care recommendations in this book, you should call the advice nurse.

USING THE EMERGENCY DEPARTMENT

The hospital emergency department serves three important functions. First, it provides life-saving medical care to critically ill or injured people brought there by ambulance (see When to Call 911, below). Second, the emergency department is a place where patients with illness or injuries too severe to be handled in a medical provider's office can be evaluated and treated. And, third, it provides medical services at night or on weekends when ordinary medical providers' offices are closed.

People sometimes go to the hospital emergency department with relatively minor problems such as the flu, small cuts, and scrapes. These are not usually problems requiring emergency attention, but often people do not know where else to go to get help. Although the emergency department can treat non-life-threatening conditions such as these, care in an emergency department is not medically necessary. Plus, emergency department care for these types of conditions can be an expensive option. The most efficient use of medical services is to reserve the emergency department for serious illnesses or injuries and to treat other kinds of medical problems in non-emergency department settings.

For these reasons, **urgent care centers have been created** to treat non-life-threatening conditions. These centers can treat patients who do not need the elaborate facilities of a hospital-based emergency department. Many urgent care centers also have night and weekend hours.

Another option for care is **after hours clinics**. These clinics are available for minor illness such as earaches, where evaluation by a medical provider is necessary but emergency care is not required. These facilities also have night and weekend hours. Both urgent care centers and after hours clinics can effectively treat non-life-threatening problems at a lower cost than the same treatment in an emergency department visit.

To determine if you need to go to the emergency department, an urgent care center, or an after hours clinic, call the advice nurse. The advice nurse service is available 24 hours a day so you can call at the first sign of illness or injury. The nurse will have information on all local facilities and will be able to direct you to the most appropriate setting for your problem.

WHEN TO CALL 911

In most parts of the United States, dialing 911 means that emergency medical care is no farther than a phone call away. For certain new symptoms or injuries, using this emergency medical service means lives are saved and long-term disabilities avoided. In reality, most of the problems for which people use an emergency ambulance service are not urgent enough to make this kind of early intervention necessary. People often call 911 because they are not sure what to do when a medical problem occurs suddenly. In many cases people would turn to other sources of help if they had the option.

You are being provided with an advice nurse service—a valuable alternative to dialing 911 when a problem arises suddenly. The 24-hour advice nurse line is always there to help you decide what to do when faced with new symptoms or injuries. In some cases, the nurse may determine that you do need to call the emergency medical service. However, you no longer need to call 911 just because you have no other source of help.

There are a few situations where it is necessary to call 911 immediately. Examples include:

• **Major accident**—automobile accidents or other disasters involving many injured people; situations where it might be difficult to remove people without injuring them more; situations where rescuing injured people would put others in danger.

• **Newly unconscious person**—having someone lose consciousness for whatever reason and not regaining consciousness within a few seconds.

• **Severe trouble breathing**—best described as when a person has to gasp for breath not following any physical exertion.

• **Multiple people involved in a non-trauma situation**—several people affected at the same time by something other than an accident, such as an exposure to toxic substances or an epidemic of food poisoning.

• **Sudden, dramatic change in alertness**—a person suddenly becomes less than fully alert, especially if the condition lasts more than a few seconds. This is to be distinguished from other, more common reasons why a person may not be completely alert such as extreme fatigue, drunkenness, or gradual changes due to aging.

• **Seizures that do not stop**—seizure lasting more than 5 minutes (measured by the clock). Seizures, sometimes called fits, are frightening to observe, but are usually over quickly and rarely, in themselves, dangerous.

• **Unusual headache with new symptoms**—severe headache unlike those commonly suffered; headache accompanied by new muscle paralysis or weakness, new trouble speaking or thinking; headache that develops suddenly within 24 hours of a head injury.

• **Dangerous bleeding**—rapid bleeding that does not stop after 10 minutes of direct pressure on the wound; bleeding heavy enough to create puddles of blood. A lot of bleeding by itself may not be a reason to call 911 since an otherwise healthy adult can lose up to a quart of blood in a short time without serious, long term effects.

• **Imminent delivery of a baby**—the baby's head is visible between the mother's legs or the birth has already occurred.

• **Domestic abuse**—violent, abusive, physical harm being inflicted as a result of a domestic dispute.

• **Suicide attempts**—by any means capable of inflicting serious harm including hanging, strangulation, and suffocation.

• **Stabbing or gunshot wound**—to the head or trunk.

DIAL 911

Dial 911 if you need emergency medical providers and equipment to save a life or limb.

If you are unsure whether you need emergency medical service, call the advice nurse.

EMERGENCIES AND FIRST AID

Self-care education offers recommendations about caring for illnesses by yourself. *All true emergencies need to be evaluated by an appropriate medical professional.* The self-care guidelines in this section are only appropriate for use when medical professionals are not immediately available and before you can get to an emergency department. This section offers advice on how to assess the needs of a person who has suffered an accident, how to offer life support if needed, and when to offer first aid.

Learning first-aid skills is your first step in being prepared to help keep someone alive in an emergency or knowing how to keep injuries from getting worse. Many communities have American Red Cross agencies that offer first-aid classes. First-aid instruction also is often available through community education programs or local community colleges and universities. These first-aid courses teach you how to identify medical emergencies; understand causes, symptoms, and signs of injuries; and apply first aid. The more you

know about first aid, the more likely you are to stay calm when helping yourself or someone suffering from an accident.

Before trying to help someone who is hurt, you should, if possible, ask his or her permission or the permission of a guardian. You are legally protected for trying to help someone if you do so in good faith and are not guilty of willful misconduct. Legally, you can assume you have the individual's consent to help if the person is unconscious or so badly hurt that he or she cannot give permission.

Many diseases can be spread through contact with the blood of an injured person. These infections do not penetrate intact skin, but you may have cracked or scratched skin that is vulnerable.

Latex gloves offer the best protection if you are giving first aid. Otherwise, keep plastic wrap, several layers of gauze pad, or other barriers between you and the person's blood.

FIRST-AID SUPPLIES

Also see Equipping Your Home for Self-Care, p. 18.

First-aid kits should contain the things you might need in an emergency. Keep them organized and in an easy-to-find place in your home and vehicles.

Check your first-aid kits periodically to be sure they are up-to-date and well stocked. Discard and promptly replace any outdated medicine or ointment. Store your first-aid kit on an upper shelf out of reach of small children. Don't store in a hot or cold area, or in a bathroom. You can buy complete first-aid kits from a drug store or medical supply outlet. You can also assemble your own from individual components. (See Stocking Your Own First Aid Kit, below.)

Everyday items that can be used in an emergency

- Disposable or regular diapers for compresses, bandages, or padding for splints
- Sanitary napkins (same uses as above)
- Magazines, newspapers, or umbrella for use as a splint for broken bones
- Clean dish towel, scarf, or handkerchief for bandages or slings
- Table leaf or old door for stretchers *Note: Do not move people with head and neck injuries unless they are in a life-threatening situation.*

STOCKING YOUR OWN FIRST-AID KIT

To assemble your own complete first-aid kit, place a copy of this book in a small tote bag or sturdy, easily carried box, along with the following items:

Dressings
- Adhesive bandage strips (assorted sizes)
- Butterfly bandages and tincture of benzoin
- Elastic bandages, 2 or 3 inches wide
- Adhesive dressing tape
- Sterile cotton balls
- Sterile eye patches
- Sterile gauze pads, 4 by 4 inches
- Sterile nonstick pads for use with sterile gauze pads
- Stretchable gauze, one roll
- Triangular bandage for sling or dressing cover

Instruments
- Bulb syringe to rinse eyes or wounds
- Sharp scissors
- Tweezers

Medication
- Antiseptic ointment
- Antihistamine tablets for allergic reactions

- Aspirin or acetaminophen
- Syrup of ipecac to induce vomiting. Follow directions of poison control center or health care provider.

Miscellaneous items
- Airtight packages of hand wipes
- Candle and waterproof matches
- Instant chemical cold packs
- Cotton swabs
- Disposable latex gloves
- Flashlight—store batteries separately to prevent corrosion or accidental discharge
- Paper and pen or pencil
- Soap
- Tissues
- Safety pins
- Blanket
- Sterile eye wash and/or plastic cup

Special needs items (*Stock these items if you or someone in your family is diabetic, has heart disease, or suffers severe reactions to insect bites or stings.*)
- Insulin (may require refrigeration) and sugar, nitroglycerin, or adrenaline or epinephrine

EMERGENCY FIRST-AID TECHNIQUES: CHOKING, CPR, POISONING

Choking

Choking occurs when a piece of food or other object becomes lodged in the throat, blocking air flow. When choking, a person may react by coughing hard in an effort to dislodge the object. If the airway is completely blocked, the person will not be able to speak, breathe, or cough, and may clutch his or her throat.

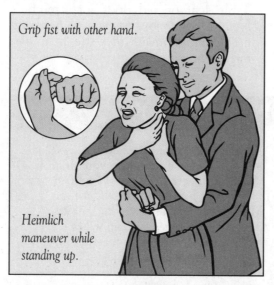

Grip fist with other hand.

Heimlich maneuver while standing up.

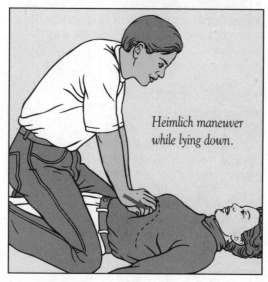

Heimlich maneuver while lying down.

SELF-CARE STEPS FOR CHOKING

Choking is life threatening and requires immediate action. If the person can speak, cough, or breathe, this means air is still passing through the airway. **In this situation, do not interfere in any way with the individual's efforts to expel the object.** Reassure the person and advise him or her to breathe deeply and slowly. This will help relax the muscles surrounding the windpipe.

Heimlich Maneuver for Adults or Children Age 1 and Older

When the Person Is Standing or Sitting

If the person is unable to breathe or make sounds, it means the airway is completely blocked. Have someone call 911. Meanwhile, perform the Heimlich maneuver using the steps below:

• Stand behind the person who is choking and wrap your arms around his or her midsection. Place the thumb side of your fist against the person's stomach slightly above the navel.

• Grip your fist with your other hand and press the doubled fist into the person's abdomen with a quick upward thrust. Repeat the thrusts until the object is expelled from the airway.

• Do not squeeze the person's ribs with your arms. Use only your fist in the abdomen. Each thrust should be a separate and distinct movement.

When the Person Is Lying Down

• If the individual is lying down and still conscious, turn him or her onto the back.

• Kneel and straddle the person, placing the heel of your fist on his or her stomach above the navel and below the ribs. Place your other hand over the fist.

• Keeping your elbows straight, give four quick, strong, downward thrusts toward the chest.

• Repeat this procedure as needed until the object is cleared from the airway.

SELF-CARE STEPS FOR CHOKING

Self-Application

The Heimlich maneuver can also be self-applied if no one else is around.

• Make a fist and place the thumb side on your abdomen above the navel.

• Grasp the fist with the other hand. Press inward and upward with a quick motion.

• If this is unsuccessful, press your upper abdomen over any firm surface such as the side of a table or the back of a chair. Repeat these single thrusts until the object is cleared from your airway.

Heimlich Maneuver for Infants—*small enough to be supported on your forearm or up to 1 year old*

• Ask someone to call 911 immediately. Meanwhile, rest the infant face down on your forearm. Support the infant's head by firmly holding the jaw.

• Give four quick back blows between the shoulder blades with the heel of your hand. If this is unsuccessful, perform the Heimlich maneuver as described below.

• Place two fingers 1 fingerwidth below the infant's nipples in the center of the chest on the breastbone, avoiding the tip of the breastbone.

• Push forward and downward. These thrusts should be more gentle than those used on an adult. Repeat both procedures if necessary.

If the Heimlich maneuver is not successful, follow CPR instructions for blocked airway (p. 13).

Call your health care provider after a rescue using the Heimlich maneuver. Some internal injuries can result from the thrusting motion; however, the risk of injury is reduced by correctly positioning your hands.

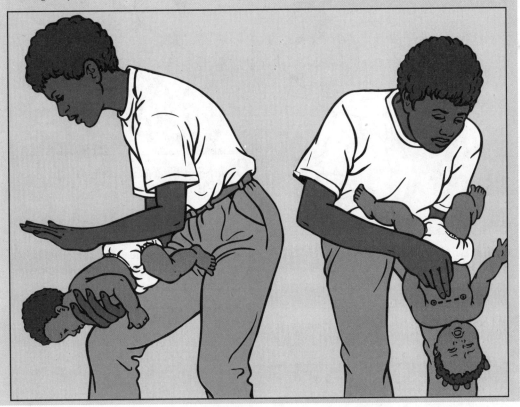

Cardiopulmonary Resuscitation (CPR)

This is meant to be a review and is not intended to replace an American Heart Association-certified CPR class.

Cardiopulmonary resuscitation (CPR) is a basic life-support technique that is used when a person is not breathing and the heart may have stopped. CPR allows you to manually perform the functions of the heart and lungs, which send blood and oxygen to all parts of the body.

All the body's cells, especially the brain cells, need a steady supply of oxygen. CPR opens and clears the person's airway and restores breathing and blood circulation through mouth-to-mouth breathing and repeated pressure on the chest.

SELF-CARE STEPS FOR CPR

Adults and Children Age 8 and Older
Check for consciousness. Gently shake the person and shout, "Are you OK?" If there is no response or the individual is not breathing, shout for help and ask someone to **call 911 immediately.** The order of action to take in an emergency can be remembered as the **ABCs—Airway, Breathing, and Circulation.**

• Place two fingers of your other hand on the bony part of the person's chin. Pull the person's chin forward and support the jaw, helping to tilt the head back.

Airway: *Open the Airway (Head Tilt/Chin Lift)*
• Tilt the person's head back if no neck/spinal injuries are suspected.

• Place one hand on the forehead and apply firm, backward pressure to tilt the head back.

• Push down on the forehead and lift the person's chin.

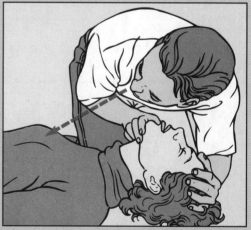

Breathing: *Check Breathing/Perform Rescue Breathing*
Place your ear over the person's mouth and nose while keeping up an open airway. Look for the chest to rise and fall; listen for air escaping during exhalation; and feel for the flow of air. Watch for 5 seconds. If there is no sign of breathing, perform rescue breathing as follows:

• Keep the airway open by using the head tilt/chin lift maneuver described above. Gently pinch the person's nose shut using the thumb and index finger of the hand on the forehead.

CONTINUED SELF-CARE STEPS FOR CPR

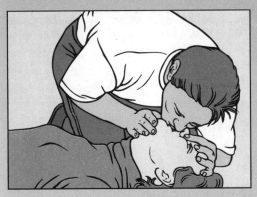

- Take a deep breath and seal your lips tightly around the person's mouth.

- Give two full breaths—1^1/2 to 2 seconds per breath, 10 to 12 breaths per minute. Take a breath for yourself after each two breaths for the other person. Watch for his or her chest to rise with each breath. Let the person's chest fall between breaths.

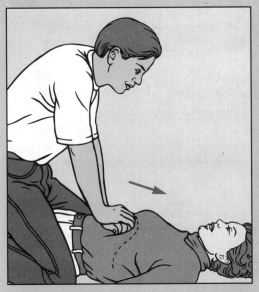

Clearing a Blocked Airway

If the person's chest doesn't rise during rescue breathing, the airway is blocked. Retilt the person's head and try again. If the airway is still blocked, perform the Heimlich maneuver as follows:

- Kneel and straddle the person, placing the heel of your fist on his or her stomach above the navel and below the ribs.

- Place your other hand over your fist. Keeping your elbows straight, give four quick, downward thrusts toward the chest.

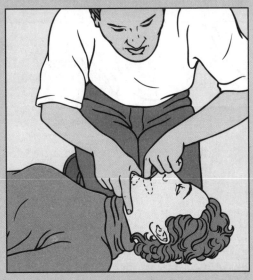

- Open the person's mouth by grasping both the tongue and lower jaw between the thumb and fingers and lift. This will draw the tongue away from the back of the throat and away from any object that might be lodged there. Look to see if an object is visible in the back of the throat.

- Next, perform the **finger-sweep maneuver** as follows: Insert the index finger of the other hand down along the inside of the cheek and deeply into the throat to the base of the tongue. Use a hooking action to dislodge the object and move it into the mouth so that it can be removed.

- Attempt rescue breathing again. If you are still unable to breathe air into the person's lungs, reposition the head and try again. Repeat the sequence of Heimlich maneuver, finger sweep, and rescue breathing. Perform this cycle until the object is dislodged, and you are able to continue rescue breathing.

Continued on next page

CONTINUED SELF-CARE STEPS FOR CPR

*C*irculation: *Check for Pulse*
While keeping the person's head tilted back, move two fingers from the Adam's apple to the side of the neck between the windpipe and the neck muscles. Press down gently and gradually for 5 to 10 seconds. A pulse shows that the heart is beating.

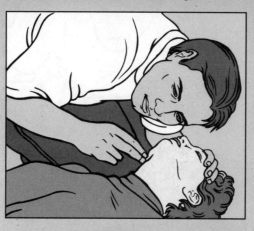

Don't rock back and forth or pause between compressions. Lock your arms straight and press hard on the breastbone to $1\frac{1}{2}$ to 2 inches or one-third of the chest depth.

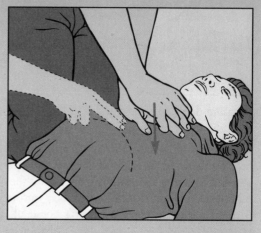

If the person has a pulse but is not breathing, continue rescue breathing at a rate of 10 to 12 times per minute, or once every 5 or 6 seconds. If the person has no pulse and is not breathing, begin chest compressions.

• Find the notch where the individual's ribs meet the breastbone in the center of the chest. Place the heel of your flattened hand 2 finger-widths up toward the chest from the notch. Place your other hand on top of this hand, interlocking your fingers.

• Lean forward until your shoulders are directly over your hands. Your body weight falling forward provides the force to depress the breastbone.

• Do 15 chest compressions (at a rate of 80 to 100 per minute), continuing to lean over the person so your shoulders are over your hands.

• Count out loud "one and, two and, three and, four and," as you push straight down. Allow the chest to return to its normal position after each compression. Do not lift your hands from the chest or change position, or correct hand position may be lost.

• Open the airway again using the head tilt/chin lift and give two slow rescue breaths. Watch for the chest to rise. Repeat this sequence of 15 compressions and two breaths for four cycles. Recheck for pulse.

• When the person is breathing and has a pulse, stop performing CPR. If the person has a pulse but is not breathing, continue rescue breathing. Recheck the pulse every 60 seconds. Start chest compressions again if pulse stops. If the person has no pulse and is not breathing, repeat sequence of 15 compressions and two breaths, checking for pulse every four cycles. Continue until the person revives or help arrives.

SELF-CARE STEPS—CPR FOR CHILDREN

Children under 8 Years Old

Shout for help and ask someone to **call 911 immediately**. Then provide the basic ABCs (*Airway, Breathing, Circulation*) of life support.

Airway: *Open the Airway*

If no neck/spinal injuries are suspected, open the airway by placing one hand on the child's forehead and tilting the head back into a neutral position. Place the fingers of your other hand under the bony part of the lower jaw at the chin and lift upward and outward.

Breathing: *Check Breathing/Perform Rescue Breathing*

• After the airway is opened, check if the child is breathing. Look for a rise and fall of the chest and abdomen; listen for exhaled air; and feel for exhaled air flow at the mouth.

• If no spontaneous breathing is detected, begin rescue breathing while keeping the chin lifted. If the child is under 1 year old, place your mouth over the infant's mouth and nose. If the child is 1 to 8 years old, make a mouth-to-mouth seal and pinch the child's nose tightly with the thumb and forefinger of the hand maintaining head tilt.

• Give two slow breaths (1 to 1^1/2 seconds per breath) to the child. Pause to take a breath in between the first and second breaths. If the air enters freely and the chest rises, the airway is clear. If air does not enter freely or if the chest does not rise, either the airway is blocked or more breath pressure is necessary.

Improper opening of the airway is the most common cause of airway blocks. Reattempt to open the airway and try rescue breathing again. If you suspect an object is blocking the airway, see Choking (p. 8). If a child loses consciousness or has more difficulty breathing, have someone **call 911** immediately and perform the Heimlich maneuver (see p. 8 for children; p. 9 for infants).

Circulation: *Check for Pulse*

Spend only a few seconds trying to get a pulse in a nonbreathing infant before starting chest compressions.

• In infants under 1 year old, gently press your index and middle fingers on the inside of the upper arm, between the infant's elbow and shoulder. In children 1 to 8 years old, find the Adam's apple with two or three fingers. Slide your fingers into the groove on the side of the neck between the windpipe and neck muscles.

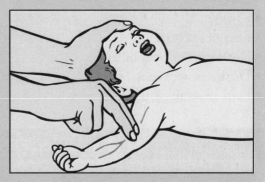

• If a pulse is present but the child is not breathing, do rescue breathing at a rate of 20 breaths per minute (once every 3 seconds) until spontaneous breathing resumes.

• If pulse is nonexistent, do chest compressions as follows: Use one hand to maintain child's head position. Use the other hand to compress the chest. Place the index finger just below the level of the child's nipples. Place the middle fingers on the breastbone next to the index finger. Using two or three fingers, compress the breastbone by about one-third to one-half the depth of the chest—about ^{1}/2 to 1 inch. Do compressions at a rate of at least 100 per minute. Coordinate with rescue breathing by doing five compressions to each breath. Continue until medical help arrives. If the child starts breathing, place the child in the recovery position (on one side with the arm supporting the head).

Poisoning

Poison can enter the body in many ways, including swallowing, breathing in, injection, or skin contact. Suspect poisoning if someone suddenly becomes ill for no apparent reason, acts strangely, or is found ill near a toxic substance.

Different poisons affect body functions differently. Some poisons interfere with the blood's ability to carry oxygen, while others burn and irritate the digestive tract and respiratory system.

Poisoning symptoms can include:

- Fever
- Chills
- Loss of appetite
- Headache or irritability
- Dizziness, weakness, or drowsiness
- Pain in swallowing or more saliva
- Abdominal pain, vomiting, diarrhea, or nausea
- Skin rash or chemical burns around the nose or mouth
- Seizures, stupor, or unconsciousness
- Double vision or blurred vision
- Muscle twitching

Poison Fumes

Many substances or combinations of substances can produce fumes that can be especially toxic in a closed area. Remove the individual from the area before starting treatment.

Take a few deep breaths of fresh air, then hold your breath before entering the area. Drag or pull the person to fresh air. If possible, quickly shut off any open source of fumes. Do not flip a switch or light a match. In some situations either action could produce a spark or a flame and cause an explosion.

SELF-CARE STEPS FOR POISONING

Poisoning is a life-threatening situation. If you suspect poisoning, even if there are no symptoms, call the poison control center. Be prepared to give the following information:

- Information from the label of the substance container (keep the original container)
- The person's age
- Name of the poison and how much was swallowed
- When the poison was swallowed
- Whether or not the person has vomited
- How long it will take to get the person to a hospital

If the individual is unconscious, keep the airway open. Be prepared to begin artificial respiration (for CPR for adults and older children, see p. 10; for children under 8 years old, see p. 13), if necessary. Do not induce vomiting unless told to do so.

Signs and symptoms of poisoning can vary widely, depending on the type of poison involved, the size and general health of the person, and how much time has elapsed. Symptoms can also take time to develop. Do not wait for them to become obvious. **Seek immediate medical attention if you suspect poisoning has occurred.**

If you have been told to induce vomiting, use syrup of ipecac, if available. Follow the directions on the label. Do not attempt to give it to an individual who is not alert enough to swallow it. Save a sample of vomit and the poison container for analysis. **Do not induce vomiting if you are unsure what poison is involved.**

For Poison Fumes

- Check breathing and pulse (for adults and older children see breathing p. 10, pulse p.12; p. 13 for children under 8 years old). If the person is not breathing, have someone call 911 and begin CPR (see p. 10 for adults and older children; p. 13 for children under 8 years old). Continue until medical help arrives. If the person is conscious and breathing, cover him or her with a blanket and check on breathing until help arrives.

EMERGENCY CARE FOR BEHAVIORAL OR EMOTIONAL PROBLEMS

Sudden changes in behavior or mood can constitute a medical emergency. Extreme disorientation, confusion, or violent, aggressive, or threatening behavior require prompt attention especially when these symptoms put the individual or others in danger. Reasons for this kind of behavior can range from drug or alcohol use, to a reaction to severe stress, or an existing mental illness such as schizophrenia. Physical problems such as a high fever or an insulin reaction can also be to blame. Whatever the reason, this type of frightening, sudden behavior change requires immediate attention.

Unpredictable, Aggressive, or Threatening Behavior

If you find yourself faced with a situation where a person is exhibiting bizarre or threatening behavior, remember that your own safety is of primary importance. Do not do anything that would put you or others in additional danger. You can try the following steps to help the situation:

• Talk to the person in a calm tone, speaking more slowly than usual, and reassure him or her that you are trying to help. As much as possible, try to reassure the person that you can be trusted and that you do not pose a threat.

• Make sure you and the other person are both safe. Look around for potentially dangerous items or weapons within the person's reach.

• If you see any kind of potentially lethal weapon, move away from the person and call 911 immediately.

• Do not try to restrain a person who is displaying aggressive or threatening behavior. Individuals in an agitated state are unusually strong and can become violent very quickly.

Threats of Suicide or Self-injury

All threats of suicide or self-injury should be taken seriously. When confronted with someone threatening harm to him or herself, you can help in the following ways:

• Try to engage the person in conversation and build a rapport. Talk in a calm tone, speaking more slowly than usual, and assure him or her that you are trying to help. As much as possible, try to reassure the person that you can be trusted and that you do not pose a threat.

• Do not try to restrain or subdue a person who is threatening suicide or self-injury. Individuals who are in an agitated emotional state behave unpredictably. Sudden attempts at subduing a violent individual can prompt the person into carrying out the threatened action. It could even lead to violence to others.

• Call 911 or have someone else call as soon as possible.

SECTION TWO
SELF-CARE FOR COMMON
MEDICAL SYMPTOMS

MEDICAL SELF-CARE

The more you know about common health problems, the more likely you will be to use the health care system well. Even though your medical provider's office tries to give good customer service—with friendly staff and compassionate care—the fact remains, most people don't want to go to the medical provider—it's no fun being sick, and it's often inconvenient to go to the office for treatment. That—along with cost and time—is why it is important to know when you or a family member has symptoms that can be cared for at home and when symptoms are serious enough to be evaluated by a medical provider.

Studies show that when patients read self-care information, they make better choices about when they need to see a medical provider. This means that for serious problems, they are more likely to get care when they need it. For problems that do not require a visit to the provider's office, informed patients are more likely to use the right home remedies. Follow-up telephone interviews with patients who know about self-care show that 80 percent continue to refer to self-care materials when appropriate.

To help you make decisions about how to relieve symptoms, we offer self-care tips whenever possible. For some health problems, only a few self-care remedies are suggested. This is because we try to recommend only remedies that have been proven effective. It is better to do nothing and be wrong than to do something and be wrong. After all, the medical credo is: "First, do no harm."

For a quick review of symptoms, check the Decision Guide at the end of each medical topic. You will see that for many symptoms, we recommend that you call the advice nurse. In many cases, the advice nurse can decide if symptoms warrant a visit. Much of this can be done over the phone, saving you the time and expense of an office visit. (See Using the Advice Nurse Service, p.2.)

The instructions in this book apply to people from ages 3 months to those 65 years and older. In some places you will find special information for children, women, men, or seniors contained in boxes or under separate headings.

Remember, these self-care guidelines are not intended as a substitute for the advice of your medical provider. If you are not sure if these guidelines apply to you or if your symptoms do not seem to get better with self-care methods, call the advice nurse.

EQUIPPING YOUR HOME FOR SELF-CARE

Also refer to p. 6, for information on preparing a first-aid kit.

Stocking your home with some special tools and equipment is the first step in handling health problems successfully. Some of these tools prepare you for treating minor health problems at home. Others give you the information you'll need to decide whether a phone call to the advice nurse is necessary. Here are some basic home medical supplies to keep on hand.

- Medical and self-care reference books (many are available at bookstores)

- Thermometer

- A heating pad for treating sore or tense muscles

- An assortment of adhesive bandages, including butterfly-shaped bandages for closing cuts; tincture of benzoin to help butterfly bandages stick

- Sterile gauze pads for cleaning cuts and scrapes and covering larger wounds

- Paper tape—which pulls off painlessly—for holding gauze pads in place

- An elastic bandage for wrapping sprained ankles or wrists or for supporting and putting pressure on injured, swollen, or sore knees

- A cold-water vaporizer for relieving congestion of colds and coughs (clean vaporizers daily when in use to avoid spreading germs)

- A penlight for examining sore throats

- Two pairs of tweezers: a blunt-tipped pair for such things as removing an object from a child's nose, and a pair with pointed ends for removing splinters

- An ice pack, either the type that holds ice cubes or the newer "cold/hot" packs that can be kept in the freezer

- Over-the-counter medications such as pain killers (acetaminophen, aspirin, ibuprofen) and antibacterial ointment

(Consult the chart below for help in choosing the appropriate pain medication.)

PAIN MEDICATION CHART			
	Acetaminophen	**Ibuprofen**	**Aspirin**
	Tylenol Tempra	Advil, Nuprin, Motrin IB	Many brand names
Use	Fever, headache, mild burns, stings; will not decrease inflammation associated with muscle pain	Muscle overuse, sports injuries, menstrual cramps	Stroke/heart attack prevention; fever in adults
Warnings/ Side Effects	Do not give to children under 3 months old without talking to medical provider	May cause upset stomach; don't give to children under 3 months old without talking to medical provider	Do not give to children or adolescents unless prescribed by medical provider

Be careful of combination products; some may have caffeine and some mix these drugs.
Do not take with cold medicines. Always follow package directions when taking medications.

DIGESTIVE, URINARY, AND STOMACH PROBLEMS

Humans eat and digest hundreds of pounds of food every year—including a huge variety of meats, produce, grains, and drinks. Your body does an impressive job of processing these foods every hour of the day. This section describes common problems related to your vital digestive and urinary organs and suggests how to take care of nonurgent health problems at home.

Your medical provider can offer advice and treatment for most digestive or urinary problems. If your condition is especially difficult to handle, your medical provider may bring in other professionals who specialize in the diagnosis and treatment of these problems.

Use the Decision Guides to see if your symptoms clearly need emergency medical services, require a call to the advice nurse, or can be treated using self-care. It is important to consider your own medical history and your current health when deciding what kind of care is right for you. If you have any conditions that do not seem to be healing normally, if the Self-Care Steps provided do not seem to help, or if you are uncertain about your symptoms, call the advice nurse. The advice nurse will evaluate your symptoms and recommend the next best steps for you to take.

ABDOMINAL PAIN

We all know the kind of abdominal pain caused by an occasional attack of vomiting and diarrhea or "stomach flu."

Abdominal pain can also point to many other conditions.

However, most stomachaches in adults are from common problems like emotional distress, overeating, or the flu (for stomachaches in children, see box on next page). If you are concerned about stomach pain you are experiencing, call the advice nurse.

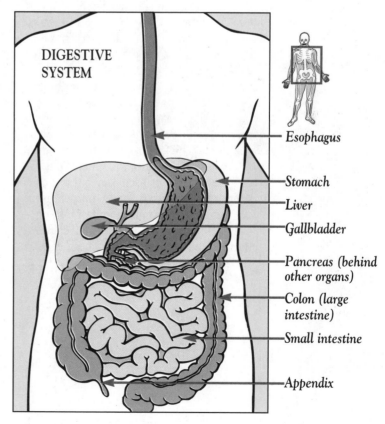

DIGESTIVE SYSTEM

— Esophagus

— Stomach

— Liver

— Gallbladder

— Pancreas (behind other organs)

— Colon (large intestine)

— Small intestine

— Appendix

My stomach often hurts if I go too long without eating. Turns out I have an ulcer.
José

SELF-CARE STEPS FOR MILD ABDOMINAL PAIN

- Eat bland, not spicy, foods.
- Eat less solid food for several hours.
- Use acetaminophen (Tylenol, Tempra or a generic) for pain relief. Do not give aspirin to children or teenagers.
- Avoid irritants such as alcohol, nicotine, caffeine, aspirin, and ibuprofen.
- Take warm baths, or apply a warm water bottle to the abdominal area for comfort.

SPECIAL CONCERNS FOR CHILDREN

Abdominal pain in children can have almost as many different causes as it does in adults. Many stomach upsets in children are caused by overeating or constipation. Often children will complain of a stomachache right before getting a cold, a sore throat, or the flu. Because the digestive tract is sensitive to emotions, children may get "tummy aches" when they are feeling stress or anxiety. If possible, talk to your child about the worries he or she might be feeling. Putting a child's mind at ease may ease the stomach pains. Always consider diet, too, when a child's stomach hurts. Some studies say too much fruit or fruit juice can cause abdominal cramps and diarrhea. Intolerance to dairy products, wheat, eggs, or other foods may also be the culprit.

DECISION GUIDE FOR ABDOMINAL PAIN

SYMPTOMS/SIGNS	ACTION
Pain that comes and goes for more than 4 weeks	
Sudden, sharp abdominal pain, lasting longer than 4 hours	
Abdominal pain and fever; jaundice; pale, pasty stools; or dark urine	
Very bad, constant abdominal pain after an injury or sudden black, tarry stools	
Abdominal pain and sudden bright red rectal bleeding or vomiting of blood or a substance that looks like coffee grounds	
Mild pain that comes and goes for less than 4 weeks	
Mild abdominal cramping associated with constipation	

 Call the advice nurse

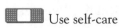 Use self-care

For more about the symbols, see p. 3.

BLACK OR BLOODY STOOLS

Stools that look tarry, black, or bloody can be caused by a number of things. Foods or medicines such as Pepto-Bismol, iron pills, or iron-rich foods like spinach can cause stools to temporarily turn black. Occasionally, stools that appear black or bloody are a sign of a more serious problem. If you are concerned about your symptoms, call the advice nurse.

Hemorrhoids—swollen blood vessels in the anal canal and lower rectum—are a common cause of pain, itching, and rectal bleeding, especially during bowel movements. People with hemorrhoids may notice bright red blood on the toilet tissue or on the stool itself. Hemorrhoids can usually be treated with self-care.

Symptoms of bloody stools accompanied by fever and weight loss or lower abdominal pain can indicate a more serious problem. If you are experiencing any of these symptoms, call the advice nurse.

SELF-CARE STEPS FOR BLACK OR BLOODY STOOLS

• Avoid nonsteroidal anti-inflammatory pain relievers, including over-the-counter ibuprofen (Advil, Motrin or a generic), naproxen (Naprosyn), and aspirin. They may cause intestinal irritation and bleeding.

To avoid constipation that can irritate hemorrhoids:

• Use a stool softener such as Colace combined with a fiber supplement such as Metamucil, Fibercon, or Citracil.

• Drink at least six to eight glasses of water each day.

• Eat plenty of fresh fruits, vegetables, and fiber.

To relieve hemorrhoid symptoms:

• Use an over-the-counter rectal ointment such as Anusol HC, Nupercainol (do not use if allergic to novocaine), or Preparation H.

• Soak in a tub of warm water for 10 to 15 minutes three times a day to help relieve pain and to clean and heal the area.

• Apply Tucks pads to the rectal area twice a day and after bowel movements.

• Take acetaminophen (Tylenol, Tempra, or a generic) for pain relief. Do not take aspirin, which may make bleeding worse.

I was relieved to find out that my black stools were caused by the iron pills I'd started taking, and not by a serious illness.

Shirifa

Ever since the births of my children, I've had bouts of hemorrhoids. They're uncomfortable and aggravating, and, quite frankly, embarrassing. I'm still trying to lose weight but I don't have the best diet, which might be making the problem worse.

Lois

DECISION GUIDE FOR BLACK OR BLOODY STOOLS

SYMPTOMS/SIGNS	ACTION
Bright red rectal bleeding and abdominal pain (p. 19), fever, changes in bowel habits, or recent weight loss	
Red blood in the stool of a person taking a blood thinner (anticoagulant)	
Sudden onset of heavy, continuous, bright red rectal bleeding or black, tarry stools and dizziness; lightheadedness	
Symptoms last longer than 24 hours	
Black, tarry stools unrelated to food or medicine	
Symptoms of hemorrhoids (p. 21)	

 Call the advice nurse   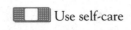 Use self-care

For more about the symbols, see p. 3.

CONSTIPATION

If you believe what you see on television, constipation is the scourge of modern life, to be banished at first suspicion by laxatives and fiber supplements. In reality, constipation is the passage of hard, dry, or infrequent stools and is usually easy to cure naturally.

Emptying one's bowels ought to be fairly easy. After all, the bowels send a signal when they're ready to pass a stool. Most frequently, the cause of constipation is ignoring this signal. The large intestine draws water from stools, so the longer stools remain there, the more water the large intestine will absorb, making the stools harder and more difficult to pass.

The myth that one should have a bowel movement every day is just that: a myth. Each person has his or her own natural schedule. Some people may move their bowels two or three times a day, while others may have a bowel movement once every three to five days. How often doesn't matter (unless the frequency has changed a lot); it is the consistency of the stool or the discomfort that tells you if you're constipated. If you are worried about constipation, discuss these concerns with your medical provider.

Children sometimes become constipated, although their parents usually are more worried about it than the children are. Stress triggered by toilet training can lead to constipation. Seniors, who may become less active as they age, sometimes complain of constipation. With both age groups, a change in diet can get the bowels back on course. Fresh fruits and vegetables have a natural laxative action and also provide fiber. Foods such as bran, celery, and whole-wheat breads also add fiber, which draws water to the stool. Extra fluids also are a good idea, particularly plain water and fruit juices. Replace soda pop and coffee with plain water. Seniors also may want to exercise more. Walking is an excellent choice.

Sometimes constipation signals an underlying, more serious problem. One common health problem is an irritable colon, causing alternating bouts of diarrhea and constipation.

Mild laxatives, such as milk of magnesia, or enemas, such as Fleets, can relieve temporary symptoms of constipation but should not be used often as an aid to regular bowel movements. Diet, particularly adding natural fiber, will work as well. Fiber supplements, such as Metamucil, can also be used.

SELF-CARE STEPS FOR CONSTIPATION

• If you have no other symptoms, relax and wait it out. It's not unusual for bowel movement frequencies and consistencies to vary from time to time.

• Learn to heed the call. Your body will signal you when it's ready for a bowel movement. When you discover the natural time during the day for you to have one, try to set aside that time each day. Relax while sitting on the toilet.

• Change your diet. Increase your liquid intake; plain water and fruit juices are best. Prune juice is especially good for relieving constipation. Add fresh fruits and vegetables and whole-grain breads to your diet.

• Decrease the amount of milk and dairy products you eat every day.

• Exercise more. Exercise not only helps your bowels move more freely, it helps reduce the stress that may make you temporarily constipated.

• Use a stool softener, mild laxative, or nondietary fiber product to relieve temporary symptoms. Once your bowel movements have returned to normal, use diet modification, exercise, and stress reduction techniques to stay regular.

• Take 2–3 teaspoons of mineral oil at bedtime for up to 3 days to help ease constipation. (Mineral oil is available at most drug stores without a prescription.)

When I was having a very stressful time at work, I began to notice I was having a really hard time having a bowel movement. I didn't have the time, and that was probably the biggest problem. My solution was to bring a lot of fresh fruit and vegetables to work and put them right on my desk. I'd eat those as I worked and it really helped.

Dena

DECISION GUIDE FOR CONSTIPATION

SYMPTOMS/SIGNS	ACTION
Constipation and abdominal pain (p. 19), vomiting (p. 34), fever, or loss of appetite	☎
Persistent pencil-thin stools	☎
Suspicion that a drug is causing the constipation (antacids, antidepressants, antihistamines, antihypertensives, diuretics, and narcotics all can cause constipation)	☎
Bowel movement becomes impacted in the rectum; only mucus and fluids will pass	☎
Self-care steps do not help after a week, or discomfort increases	☎
Constipation without other symptoms	▭

☎ Call the advice nurse   ▭ Use self-care

For more about the symbols, see p. 3.

DIARRHEA

Diarrhea is perhaps the world's least favorite traveling companion and most unwelcome houseguest. Yet, it seems everyone is occasionally visited by it.

Diarrhea is frequent, loose, or watery stools, often with abdominal cramps, vomiting, or fever. Stools move so quickly through the intestines that the body is unable to absorb the water in them. Because of this loss of fluid, it is possible for diarrhea to lead to dehydration. Therefore, it is important to drink extra liquids at the first sign of diarrhea.

Diarrhea can be caused by bacteria, viruses, emotional upset, stress, certain drugs, and some chronic bowel diseases. With bacterial infections of the colon, however, diarrhea is usually more severe, lasting longer than usual. Prolonged diarrhea may also be a symptom of conditions such as giardiasis (if you have been traveling), amoebic dysentery, Crohn's disease, ulcerative colitis, or food intolerances.

Most diarrhea goes away on its own or with self-care within 2 days. When a diet of clear liquids doesn't help, your medical provider may prescribe a prescription drug, such as Lomotil, that will slow down activity of the bowel. These drugs usually aren't recommended for children.

Diarrhea is always unpleasant, but it's usually not a major health concern for healthy adults. If severe, however, it can seriously weaken young children and older people.

SELF-CARE STEPS FOR DIARRHEA IN ADULTS

• Drink enough liquids so that the amount of urine you pass stays at the normal level or is slightly more.

• Avoid alcohol, smoking, caffeine, milk, and fruit juice.

• Don't eat if your stomach feels very upset or crampy.

• Drink only clear liquids such as water, flat nondiet soda (ginger ale, 7 Up, Sprite), clear chicken or beef broth, or Gatorade. Sip a few ounces a bit at a time throughout the day.

• Suck ice chips or popsicles if other liquids can't be kept down.

• When your appetite returns but diarrhea continues, choose the following foods: ripe bananas, rice, applesauce, white toast, cooked cereal, potatoes, chicken, turkey, cooked carrots.

• Avoid until diarrhea is gone: fresh fruits, green vegetables, alcohol, greasy or fatty foods (cheeseburgers, bacon), highly seasoned or spicy foods.

• Take over-the-counter drugs such as Pepto-Bismol, Kaopectate, or Immodium, following the product instructions. Note that Pepto-Bismol may temporarily darken the stools or tongue.

• Call the advice nurse if you believe the diarrhea could be caused by a drug. Diarrhea is a common side effect of many drugs.

I had a mild case of diarrhea when I was on a business trip. I took Pepto-Bismol and felt better. The next morning when I went to brush my teeth, I noticed the black coating on my tongue. It really shocked me. I thought I had come down with some strange and horrible disease. I can't tell you how relieved I was to find out it was just something that occurred occasionally as a normal part of taking Pepto-Bismol.
Larry

PREVENTIVE STEPS

• Washing your hands after using the toilet or diapering a baby and before eating or preparing food is an important way to prevent the spread of organisms that can cause diarrhea.

• Unpasteurized dairy products and undercooked fish, poultry, eggs, and meat—especially hamburger—can also have bacteria that can cause diarrhea and other gastrointestinal problems. Always cook foods thoroughly and wash cutting boards, utensils, and hands that have touched uncooked meat products in warm, soapy water. Eat only pasteurized dairy products. Be sure to keep hot foods hot and cold foods cold. Harmful bacteria can grow in foods left at room temperature for too long.

• If you have diarrhea, don't prepare food for others unless you first wash your hands thoroughly. Do not work as a waiter, waitress, or cook or in any food-handling position until

your diarrhea and upset stomach are completely gone and you know you are not contagious.

• Foreign travelers often get diarrhea. About half of North Americans and Northern Europeans who travel to less well-developed areas of the world will get some type of diarrhea during or just after their trip.

• Travelers to foreign countries should avoid drinking or cooking with unpurified water. Water can be purified by boiling it for 15 to 20 minutes or by adding special iodine or chlorine drops or tablets. It's very important to follow product directions exactly when using water-purifying products. Travelers should also avoid fresh fruits and vegetables unless the foods have been thoroughly washed in purified water or can be peeled. Be wary of foods such as melons, which are often injected with water (sometimes contaminated) to increase their weight.

DECISION GUIDE FOR DIARRHEA IN ADULTS

SYMPTOMS/SIGNS	ACTION
Is associated with severe, constant abdominal pain (p. 19) lasting longer than 4 hours	☎
Is accompanied by breathing difficulty	☎
Is associated with recent international travel; ingestion of untreated water from lakes, streams, or wells; or blood streaking on toilet paper and no history of hemorrhoids	☎
Person is elderly or has a chronic illness, such as diabetes	☎
Persistent mucus or blood in stool	☎
Intermittent abdominal pain or cramping that lasts 24 hours or longer	☎
Symptoms of diarrhea accompanied by what you believe to be a high fever	☎
Black and sticky or dark red stools (p. 21), dizziness, sweatiness	☎
Lasts longer than 1 week	☎
Lasts less than 48 hours with mild cramping that's relieved by bowel movements	▭

 Call the advice nurse

 Use self-care

For more about the symbols, see p. 3.

In Children

Diarrhea is common in infants and young children because their digestive systems are still developing. Diarrhea in children most often goes away on its own. The parents' job is to closely watch the child with diarrhea and to see that the child gets enough liquids, the right diet, and lots of tender loving care.

Just as in adults, the major concern for children with diarrhea is dehydration. Because of their smaller body size, children can become dehydrated more rapidly than adults. **Be alert to the following signs of fluid depletion in children:**

- No urination (more than 8 hours without urinating for children under 1 year old; more than 12 hours without urinating for children 1 year and older)

- Unusually dark yellow or strong-smelling urine

- Dry mouth

- Absence of tears

- Dizziness or disorientation

- Dry skin that doesn't spring back after being touched

- In an infant, a sunken soft spot (fontanel) on the top of the head

SELF-CARE STEPS FOR DIARRHEA IN CHILDREN

• Make sure children get lots of fluids. Avoid fruit juices and highly colored drinks (food dyes may make the problem worse). Infants may have breast milk or soy formula. Also offer water and electrolyte solutions such as Pedialyte, Ricelyte, or Gatorade. Older children can have light-colored Kool-aid or flat, clear soda pop. Give small amounts of fluids often—every half hour or so.

• If the child doesn't have an appetite, don't encourage solid foods. When appetite returns, offer small amounts of starchy, easily digested foods such as: white rice, bread, and crackers; potatoes; ripe bananas; cooked carrots, squash, and sweet potatoes; noodles; bland soups such as chicken rice or chicken noodle; turkey or chicken, cooked without the skin.

• Don't give Pepto-Bismol to children or teenagers. It contains aspirin, which has been linked to serious conditions in children.

• Diarrhea can be very hard on the tender skin of young children, especially those still in diapers. To protect the skin, change diapers quickly after each stool. Wash the bottom with plain water or sit the child in a tub with a few inches of warm water (a sitz bath). (You don't need to use soap, but if you do, use mild soap in small amounts and rinse it off well.) For cleanup, use a soft washcloth and plain water or a commercial diaper wipe that has been rinsed out well with water. Dry the area completely by patting with a soft cloth or towel or using a blow dryer on the low/cool setting. A generous layer of petroleum jelly or other ointment will help protect the skin. Since cloth diapers are more gentle on the skin than disposables, consider switching to cloth diapers or lining disposable diapers with cloth ones during prolonged bouts with diarrhea.

DECISION GUIDE FOR DIARRHEA IN CHILDREN

SYMPTOMS/SIGNS	ACTION
Diarrhea and breathing difficulty, severe and constant abdominal pain or cramps, blood in stools, more than one stool per hour, child acting very sick	
Three or more loose stools per day for more than 1 week with no other symptoms	
Diarrhea accompanied by a temperature of a level you believe to be a fever	
Eight or more stools per day over 48 hours with no improvement after dietary changes	
Intermittent abdominal pain and cramps for more than 24 hours	
Signs of dehydration (p. 26)	

Call the advice nurse

For more about the symbols, see p. 3.

I never even knew what heartburn was until I was pregnant. My daughter was breech, with her hard little head pushing up against my stomach and esophagus. In my ninth month, everything gave me heartburn, even water.

Roberta

HEARTBURN

That hamburger topped with tomatoes and raw onion with a big basket of fries sure tasted good, but 2 hours later, you feel like it's ripping a hole in your chest. Is it your stomach taking revenge? Nope—it's probably heartburn.

When you eat, a muscle, called a sphincter, at the lower end of your esophagus relaxes and opens to admit food to your stomach. The sphincter then closes to prevent stomach acid from washing back up the esophagus. Heartburn occurs when the sphincter at the end of the esophagus doesn't close completely. Acid and bile from the stomach then come back up the esophagus, causing a burning sensation.

Nearly everyone has heartburn once in a while. Although heartburn can be treated easily with changes in diet and over-the-counter drugs, it also can be a symptom of more serious problems. Heartburn that just won't go away needs medical attention, because it may be a sign of ulcers or other gastrointestinal problems.

People sometimes confuse symptoms of more serious diseases with heartburn. If you are over 35 and have never discussed your symptoms with your medical provider, it is important to call the advice nurse to talk about them.

There are many things you can do that will reduce or relieve the symptoms of heartburn. Using the Self-Care Steps to the left can help cut down acid levels in your stomach, reduce pressure on your stomach or esophagus, and neutralize the effects of acid.

SELF-CARE STEPS FOR HEARTBURN

- Don't smoke.

- Don't overeat. Try eating smaller meals, more often. And don't eat within a few hours of going to bed.

- Make mealtimes relaxed. Eat slowly and chew thoroughly.

- Lose weight if you're overweight. Often, losing as little as 10 pounds can decrease symptoms.

- Loosen or remove tight-fitting clothing when you eat.

- Don't lie down for 2 hours after eating.

- Sleep with the head of your bed elevated.

- Avoid alcohol, caffeine, decaffeinated coffee, and any other drinks or foods that regularly cause heartburn for you.

- Avoid aspirin, ibuprofen (such as Advil), naproxen (Naprosyn), and other arthritis medications except acetaminophen (Tylenol, Tempra, or a generic).

- If needed, use over-the-counter antacids to relieve heartburn symptoms.

DECISION GUIDE FOR HEARTBURN

SYMPTOMS/SIGNS	ACTION
Heartburn-like symptoms that occur more often during exercise than at other times, especially if symptoms resolve within minutes of stopping exercise	
Persistent symptoms and over age 35 and have never discussed symptoms with medical provider	
No relief after 2 weeks of self-care	
Occasional mild heartburn	

 Call the advice nurse

 Use self-care

For more about the symbols, see p. 3.

RECTAL PAIN

Rectal pain may be linked with intense itching, fever, and rectal bleeding with bowel movements. Obesity, pregnancy, chronic diarrhea or constipation, and some infections—especially of the bowel—may contribute to the problem.

Hemorrhoids, or "piles," (very swollen veins in the rectal area) or *fissures* (cracks in the skin around the rectum) are the most common causes of rectal pain.

Rectal itching is usually not a medical emergency and, in many cases, can be prevented. Wearing cotton, breathable underwear and loose clothing will help. Also have plenty of water, fresh fruit, and high-fiber foods to soften stools and avoid constipation. Try avoiding certain foods that may contribute to irritation, such as highly spiced or acidic foods, coffee, alcohol, or chocolate.

SPECIAL CONCERNS FOR CHILDREN

Sometimes a child will suddenly awake with rectal pain and itching. This often means pinworms. Seldom visable—but quite common and harmless—these small worms are contagious and may be picked up from contaminated food or from household pets. If you suspect someone in your household has pinworms, take extra care to wash hands thoroughly after using the bathroom and before preparing food, and call the advice nurse.

Home care is highly effective in relieving rectal pain and itching. Patients with frequent hemorrhoids and bleeding should see a medical provider for an examination of the anus and rectum. The hemorrhoids may be treated through one of several outpatient methods. Major hemorrhoid surgery is reserved for the most persistent problems.

Internist

SELF-CARE STEPS FOR RECTAL PAIN

- Avoid straining during bowel movements.

- Cleanse rectal area well after each bowel movement. Try Tucks pads instead of, or after, toilet paper. Or use a soothing lotion like Balneol on the toilet paper.

- Use a soft, white, unscented toilet tissue to reduce irritation.

- Try dusting the area with unscented cornstarch or talcum powder.

- Use zinc oxide ointment to decrease chafing and absorb excess moisture.

- Avoid prolonged sitting.

- Raise legs when sitting, especially if obese or pregnant.

- Apply cold compresses (ice packs, Tucks pads, or witch hazel) four times a day for pain.

- Follow cold compress with a warm bath or sitz bath to soothe and cleanse.

- If needed, take aspirin or use medicated suppositories to relieve discomfort. Do not give aspirin to children or teenagers.

Note: Anal ointments with a local anesthetic may cause an allergic reaction. These medicines will have the suffix "caine" in the name or ingredients.

DECISION GUIDE FOR RECTAL PAIN

SYMPTOMS/SIGNS	ACTION
Pain lasts longer than 2 weeks with self-care, or itching occurs with bleeding or pain	
Bleeding from hemorrhoids is heavy or dark in color	
Heavy bleeding	
Pain is severe or lasts longer than 1 week	
Pain lasts less than 1 week	

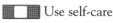 Call the advice nurse   Use self-care

For more about the symbols, see p. 3.

URINARY INCONTINENCE

It's one of those embarrassing problems people don't like to talk about—even with their medical provider. But there is help for incontinence. In most cases, the problem is treatable. It can usually be improved if not completely cured.

The first step is understanding the problem. Urinary incontinence is not being able to control leakage of urine. It affects more than 10 million Americans, and is more common in older people. Childbirth, being overweight, and aging can all weaken the muscles of the pelvic floor, causing incontinence in women. As men age, the prostate gland can enlarge and block the flow of urine, which can build up in the bladder until it overflows.

Families who care for elderly relatives sometimes worry that they will be unable to handle the problems of incontinence. But these problems are often reversible, and families can learn about treatment options together.

Symptoms of incontinence are:

- Urine leaks when coughing, sneezing, laughing, lifting, or getting up from a chair
- Urinate often to avoid accidents
- Get up several times at night to use bathroom
- Urinate in a dribbling, weak stream with no force
- Urine leaks during the day, unrelated to lifting or other stresses
- Sometimes can't urinate despite the urge to do so
- Don't feel empty after urinating
- Urinate only in small amounts
- Wet bed during the night
- Feel urgent need to urinate, and sometimes can't get to toilet in time
- Strong need to urinate at least every 2 hours
- Urge to urinate shortly after drinking
- Urine leaks a minute or so after urinating, especially in men

I have suffered with incontinence for more than 20 years. It's gotten worse recently. I use disposable underwear and try to avoid drinking large amounts of liquid or stressing myself. Sometimes I wish I could talk with my medical provider about this, but I just can't imagine discussing it with anyone.

Joe

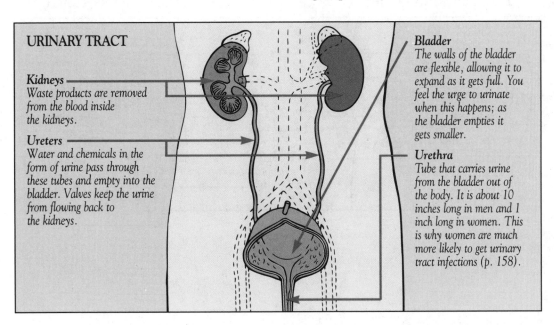

URINARY TRACT

Kidneys
Waste products are removed from the blood inside the kidneys.

Ureters
Water and chemicals in the form of urine pass through these tubes and empty into the bladder. Valves keep the urine from flowing back to the kidneys.

Bladder
The walls of the bladder are flexible, allowing it to expand as it gets full. You feel the urge to urinate when this happens; as the bladder empties it gets smaller.

Urethra
Tube that carries urine from the bladder out of the body. It is about 10 inches long in men and 1 inch long in women. This is why women are much more likely to get urinary tract infections (p. 158).

For several years, I could control my incontinence by doing pelvic floor exercises. Then, after my third child, it seemed the exercises didn't help much anymore. I've got three youngsters to keep up with, and I can't let a problem like this slow me down. I had surgery to correct the problem.

Beth

Stress incontinence is caused when activities place pressure on the bladder, and the muscles that are designed to prevent leaks are weak. People who suffer from stress incontinence leak small amounts of urine when they cough, sneeze, laugh, lift heavy objects, exercise, or even get up from a chair.

Urgency incontinence affects people who suddenly feel the need to urinate so badly that they can't hold back. A bladder infection may be the cause, especially if symptoms of pain and burning accompany urination.

Overflow incontinence occurs when the bladder never completely empties. People with overflow incontinence tend to leak small amounts of urine throughout the day. They often feel the need to go to the bathroom—especially at night—but can only produce small amounts of urine. They don't feel completely "empty" after urinating.

Treatments for incontinence may include exercises, drug therapy, or surgery. Exercises can tone and strengthen sphincter muscles. "Bladder training" techniques help patients empty their bladders as completely as possible and help lengthen the time between trips to the bathroom. Various drugs can help correct some types of incontinence. In postmenopausal women, for example, estrogen may help reduce stress incontinence.

Surgery can help some types of incontinence. One operation for women moves the bladder, allowing the bladder neck (where the bladder opens into the urethra) to return to its normal, closed position. In men, an operation to remove the part of the prostate gland that blocks urination can relieve symptoms of overflow incontinence.

The Self-Care Steps on the following page have special exercises and techniques that may help control incontinence.

FEMALE URINARY TRACT   **MALE URINARY TRACT**

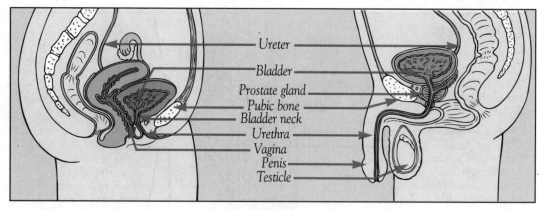

Ureter
Bladder
Prostate gland
Pubic bone
Bladder neck
Urethra
Vagina
Penis
Testicle

SELF-CARE STEPS FOR URINARY INCONTINENCE

- Practice starting and stopping the flow of urine several times.

- Tighten the muscles around the anus and urinary sphincter, hold for a few seconds, then relax the muscles. Repeat 20 times. Perform exercises during a daily routine activity—while brushing your teeth, doing dishes, or reading the paper. Doing a set of 20 exercises several times during the day should improve symptoms of incontinence within a few months.

- Set a specific schedule for going to the bathroom—every 3 hours, for example—even if there's no urge to go. Use an alarm or timer to help stay on schedule.

- After urinating, wait a minute, then try to empty the bladder again. People often find they are able to release additional urine this way.

- Try to resist the urge to urinate more often. If this isn't possible without risking an accident, reduce the timing to every 2 hours, and then try to increase to every 4 hours.

- The time between bathroom trips can be extended this way. When you feel the urge to go to the bathroom, contract the muscles of the pelvic floor until the urge goes away. Try to hold off going to the bathroom a little longer each time. Keep track of how long you can wait between urinating. Within 2 to 3 weeks, you should see an improvement.

- If your problem occurs mainly at night, avoid drinking after the evening meal.

- Avoid stimulants such as caffeine-containing beverages (coffee, cola drinks, etc.), especially after dinner.

- Don't stop drinking water—especially when it's hot or when you are working or playing in a hot climate. It is important to drink fluids regardless of the weather.

- If getting to the toilet in time is a problem, keep a portable urinal nearby (you can buy one at a drugstore or medical supply store). Drugstores also carry a variety of absorbent undergarments.

- Keep a record of the symptoms. A record can help your medical provider understand the specific problem and recommend the right treatment. For several days, keep a record of each time you drink fluids, each time you urinate, and each time you leak urine—even during the night. Use "D" for drink, "U" for urinate, and "L" for leak. Note the time next to each letter. For every "L," also note the circumstances, for example, "while coughing," or "couldn't get to bathroom in time."

- Call the advice nurse if incontinence interferes with your lifestyle. Some people prefer to try self-care techniques before consulting a doctor. Whatever approach you choose, know that incontinence often isn't something you just have to live with.

My incontinence was related to an enlarged prostate. I'd heard most men face that problem sooner or later, so I didn't give it much thought. I assumed it was just part of the natural process of aging. My medical provider told me that even though it's very common, prostate problems shouldn't be ignored. My medical provider and I have chosen "watchful waiting" as the best approach for me at this time.

Clarence

DECISION GUIDE FOR URINARY INCONTINENCE

SYMPTOMS/SIGNS	ACTION
Symptoms are frequent and troublesome and interfere with your lifestyle	
Self-care doesn't improve the problem	
Symptoms are occasional, manageable	

 Call the advice nurse

 Use self-care

For more about the symbols, see p. 3.

Many parents worry about dehydration when their children have an upset stomach. Be patient. Give fluids in very small amounts at first, and solid foods only after eight hours without vomiting.

Pediatric Nurse

There is no magic choice of foods that will settle an upset stomach. While it is commonly believed that milk can coat the stomach and have a calming effect, the opposite is just as likely. Be careful of caffeinated drinks—such as colas, coffee, and tea— which can irritate the stomach.

Dietitian

VOMITING

Vomiting is usually the result of an infection located anywhere from the stomach to the large intestine.

More rarely, it is caused by a bacterial infection that would benefit from medical treatment. But in most cases, an upset stomach is a simple virus that will disappear by itself in a few days.

Vomiting can also be the body's reaction to eating spoiled food—for example, food left at room temperature for too long before being refrigerated. Or it can be the side effect of a drug or drinking too much alcohol. Nervousness, emotional stress, or tension can also cause an upset stomach. And, particularly in children, these upsets can be brought on by motion sickness, too much excitement, or too much sun.

It's very important to prevent dehydration while recovering from vomiting. **Be alert to the following signs of fluid depletion:**

- Less than normal urination (In children, more than 8 hours without urinating for children under 1 year old; more than 12 hours without urinating for children 1 year and older)

- Unusually dark yellow or strong-smelling urine

- Dry mouth

- Absence of tears

- Dizziness or disorientation

- Dry skin that doesn't spring back after being touched

- In an infant, a sunken soft spot (fontanel) on the top of the head

Fortunately, there are sensible and safe home remedies that can satisfy your body's need for fluids and provide relief. Although over-the-counter drugs may make you more comfortable, they won't speed your recovery, and you will get well without them.

SELF-CARE STEPS FOR VOMITING

- Let your stomach rest. Adults should eat nothing for several hours and gradually add liquids as the nausea stops.

- Stay on clear liquids for the first full day. Try water, cracked ice, bouillon, gelatin, chicken soup, popsicles or flat nondiet soda, sipping a little at a time during the day.

- Add bland foods on the second day. Choose foods like bananas, rice, applesauce, unbuttered toast, soup, dry crackers, or dry cereals without milk. Eat these foods in small amounts as comfortably tolerated.

- Avoid milk and dairy products. They may prolong the illness. Cigarettes, caffeine, and alcohol should be avoided also.

- Get plenty of rest.

DECISION GUIDE FOR VOMITING

SYMPTOMS/SIGNS	ACTION
Vomiting blood or a substance that looks like coffee grounds	
Temperature at a level you believe to be a fever	
Possibly pregnant	
Listless, less-than-normal activity level	
Early signs of dehydration (see p. 34)	
Severe, constant stomach and abdominal pain	
Yellowish look to the skin or the whites of the eyes and vomiting or diarrhea, dark brown urine, and light stools	
Person has diabetes	
Possible motion sickness	
After eating too much	
After drinking too much alcohol	
Possibly stress or tension related	

SPECIAL CONCERNS FOR CHILDREN AND SENIORS

Because dehydration is especially serious for young children and seniors, limit fluids for the first 2 hours only. Then, begin offering fluids by the teaspoon, gradually increasing the amount. For some children, fruit juices can make symptoms worse. Limit or dilute juices if symptoms persist.

When a child younger than 2 years of age keeps vomiting for more than 8 hours or has diarrhea (more than five runny stools a day) for more than 2 days, call the advice nurse.

Dehydration (loss of fluids), fever, or loss of appetite can lead to serious problems, so it is important to keep enough fluids in the body. Frequent, small sips of clear liquids will ensure that you are getting adequate fluids.

Family Practitioner

 Call the advice nurse

Use self-care

For more about the symbols, see p. 3.

EYE, EAR, NOSE, AND THROAT PROBLEMS

This section describes common problems related to your eyes, ears, nose, and throat and suggests ways to take care of nonurgent conditions at home.

Your medical provider can offer advice and treatment for most eye, ear, nose, and throat problems. If the condition is very hard to handle, your medical provider may involve other professionals who specialize in these problems.

Use the Decision Guides to see if your symptoms clearly need emergency medical services, require a call to the advice nurse, or can be treated using self-care. It is important to consider your own medical history and your current health when deciding what kind of care is right for you. If you have any conditions that do not seem to be healing normally, if the Self-Care Steps provided do not seem to help, or if you are uncertain about your symptoms, call the advice nurse. The advice nurse will evaluate your symptoms and recommend the next best steps for you to take.

BAD BREATH

It's one of nature's cruelest tricks. People who suffer from bad breath often aren't aware of it, and few people are willing to tell them that their breath has, well, quite an impact.

Although there are dozens of possible causes of bad breath (often referred to as "halitosis"), often it is caused by poor dental hygiene. Without proper brushing and flossing, food particles and plaque build up on the teeth, gums, and tongue. Bacteria begin to grow and produce bad mouth odors.

Smoking is another leading cause of foul-smelling breath. Tar and nicotine residues coat the teeth, tongue, inside of the mouth, and lungs, making breath especially smelly.

Bad breath can also be caused by tonsillitis, pneumonia, mouth sores, sore throats, sinus infections, and even the common cold. Stomach problems such as heartburn can produce bad breath, and so can certain drugs. When bad breath is associated with a sore throat or with mouth ulcers it may require medical care.

Breathing through the mouth, talking for long periods, or sleeping with the mouth open can dry out the mouth and turn breath sour. And, of course, eating garlic, onions, cabbage, or hot and spicy foods can leave breath smelling ripe for a day or so after the meal. Foods high in milk and butterfat are also culprits.

As a salesperson, it's important that my breath not offend people. Before calling on a customer, I always check my breath. I cup my hands over my mouth, exhale, and then sniff. If my breath could use some improvement, I'll brush my teeth or use a breath spray. I want customers to remember me and my products, not my breath.

Kristine

SELF-CARE STEPS FOR BAD BREATH

• The best way to fix a bad breath problem is to brush up on your dental hygiene. Brush your teeth after every meal and floss at least twice a day. See your dentist for an exam and cleaning twice a year.

• If your gums bleed when you floss or brush, you may have gum disease (gingivitis), which can cause bad breath. If the condition doesn't improve after 3 weeks of careful dental hygiene, see your dentist.

• Brush the back of your tongue with a soft toothbrush. The tongue, especially far in the back as it goes down your throat, can have bacteria that cause bad breath. Studies have shown that people who brush the top and back surface of the tongue as well as the teeth have better breath than people who brush only the teeth.

• If you smoke, stop now. You'll need to brush your teeth and tongue twice a day for 2 weeks after you stop smoking before the smelly effects of tobacco are out of your system.

• Drink plenty of fluids to avoid dry mouth. Eat apples, citrus fruits, lettuce, and other raw vegetables that cleanse the teeth. Avoid strong-smelling foods such as onions, garlic, cabbage, and hot and spicy foods.

• Parsley is a natural breath freshener. Mouthwashes, breath mints, and sprays may mask the odor of bad breath temporarily, but they don't get at the source of the problem. Avoid sugary breath mints. They can make bad breath worse. (Bacteria thrive on sugar.)

• Change your toothbrush every 2 to 3 months.

Do you have bad breath? Do a breath check (cup your hands over your mouth, exhale, and then sniff) to find out. Or, floss your back molars and then sniff the used section of the dental floss. If it smells bad, you've got a problem.

DECISION GUIDE FOR BAD BREATH

SYMPTOMS/SIGNS	ACTION
Constant or recurring bad breath that doesn't respond to self-care	
Bad breath associated with a new sore throat or mouth sores	
Bad breath from decayed teeth or gum disease	
Most cases of bad breath without mouth sores or a sore throat	

 Call the advice nurse

Use self-care

For more about the symbols, see p. 3.

BURNING EYES

Lots of different things can make your eyes burn. Smoke, pollen, or a viral infection such as a cold or the flu can cause eyes to itch, burn, water, and redden. In these cases, the burning and itching usually go away when the irritant is removed. However, age and disease can cause chronic dry eyes, which sometimes leads to burning eyes. Over-the-counter lubricating drops (artificial tears) can relieve this type of burning. Itchy, burning eyelids can also result from infection. Over-the-counter eyelid scrubs are available to treat this problem at home.

Caustic substances such as paint thinner, dish washing detergent, lye, toilet cleaner, drain cleaner, or gasoline can chemically burn the eyes. Chemical burns are painful medical emergencies that can result in decreased vision and sensitivity to light. Always wear protective eyeglasses or goggles when working with caustic chemicals.

Unprotected eyes can also be burned by the ultraviolet (UV) rays from the sun, tanning lamps, or arc welding equipment. Like sunburns to the skin, the pain isn't felt until hours later. Then the eyes and the area surrounding them swell up. UV rays can damage the retina. The risk of sunburning the eyes is very high when sunlight is reflected off water, sand, or snow. Wear sunglasses with UV protection when in the sun.

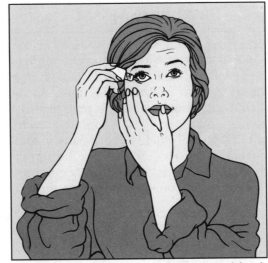

To put eyedrops into the eye, pull down lower lid and look up.

SELF-CARE STEPS FOR BURNING EYES

• If your eyes burn and water, try to trace the source of irritation and then avoid it. Smoke, cosmetics, chemical fumes, and pollen are some possibilities.

• For chemical burns to the eye, see Chemical Burns, p. 167.

• Apply a cool compress to sunburned eyes. Stay out of the sun until swelling is gone.

SPECIAL CONCERNS FOR CHILDREN

Make sure children wear sunglasses with UV protection. Be sure to shade your baby's eyes from the sun, too. Face infants away from the sun when outside. Store cleaning products and other caustic substances out of children's reach.

DECISION GUIDE FOR BURNING EYES

SYMPTOMS/SIGNS	ACTION
Sunburned eyes	☎
Irritated eyes that don't respond to self-care	☎
Impaired vision	☎
Colored parts of eyes appear whitish or cloudy	☎
Discharge from the eye (p. 43)	☎
Any chemically burned eyes (see Self-Care Steps for Chemical Burns, p. 167)	☎ & ▭
Irritated eyes	▭

☎ Call the advice nurse   ▭ Use self-care

For more about the symbols, see p. 3.

COUGH

Coughing is a reflex that causes the air passages to contract and prevent foreign objects from entering the lungs. It also serves to clear the breathing passages of secretions. Coughing is a normal, healthy process as long as these tasks are carried out effectively. However, harsh and forceful coughs can irritate the linings of the airways. This causes the membranes to become inflamed and leads to further coughing.

When coughing lasts for several days, it is usually a symptom of an underlying upper respiratory problem such as a cold (p. 64). Chronic coughing that continues for several months is usually associated with a long-term habit such as smoking, with a chronic illness such as asthma, or with allergies.

DECISION GUIDE FOR COUGH

SYMPTOMS/SIGNS	ACTION
Cough that leads to vomiting	
New cough accompanied by a temperature at a level you believe to be a high fever	
Cough that persists for longer than 3 weeks	
Cough accompanied by swollen glands, with or without a fever	
Cough accompanied by persistent inability to catch one's breath	
Cough with sore throat	

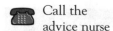 Call the advice nurse

For more about the symbols, see p. 3.

SELF-CARE STEPS FOR COUGH

• Try to cough as little as possible. The less coughing you do, the less you will aggravate the lining of your throat.

• If you are coughing at night, raise the head of the bed to prevent stomach contents from being regurgitated and accidentally breathed into the lungs. This is especially important for elderly people.

• Relieve the sore throat that often comes with a cough by sucking on hard candy (butterscotch is a good choice), throat lozenges, or honey.

• Drink warm liquids such as tea, broth, or hot lemonade.

• You can suppress the cough with over-the-counter cough syrups that contain the ingredient "dextromethorphan." The drug "diphenhydramine," a component of many over-the-counter antihistamines, also acts as a cough suppressant.

EARACHES

There are many possible causes for earaches—the most frequent is an infection of the middle ear. Although uncommon in adults, middle ear infections are an increasing problem for young children. For parents, it's important to be well informed about the care and treatment of children's ears, particularly if their child often has ear pain.

Middle Ear Infections

Middle ear infections result from a buildup of infected fluid in the middle ear (see illustration on next page). Fluid buildup is caused when congestion blocks the natural channel (eustachian tube) and fluid is not allowed to drain from the middle ear. Once the fluid is infected with bacteria, a middle ear infection develops. This condition may require medical attention.

Colds or allergies are almost always to blame for the congestion and fluid accumulation. That's why ear infections often occur on the second or third day of a cold. When children tug at their ears, act very irritable, or have a fever after a cold, suspect an ear infection, and call the advice nurse.

For children with chronic ear infections, regular treatment with low doses of antibiotics is sometimes recommended. The insertion of ear tubes, which drain the inner ear through a hole in the eardrum, may also be considered for recurring problems. With ear tubes, drainage from the ears during a cold is considered "normal" although it may cause some people concern.

Swimmer's Ear/Earwax Buildup

An infection of the outer part of the ear canal, known as "swimmer's ear," usually results from water in the ear that gets infected. The symptoms are an itchy feeling, redness of the outer ear or ear canal, and pain from simply wiggling the ear. Ear pain may also result from a buildup of earwax in the ear canal. Although earwax is normally protective, it can sometimes become impacted and hard to remove.

Avoid smoking at all, but especially near children. Cigarette smoke is irritating to breathing passages and can increase the chance of congestion—and ear infections—in your children.

Family Practice Physician

SELF-CARE STEPS FOR MIDDLE EAR INFECTIONS

• If your medical provider has prescribed an antibiotic, *it is important to take it as directed.* That means not skipping doses, measuring doses carefully, and taking all the prescribed amount *even if the symptoms have gone away.* Store the antibiotic as directed—some require refrigeration.

• Follow your medical provider's recommendations for follow-up exams or other measures to prevent future ear problems.

• For relief from pain or help with sleep, *use acetaminophen* (Tylenol, Tempra, or a generic) instead of aspirin. (Do not give aspirin to children or adolescents.)

• Apply heat to the area around the ear to soothe pain.

• Avoid swimming, airplane flights, or trips to the mountains.

• Since colds are a common cause of ear infections, *teach your children to prevent colds* by avoiding contact with people with a cold. Teach children to wash their hands after contact with someone with a cold.

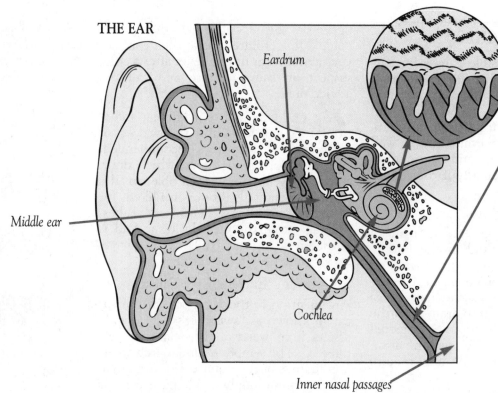

THE EAR

Eardrum

Middle ear

Cochlea

Inner nasal passages

Hair cells in the inner ear can be damaged by long exposure to noise above 86 decibels or one exposure above 140 decibels.

Eustachian tube—
Plugging of the eustachian tube leads to fluid buildup in the middle ear. Fluid can build up in this tube from congestion caused by colds or allergies. This fluid can become infected with bacteria, resulting in a middle ear infection. Middle ear infections may require medical attention.

SELF-CARE STEPS FOR SWIMMER'S EAR/EARWAX BUILDUP

• To prevent swimmer's ear, dry your ears after a swim with a clean towel or hair dryer. You may also want to use drying ear drops if your doctor recommends them.

• If earwax has built up, *do not probe in the ear with swabs like Q-tips—they often jam earwax farther into your ear, causing even more problems.* Instead, direct a warm (never hot) shower at your ear to loosen the wax and then wipe it out with a clean towel. Sometimes gently squeezing warm water into the ear using a soft rubber-nose syringe helps. Don't try to wash your ear if you think you have ruptured your eardrum or if you have ear drainage.

• A heating pad or a warm cloth on the ear may also provide relief.

DECISION GUIDE FOR EARACHES

SYMPTOMS/SIGNS	ACTION
Discharge of fluids from the ear or any type of severe, constant ear pain	☎
Symptoms of a middle ear infection (p. 41)	☎
Ear stuffiness or blocked ear passages that do not respond to self-care within 3 days	☎
Temperature at a level you believe to be a fever	☎
Child with ear pain	☎
Painful, itchy outer ear	☎
Earwax can't easily be dislodged	☎
Hearing loss	☎
Swimmer's ear (p. 41)	▭
Mild wax buildup (p. 41)	▭

☎ Call the advice nurse

▭ Use self-care

For more about the symbols, see p. 3.

EYE DISCHARGE

Have you ever awakened in the morning with your eyes stuck shut? That memorable experience is most often caused by **conjunctivitis,** also known as pinkeye. This eye infection can produce a sticky discharge that leaves eyelids crusty when it dries.

Conjunctivitis is an infection of the membrane that lines the inside of the eyelids and covers the surface of the eye. Along with discharge, conjunctivitis can cause red, swollen, itchy, watery eyes. Eyes may burn or feel like they have sand in them.

Conjunctivitis can be caused by viruses, bacteria, allergies, pollution, or other irritants. Some forms of pinkeye can be contagious. Conjunctivitis caused by allergies, pollution, or irritants is not contagious, but viral or bacterial forms of pinkeye can be very contagious. Medical providers treat bacterial conjunctivitis with antibiotic ointments or eye drops (antibiotics have no effect on viruses), but the infection will often clear up on its own within 5 days. However, if left untreated for long, some forms of conjunctivitis can seriously damage the eyes. The most common form of conjunctivitis is caused by a virus similar to the type that causes a cold.

SELF-CARE STEPS FOR EYE DISCHARGE

• Warm compresses applied to the eyes will help relieve irritation and buildup of the discharge.

• A cold compress will help relieve itching.

• Wipe away the discharge or crust with a washcloth or cotton ball and warm water.

• Don't rub your eyes. It can spread the infection from one eye to the other.

• Keep it to yourself. Don't share towels, washcloths, or anything else that touches the eyes. Wash these items separately in hot water. Wash your hands frequently and thoroughly if you have conjunctivitis, if you are caring for someone who does, or even if you are around someone who has the infection.

SPECIAL CONCERNS FOR CHILDREN

It may be necessary to take your child out of school or day care when you notice symptoms of conjunctivitis. Follow your school or day care policy on attendance. Be very careful to limit as much as possible the contact between an infected child and infants, other children, elderly people, and those with chronic illnesses or damaged immune systems.

DECISION GUIDE FOR EYE DISCHARGE

SYMPTOMS/SIGNS	ACTION
True pain, rather than irritation, in the eye	
Pupils are different sizes	
Eyes are sensitive to light	
Pinkeye and cold sores	
Discharge is thick and yellow or greenish	
History of recent eye injury or foreign object in eye	
Infection is worse rather than better after 3 days	
Unclear vision	
Infection recurs	
Infection is mild and lasts less than 5 days	

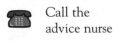 Call the advice nurse

 Use self-care

For more about the symbols, see p. 3.

EYELID PROBLEMS

A sty is a red, tender bump on the eyelid. It can make the lid swell and feel itchy. Sties are normally smaller than a pebble, but the discomfort and swelling tend to make them feel huge.

A sty appears when an oil gland at the base of an eyelash becomes clogged. Over a few days, a sty usually comes to a head —like a pimple—and drains on its own.

Sometimes a sty will persist for weeks without coming to a head. In these cases, a medical provider may choose to open and drain the sty. Good hygiene can help keep hair follicles from becoming clogged and forming sties.

Growths on the eyelid that are not red and painful are usually cysts, rather than sties. Although any unusual lump or growth should be checked by a medical provider, most eyelid cysts are harmless and do not need to be removed.

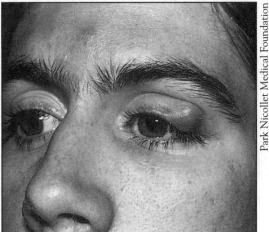

Park Nicollet Medical Foundation

A sty on the upper eyelid.

An eyelid sometimes becomes swollen for no apparent reason. This is usually caused by something in the air that irritates the eyelid or causes an allergic reaction. Although uncomfortable, it is almost never a dangerous condition. Occasional crusting on the eyelid is also fairly common. Crusting appears when irritation or allergy causes fluid to leak from small blood vessels. The fluid then dries much like a scab on a cut. Eyelid crusting can usually be treated with self-care.

SELF-CARE STEPS FOR STIES

 • Hot compresses will help a sty come to a head and drain. Place a clean washcloth in water as hot as you can stand it without burning yourself. Wring out the cloth and place it on your eye for 5 to 10 minutes. Repeat three or four times a day.

• If pus discharges on its own or during the self-care process, carefully clean the entire area.

SPECIAL CONCERNS FOR CHILDREN

A child's skin is much more sensitive to heat than is an adult's. Use lukewarm compresses instead of hot ones to treat a child's sty. Allow the child to test the temperature of the compress before you apply it.

DECISION GUIDE FOR EYELID PROBLEMS

SYMPTOMS/SIGNS	ACTION
Lump on eyelid that isn't painful	
Sty persists and remains painful for a week or more	
Sty returns	
New vision changes	
Red, swollen, itchy lump on eyelid	
Swelling on surface of eyelid	
Eyelid crusting	

 Call the advice nurse   Use self-care

For more about the symbols, see p. 3.

SELF-CARE STEPS FOR EYELID CRUSTING & SWELLING

• Apply cold, moist compresses to your eyes for 20 minutes. Repeat several times a day.

• As much as possible, avoid substances in the air that may cause irritation or allergic reactions in the eyes.

• Avoid wearing contact lenses while you have symptoms of crusting or swelling.

FOREIGN OBJECT IN THE EYE

Pain is the body's way of getting our attention, and nothing grabs attention quite like an object that becomes trapped on the eye or under the eyelid. It simply cannot be ignored.

If you feel something in your eye, don't rub it. Rubbing can damage the cornea, the clear tissue covering the colored part of the eye.

Wash your hands and take a look in the eye. If you find any of the following, put a patch over your eye (without putting pressure on the eyeball), and see the doctor right away: **a piece of glass or metal; an object that has penetrated the eyeball or is stuck on or embedded in the eye; or an object floating or stuck on the colored part of the eye—the iris or pupil.**

If the **object is on the cornea** (the clear layer covering the iris and pupil), you need to be seen by a medical provider at once.

If the object is on the white part of the eye, try the Self-Care Steps on the next page.

Always wear eye protection when working around flying objects or caustic chemicals.

I was working on a carpentry project in my basement and got some wood shavings in the white part of my eye. I got them out with the corner of a handkerchief and everything was fine. But it was a painful reminder. Now I never forget to wear my safety glasses.

Steve

SPECIAL CONCERNS FOR CHILDREN

Try to help the child understand that rubbing the eye will make the problem worse. Give the child something to squeeze or hold onto to keep those little hands occupied while you examine the eye. It's also important for the child to stay calm so he or she can follow your directions. Speak soothingly and stay calm yourself.

SELF-CARE STEPS FOR A FOREIGN OBJECT IN THE EYE

• Wash the eye with water dropped from an eyedropper or squeeze bottle. The object may loosen and flow out of the eye with the water.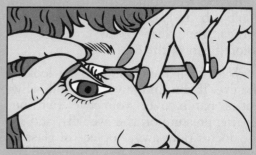

• Fill the sink or other large open container with lukewarm water. Hold your breath and plunge your face into the water with eyes open. Roll your eye and move your head around until the object floats away. (Don't try this with young children who don't know how to hold their breath.)

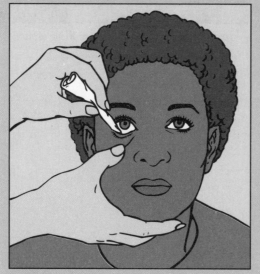

• Roll the corner of a clean handkerchief, tissue, paper towel, or other clean cloth to a point and gently push the object out of the eye with the cloth.

• If the object feels as though it is stuck on the inside of the upper lid, pull the lid out and down over the lower lashes and hold for a few seconds. This may help dislodge the object.

• The following technique works best when someone else helps you. Look up and pull the lower lid down while your helper looks under the lower lid. Then look down at your shoes and pull the upper lid up by the lashes while your helper looks under the upper lid. A Q-tip can help you grasp the upper lid (*see illustration*). **Never insert** a toothpick, matchstick, tweezers, or other hard object into the eye itself to remove an object.

• You can remove something stuck on the under surface of your upper eyelid with a moistened Q-tip if care is taken to avoid brushing the cornea (the clear layer over the colored part of the eye).

DECISION GUIDE FOR A FOREIGN OBJECT IN THE EYE

SYMPTOMS/SIGNS	ACTION
Object causes impaired vision	
Object is embedded in or penetrates the eyeball	
Self-care methods fail to remove the object	
Pain continues after the object has been removed	
Eye shows signs of infection (is red, warm, swollen; is increasingly painful; discharges a yellow/green pus)	
Object is on the colored part of the eye	
Eye is bleeding	
Object is a piece of metal or glass	
Object is on the white part of the eye	

 Seek help now

 Call the advice nurse

 Use self-care

For more about the symbols, see p. 3.

HOARSENESS/LARYNGITIS

You never realize how much you need your voice until it's gone. When laryngitis strikes, you can't talk on the phone, read the kids a bedtime story, or even join in a conversation.

Laryngitis is the inflammation of the vocal cords. It keeps the vocal cords from vibrating normally, so the sounds they produce are far from normal. The voice may sound hoarse or husky or disappear altogether.

Hoarseness or laryngitis is usually caused either by overuse of the vocal cords or a viral infection. Cheering your team on at a sporting event, shouting, singing, and speaking for long periods can all cause temporary hoarseness or loss of voice. Occasional hoarseness often afflicts teachers, singers, actors, salespeople, politicians, and others who use their voices for long periods. A cold, sore throat, or other upper respiratory infection can also rob you of your voice if the infection spreads to the voice box.

Hoarseness that is caused by overuse or by a cold or other infection will usually go away on its own within 2 weeks. To prevent attacks of hoarseness, avoid straining your voice and stop talking as soon as you begin to feel hoarse. Whispering can actually be more irritating to your vocal cords than speaking softly.

Smoking, alcohol, and air pollution can dry the vocal cords and cause hoarseness. Constant or repeated hoarseness not linked to overuse or an infection may be something more serious.

I always seem to get laryngitis at the end of a cold, when the other symptoms are almost gone. It's annoying, but it doesn't make me feel as ill as the other cold symptoms do. For me, hoarseness is a sign that it's almost over. I start to sound awful just when I'm beginning to feel better.

Rob

SELF-CARE STEPS FOR HOARSENESS/LARYNGITIS

• Give it a rest. Avoid talking and whispering as much as possible. (Whispering strains vocal cords as much or more than talking.) Use a pencil and paper and lots of hand gestures to communicate.

• Drink plenty of fluids. Water is best to keep your vocal cords well hydrated.

• Don't smoke or drink alcohol. Both can dry out and irritate vocal cords.

• Humidify your home.

• If you have to go out in extremely cold weather, wear a scarf or mask over your mouth.

• Drink warm liquids to relieve discomfort.

DECISION GUIDE FOR HOARSENESS/LARYNGITIS

SYMPTOMS/SIGNS	ACTION
Repeated bouts of hoarseness not caused by overuse or infection associated with cold symptoms	
Hoarseness that lasts longer than 1 month, particularly if you are over 40 and smoke	
Hoarseness or loss of voice caused by overuse or infection associated with cold symptoms	

 Call the advice nurse

 Use self-care

For more about the symbols, see p. 3.

MOUTH SORES

Mouth sores can be painful, unsightly, and slow to heal, but most of them go away on their own in a couple of weeks. Fortunately, people don't die from simple mouth sores, but they can be uncomfortable so we need to find ways to treat the pain, promote healing, and keep new sores from forming.

Canker sores and cold sores are the two most common types of mouth sores. **Canker sores** are found on the wet surfaces inside the mouth, on the gums, or inside the lips or cheeks. They can be red or yellowish white with a red border. No one knows what causes them.

Cold sores usually crop up outside the mouth, on or around the lips. More than half of us have had these before we are out of high school. They are caused by the herpes simplex virus type 1 and can start before or during a cold or the flu. Because cold sores can easily spread from one person to another, kissing someone with a cold sore should be avoided. Often an early warning signal is given—the affected area will itch, tingle, or burn before the sore forms.

Both cold sores and canker sores are more apt to develop when you are under stress. Fatigue, frustration, emotional upset, poor nutrition, and other stress may weaken the body's defenses enough for a mouth sore to form.

SPECIAL CONCERNS FOR CHILDREN

The virus that causes cold sores can be dangerous to newborn babies. Keep newborns away from anyone who has a cold sore or the itching, burning symptoms that precede a cold sore.

SELF-CARE STEPS FOR MOUTH SORES

• Apply over-the-counter products such as Anbesol for canker sores, and try Carmex or Blistex for cold sores. These won't make the sores heal any faster, but they may reduce the pain.

• Avoid eating acidic foods such as citrus fruits or tomatoes. Salty, spicy, or vinegary foods may irritate mouth sores, too. Also avoid foods with sharp edges, like potato chips.

• Cold sores are contagious. If you have one or feel one coming on, avoid skin-to-skin contact with anyone else until the sore has healed.

DECISION GUIDE FOR MOUTH SORES

SYMPTOMS/SIGNS	ACTION
Large, bleeding, and painful ulcers on gums	☎
Recurring mouth sores	☎
Mouth sores that don't heal within 3 weeks	☎
Small whitish, lacy sores	☎
Creamy yellow patches on inside of mouth that may be sore or painful	☎
Mouth sores caused by poorly fitting dentures or rough or broken teeth	☎
For canker sores: One or more red, craterlike sores inside the mouth, on gums, or inside of lips or cheeks	▭
For cold sores: One or more blisters on the outside of the mouth area	▭

 Call the advice nurse   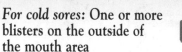 Use self-care

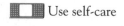

For more about the symbols, see p. 3.

SINUS PROBLEMS

The sinuses are naturally occurring cavities in the bones of the face. There are four pairs of sinuses, which are connected to the nasal cavities by small openings. The lining of the sinuses normally secretes a thin mucus that drains into the nose. Sinus problems occur when the lining in these cavities becomes inflamed and swollen, blocking the drainage of fluid. As the sinuses secrete more mucus, the trapped fluid causes increasing pressure and pain in the sinuses. If the fluid in the sinuses then becomes infected, it will thicken and take on a yellow to green color. The two most common causes of sinus problems are cold and allergies, but other things can irritate the sinuses as well.

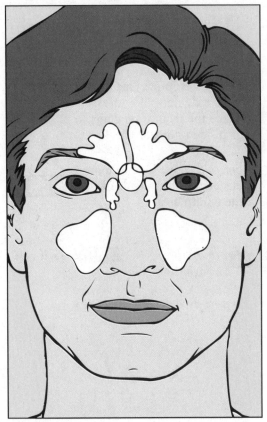

Location of sinuses

SELF-CARE STEPS FOR SINUS PROBLEMS

- Drink plenty of fluids to help dilute the secretions and allow sinuses to drain more easily.

- Stand in a steamy shower to help open sinuses and decrease pressure.

- Take acetaminophen (Tylenol, Tempra or a generic) to reduce the sinus pain.

- Avoid bending over with your head down.

- Sleep with extra pillows to elevate the angle of your head and reduce sinus pain.

DECISION GUIDE FOR SINUS PROBLEMS

SYMPTOMS/SIGNS	ACTION
Difficulty breathing through nose after 10 days of self-care	
Pain around eyes or cheeks with or without a fever	
Toothache (see p. 56)	

 Call the advice nurse

For more about the symbols, see p. 3.

SORE THROATS

Sore throats can be annoying, but they usually can be improved with a few simple self-care steps. Low humidity in your home, failing to drink enough fluids, winter dryness, or smoke may be the culprits, but often, sore throats are a sign of infection.

Two types of infections cause sore throats: the more common viral infection; and the less common—but more serious—bacterial infection. Here are the usual differences between the two:

Viral Sore Throat

- Caused by a virus
- Usually causes a dry cough and a lighter-colored mucus
- Less likely to be accompanied by a fever
- Often associated with cold or flu

Bacterial Sore Throat

- Caused by bacteria
- Throat appears very red with white patches or pus and swollen tonsils and neck glands
- Often produces a temperature of over 101° F
- Requires treatment with antibiotics

Symptoms of viral sore throats usually will go away in a few days, but it is not uncommon for symptoms to last 7 to 10 days. These do not benefit from being treated with antibiotics.

NOTES FOR CHILDREN

- Fluids are very important for children. Be sure to give them plenty of soups, juice, or water.

- Fever doesn't necessarily mean serious illness in children. Be more concerned with changes in eating or sleeping habits or an unhealthy appearance. Acetaminophen (Tylenol, Tempra, or a generic) can be used for fever. Do not give aspirin to children or adolescents.

- If a child doesn't feel too tired, staying active is fine.

- Teach your children to prevent sore throats and other infections by washing their hands often and keeping their hands away from the face. If your children have been with friends who are infected, these preventive steps may keep the illness from spreading to themselves and others.

SELF-CARE STEPS FOR SORE THROATS

- Drink fluids. Drinking at least eight glasses of fluid a day will soothe your throat and loosen mucus for a more productive cough.

- Gargle with warm salt water. Add 1/4 teaspoon of salt to 8 ounces of water. Mouthwashes don't prevent or relieve a sore throat and are no more effective than salt water.

- Suck on hard candies or cough drops and take aspirin for fever or discomfort if you need to. For children or teenagers, use acetaminophen (Tylenol, Tempra, or a generic) instead of aspirin.

- Increase the humidity with vaporizers or hot showers. However, since vaporizers can transmit infection, it is important to keep them very clean.

I take good care of my sore throat and cough by removing outside irritants such as smoke, smog, chalk dust, allergens, etc. I tell friends "yes, I do mind if you smoke" and request nonsmoking areas when I'm dining out. I also avoid the dehydrating effects of alcohol or caffeine from coffee, tea, or soft drinks.

Professional Speaker

The main problem with topical medicines used to soothe your throat is that they don't work any better than sucking on a less expensive candy. Hard candy helps to keep your throat moist—or gargle with warm salt water for relief.

Family Practitioner

Most sore throats and coughs will go away without the need for medical care. However, a frequent cough that disturbs sleep or worsens with exercise could mean lower respiratory disease such as pneumonia or asthma. These require a medical provider's attention.

Pediatrician

DECISION GUIDE FOR SORE THROATS

SYMPTOMS/SIGNS	ACTION
Difficulty breathing	☎
Inability to swallow saliva	☎
Cough that gets worse	☎
Swollen glands (see right)	☎
Throat very red with white patches or pus and swollen glands	☎
Temperature at a level you believe to be a fever that lasts longer than 48 hours	☎
Sore throat develops into chest symptoms with cough getting worse	☎
Cough that comes and goes	▭
Dry, sore, itchy throat	▭
Seems like a cold	▭

☎ Call the advice nurse   ▭ Use self-care

For more about the symbols, see p. 3.

SWOLLEN GLANDS

Swollen glands are a good news/bad news story. The good news is that your glands probably are swollen because they're busy fighting an infection in your body. The bad news is that they may be painful.

Lymph glands produce the antibodies you use to fight viruses and infections. Ordinarily about the size of a pea, lymph glands get larger quickly when fighting an infection.

When lymph glands enlarge rapidly, it may cause some tenderness. If the gland feels fairly soft and somewhat mobile, as well as tender, the infection probably is minor. The soreness will get better in a few days, although the gland may remain somewhat swollen for several weeks. It simply takes longer for it to return to its natural size than it does for it to grow.

The location of the swollen gland can tell you where the virus or infection is. An infection in the feet, legs, or genital area—and it can be as simple as athlete's foot or an ingrown toenail—will cause glands in the groin to swell. A swollen gland in the armpit might be from an infected cut on the arm or finger.

Most people connect the term "swollen glands" with the glands between the ear and the angle of the jaw, which often swell during sore throats and ear infections. Swollen glands in the neck may indicate other types of illness.

Swollen glands usually need no special treatment. Most often, swollen glands are caused by viral infections and the only treatment is acetaminophen to relieve pain. Sometimes a bacterial infection will lodge in the glands themselves, making them red, hot, very tender, and very sore. In these cases, infected glands may require antibiotics.

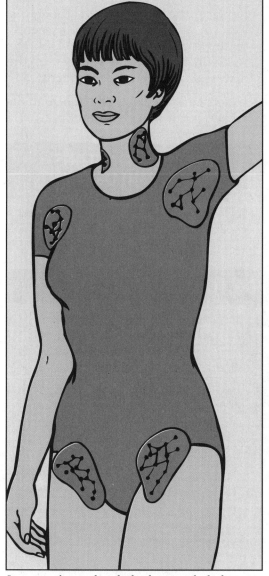

Location of major lymph gland sites in the body

DECISION GUIDE FOR SWOLLEN GLANDS

SYMPTOMS/SIGNS	ACTION
Difficulty breathing and new inability to swallow saliva accompanied by swollen glands in the neck	
Swollen glands with a sore throat and/or a temperature at a level you believe to be a fever	
Swollen glands are very tender and red	
Swelling lasts longer than 2 weeks	
Swollen glands without more serious symptoms, such as redness and extreme tenderness	

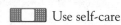 Call the advice nurse   Use self-care

For more about the symbols, see p. 3.

SELF-CARE STEPS FOR SWOLLEN GLANDS

 • Swollen glands are usually a temporary problem and require little treatment. Take acetaminophen (Tylenol, Tempra, or a generic) for any minor pain or discomfort that the glands might cause

• If you notice that the glands become red and very painful, call the advice nurse.

My toddler woke up from his nap crying, which was very unusual. When I went in to get him, he was hot and the glands under his jawline were large and tender. I called his pediatrician, who said to start him on Tylenol. The Tylenol took away the fever and eventually the glands went down in size. It was kind of weird how fast it came on, but it went away pretty quickly.

Roberta

It seemed like, when I was a kid, my glands were never the normal size. I had chronic tonsillitis. I never knew what I really looked like until my tonsils finally came out. Then I finally discovered I had a normal jawline and neck after all.

Tim

I had a throbbing toothache. Unbelievable. And even the short time that passed before I could get in for a root canal was too much. It was a good motivator. I floss daily now and brush after every meal. I never want to go through that again.

Pablo

TOOTHACHE

At the painful peak of a toothache, you may be moved to vow that you'll never go a day without flossing again. *Ever.*

Whether or not you ever feel that much pain, you should promise to floss daily (see next page for proper flossing technique) because tooth decay is at the root of most toothaches. Good dental hygiene, together with regular cleanings and dental checkups, works like nothing else to prevent decay and the toothache caused by it.

Toothache can also be caused by cracked teeth, hypersensitive teeth, food stuck between the teeth, or old and crumbling dental work. Sometimes pain in the upper teeth may be caused by sinusitis. So once again, don't put off your regular checkups.

Emergency Steps for a Lost Permanent Tooth

If you should happen to have a tooth knocked free from its normal place in your mouth, the following actions are very important.

- **Act quickly.** The longer a tooth is out of its socket, the harder it is to successfully reimplant.

- If the tooth is dirty, gently rinse under water. Do not scrub, and remember to plug the sink.

- Replace the tooth, even though it won't be securely anchored, by gently teasing it back into its socket. Hold the tooth in place while you get to the dentist or emergency department.

- If you can't replace the tooth in its socket, put it in a glass of milk.

SPECIAL CONCERNS FOR CHILDREN

Ask your dentist if dental sealants are a good preventive treatment for your child.

SELF-CARE STEPS FOR TOOTHACHE

- First figure out if your tooth pain is caused by an object or food particle wedged between your teeth. Try to remove it by flossing carefully. If this doesn't work, call the advice nurse. Don't try to remove a tightly wedged particle on your own. You could do even more damage.

- If your pain lingers, call your dentist as soon as possible. Swelling should always be seen by your dentist immediately.

- For temporary relief of pain, you may try the following techniques:

- Take acetaminophen (Tylenol, Tempra, or a generic) or ibuprofen (Advil, Nuprin, or a generic) to relieve the pain. Children and teenagers should not take aspirin. Be sure to swallow the pill. Do not rub it on the sore area, which can cause acid burns to an already sore mouth.

- Apply small amounts of oil of cloves to the tooth. Also called eugenol, oil of cloves is a nonprescription remedy available at drug stores. Over-the-counter anesthetic gels with benzocaine can also be used to numb tooth pain.

- If your gums become swollen, an infection may be present. Apply a cold pack on the outside of the cheek to reduce the swelling and pain. Ice cubes wrapped in a towel will work. If nothing else is available, hold a cold can of soda to your cheek.

- If milk is not available, place the tooth in plastic wrap or a wet towel.

- **Do not allow the tooth to dry out in the air.**

- If the tooth is a baby tooth, it will *not* be reimplanted. If you are not sure whether it is a baby tooth, call the advice nurse.

Chipped Tooth

A chipped tooth, though inconvenient, is seldom a serious medical problem. However, your "bite" may have been affected, since a blow hard enough to chip may also cause other problems. There are a variety of ways to fix this physical and cosmetic problem. Call the advice nurse if you have questions.

Wisdom Teeth

For temporary relief of pain, rinse your mouth with warm salt water and take an anti-inflammatory medication such as acetaminophen (Tylenol, Tempra, or a generic) or ibuprofen (Advil, Nuprin, or a generic) to relieve the pain. If there is any swelling, call the advice nurse.

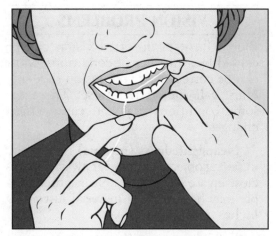

Correct Flossing Technique—*Insert floss and curve in a "C" shape against tooth; from base of tooth, shimmy floss back and forth while pulling away from gum. (The action is similar to drying the back with a towel.) Do this on either side of each tooth.*

DECISION GUIDE FOR TOOTHACHE

SYMPTOMS/SIGNS	ACTION
Toothache and fever, earache, or pain when opening mouth	☎
Loss of a permanent tooth	☎
Any toothache	☎
Dental appointment has been scheduled	▭
Unable to get to a dentist	▭

☎ Call the advice nurse   ▭ Use self-care

For more about the symbols, see p. 3.

VISION PROBLEMS

Blurry, fuzzy, or distorted vision can be caused by a number of conditions. Most can be corrected. If your vision suddenly blurs, call the advice nurse. These are some conditions that can cause vision changes.

Nearsightedness (myopia) is difficulty in seeing objects that are far away. Objects close up are seen clearly. Nearsighted people may hold reading material just a few inches from their noses.

Farsightedness (hyperopia) causes nearby objects to appear fuzzy. Objects at a distance are seen clearly. Farsighted people often hold their reading material at arms length.

Astigmatism can cause areas of blurry vision because the lens in your eye is not smooth. People with astigmatism may find it hard to see vertical, horizontal, or diagonal lines clearly.

Presbyopia is a problem of aging. As we get older, the eye lens hardens and loses its flexibility, making it hard to focus on near objects. Eyeglasses with bifocal lenses can correct most cases of presbyopia.

Cataracts cloud the lens of the eye, impairing vision. They usually start very slowly over several years. Most cataracts are a result of aging but they can also be caused by injuries, birth defects, too much heat or ultraviolet (UV) light, drugs, and diabetes. Lenses affected by cataracts can be replaced by surgery if necessary.

Diplopia (double vision) occurs when the eyes do not focus in unison. Double vision can be a sign of a more serious condition and should be evaluated by a medical provider.

Eye floaters can seem scary but rarely indicate a serious problem. At one time or another, most people see what appear to be specks or strings floating in and out of their field of vision. In reality, these objects are "leftovers" from the eye's growth process before birth and do not require treatment.

Glaucoma, a major cause of blindness, is increased pressure within the eyeball. This pressure can damage the optic nerve, which controls sight. Symptoms of glaucoma include loss of vision to each side (peripheral vision), halos around lights, pain in the eye, blurred vision, and then blindness. Glaucoma destroys peripheral vision first, so it often is not caught until a good deal of vision is lost. Early diagnosis through routine glaucoma checks after age 40 is the key to treating this problem (see Glaucoma, p. 224).

Macular degeneration is the leading cause of blindness in the United States. It causes increasingly blurred central vision and most often strikes elderly people. If diagnosed early, laser treatment can sometimes keep it from getting worse.

SPECIAL CONCERNS FOR CHILDREN

Children should have their first eye exam at 3 or 4 years of age unless you suspect a vision problem earlier. If a school-age child starts having headaches or is having trouble at school, he or she may have a vision problem.

SELF-CARE STEPS FOR VISION PROBLEMS

• Have regular eye exams—every 3 to 5 years if you don't have vision problems, every 2 years if you wear glasses, contact lenses, or have other vision problems. More frequent exams may be recommended by your medical provider or eye specialist.

• Wear safety glasses or goggles whenever you use power tools.

• Wear sunglasses with UV protection when you are out in bright sunlight. Be especially careful when sunlight is reflected by water or snow. Too much UV light has been linked to cataracts.

DECISION GUIDE FOR VISION PROBLEMS

SYMPTOMS/SIGNS	ACTION
Decreased vision began while taking medication	☎
New decrease in vision in person over age 50	☎
New double vision	☎
Tunnel vision or loss of peripheral vision	☎
Eyes protrude or bulge out of sockets	☎
Sudden loss or blurring of vision	☎
Loss of vision associated with injury to head or eyes	☎
Seeing flashing lights or black spots	☎

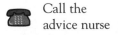 Call the advice nurse

For more about the symbols, see p. 3.

HEART AND LUNG PROBLEMS

Your heart and lungs are the organs that offer the most dramatic evidence of your body's well-being. This section describes common problems of these vital organs and suggests how to take care of nonurgent conditions at home.

Your medical provider can offer advice and treatment for most heart and lung problems. If your condition is very hard to handle, your medical provider may involve other professionals who specialize in these problems.

Use the Decision Guides to see if your symptoms clearly need emergency medical services, require a call to the advice nurse, or can be treated using self-care. It is important to consider your own medical history and your current health when deciding what kind of care is right for you. If you have any conditions that do not seem to be healing normally, if the Self-Care Steps provided do not seem to help, or if you are uncertain about your symptoms, call the advice nurse. The advice nurse will evaluate your symptoms and recommend the next best steps for you to take.

ACUTE BRONCHITIS

A cold or flu usually lasts about a week, but after all the other symptoms are gone, you may find yourself with a cough that lingers a while longer. The cough may be "productive," meaning you cough up mucus (usually yellow or gray instead of clear), or dry and hacking. A productive cough is often a sign of acute bronchitis.

Bronchitis occurs when the lining of the tubes leading to the lungs gets inflamed and begins making too much mucus. When this happens, your body must cough to clear out the extra mucus.

Acute bronchitis in an otherwise healthy person may be caused by viruses or bacteria. Airborne irritants—such as smoke, dust, chemical fumes—or even cold weather may cause bronchitis. People with asthma may also develop bronchitis more easily.

Because bronchitis is so closely related to pneumonia, it is important to see your medical provider to rule out pneumonia if symptoms get worse instead of better or if they last longer than a week. Often a chest exam is all that is needed, but your medical provider may also order chest X-rays or a sputum culture. If your provider prescribes an antibiotic, take it as directed until it is gone, even if you feel better.

SELF-CARE STEPS FOR ACUTE BRONCHITIS

The best treatment for bronchitis is to drink plenty of fluids. By drinking six to eight glasses of clear liquids (not milk) a day, you will help keep the mucus from "gumming" up your bronchial tubes. When the mucus is thin and fluid, it is easier to clear away by coughing. And when the bronchial passages are clear and the inflammation has gone away, so too will the cough.

Here are some other things you can do on your own to treat bronchitis:

• Watch for signs of pneumonia. These can include: coughing; shaking and chills; fever; white, yellow, green, blood-streaked, or rust-colored mucus; shortness of breath; chest pain; and fatigue. Because pneumonia left untreated can be life threatening, it is important to see your medical provider if your bronchitis becomes worse or you start to have the above symptoms.

• Get plenty of rest. Listen to your body. You may be able to continue your daily routine while you have bronchitis, but don't overdo it. If you feel tired, rest.

• Avoid alcohol and caffeine. Either can make you lose body fluid, which you need to keep the mucus thin.

• If you feel you need medicine, choose a cough suppressant or an expectorant. Some cough medicines contain antihistamines or other preparations you probably don't need or want when you have bronchitis. Look for a cough preparation that has only the cough suppressant dextromethorphan. If you are coughing up mucus you might also try one with the expectorant guaifenesin.

Acute bronchitis usually lasts 1 to 2 weeks. But even after the inflammation in the bronchial tubes is gone, a dry cough, sometimes with wheezing, remains for as long as 4 to 6 weeks. During this time, exposure to cold, dry air, smoke, or dust can irritate the bronchial tubes and bring on coughing. Over-the-counter cough suppressants and decongestants may help relieve this nagging cough, or your medical provider may prescribe other drugs. If a cough lasts longer than 4 to 6 weeks, call the advice nurse.

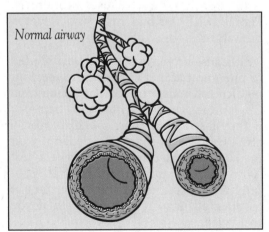

Normal airway

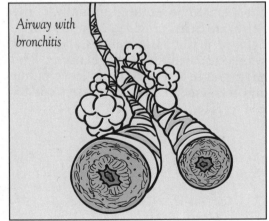

Airway with bronchitis

DECISION GUIDE FOR ACUTE BRONCHITIS

SYMPTOMS/SIGNS	ACTION
Blood in sputum	
Cough lasts longer than 4 to 6 weeks	
Shortness of breath and heavy coughing	
Person has asthma (p. 241) and gets symptoms of bronchitis	
Person has chronic obstructive lung disease (p. 245) and gets symptoms of bronchitis	
Temperature at a level you believe to be a fever	
Cough worsens or lasts longer than 1 week	
Productive or dry cough after a cold or flu, no fever, and tiredness	

 Call the advice nurse    Use self-care

For more about the symbols, see p. 3.

CHEST PAIN

Feelings of pain or pressure in the chest area could signal a problem as simple as indigestion or as serious as a heart attack. Pay attention to those signals, and call the advice nurse if you are unsure of what the symptoms mean.

Keep Your Heart Healthy

Heart-related chest pains are caused by clogged arteries in your heart. Good health habits can help prevent or correct the problem. Exercise regularly, eat a low-fat diet, don't smoke, lose weight if you are overweight, learn to relieve stress, and get your blood pressure and cholesterol levels checked. Lifestyle changes can't prevent all cases of heart disease, but they can greatly reduce your risk of heart attack.

Be Prepared

If someone in your family suffers from heart disease, learn CPR (cardiopulmonary resuscitation, p. 10) and be prepared to use it in an emergency. It could save a life.

DECISION GUIDE FOR CHEST PAIN

SYMPTOMS/SIGNS	ACTION
Unidentifiable or unusual pain or pressure in the chest area	

Frankly, when it comes to colds, my advice as a medical provider is not much better than what your mother tells you. You can spend a lot of money trying drugstore remedies, but I think you can't do better than chicken soup. Be a good citizen when you have a cold by washing your hands often and not sharing your food with others. If you have a sore throat, gargle with slightly salted, warm water.

Infectious Disease Specialist

COLDS
(UPPER RESPIRATORY INFECTIONS)

Coming down with another cold is hardly a surprise. Neither is having a runny nose, congestion, fever or cough, or feeling just plain miserable. Although myths abound about this common annoyance, the fact is you can't catch a cold by walking in the rain, failing to bundle up in the cold, or sitting by a draft. Simply put, a cold is a *viral infection*.

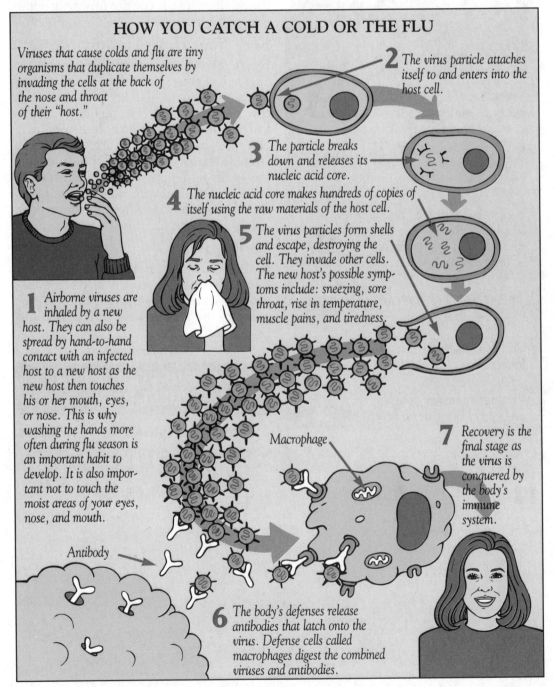

HOW YOU CATCH A COLD OR THE FLU

Viruses that cause colds and flu are tiny organisms that duplicate themselves by invading the cells at the back of the nose and throat of their "host."

2 *The virus particle attaches itself to and enters into the host cell.*

3 *The particle breaks down and releases its nucleic acid core.*

4 *The nucleic acid core makes hundreds of copies of itself using the raw materials of the host cell.*

5 *The virus particles form shells and escape, destroying the cell. They invade other cells. The new host's possible symptoms include: sneezing, sore throat, rise in temperature, muscle pains, and tiredness.*

1 *Airborne viruses are inhaled by a new host. They can also be spread by hand-to-hand contact with an infected host to a new host as the new host then touches his or her mouth, eyes, or nose. This is why washing the hands more often during flu season is an important habit to develop. It is also important not to touch the moist areas of your eyes, nose, and mouth.*

Macrophage

7 *Recovery is the final stage as the virus is conquered by the body's immune system.*

Antibody

6 *The body's defenses release antibodies that latch onto the virus. Defense cells called macrophages digest the combined viruses and antibodies.*

The easiest way to catch these viruses is from other people: by shaking their hands, being near their sneezes, or touching things they have touched. The best way to prevent the spread of the common cold is to avoid people with colds. *Wash your hands if you have physical contact with someone with a cold.*

Many parents are surprised to learn that a fever with colds is not necessarily harmful. It helps the body's immune system fight off the cold virus. If a child with a cold has fever and otherwise seems well, there is no medical reason to treat the fever. However, if a child is uncomfortable, a parent may want to use acetaminophen to bring the fever down.

Pediatrician

SELF-CARE STEPS FOR COLDS

• Raise the humidity at home. You can sit in the bathroom with a hot shower running or use a humidifier/vaporizer. If using a humidifier, empty and clean it daily following the manufacturer's instructions.

• Drink extra fluids. Warm, clear fluids are especially soothing for irritated throats.

• Sleep with your head raised on pillows to relieve nasal congestion.

• Gargle with salt water or suck hard candy. Homemade salt water (¼ teaspoon salt dissolved in 8 ounces warm water) will help relieve a sore throat. Hard candy is as effective for sore throats as cough drops. Butterscotch is a good choice.

• Try saline nose drops or sprays (e.g., Ocean or Salinex) to relieve congestion. Follow manufacturer's instructions.

• Remain up and about. You will benefit from extra rest, but generally, you'll feel better by staying moderately active.

• Over-the-counter nasal sprays and decongestants are of limited benefit but may be used for temporary relief.

• Fevers during a cold are not uncommon and usually last less than 3 days. Use acetaminophen (Tylenol, Tempra, or a generic) to ease discomfort. Symptoms usually begin to go away within a week but may last for up to 2 weeks.

SPECIAL CONCERNS FOR CHILDREN

• Children typically have colds more frequently than adults—five to eight colds each year is not unusual.

• Over-the-counter medicine is not recommended for children without a medical provider's advice. Call the advice nurse if you have questions about medications.

• Encourage children to drink a lot of clear fluids and to stay active if they do not feel too tired.

• For infants younger than 3 months of age, call the advice nurse if infant has what you believe to be a fever, is feeding poorly, can't be comforted, can't stay awake, or has a weak cry.

DECISION GUIDE FOR COLDS

SYMPTOMS/SIGNS	ACTION
Children: Less responsive, poor eye contact	☎
Bothersome cold symptoms and a fever lasting longer than 72 hours or accompanied by symptoms of ear infection	☎
Adults and children: Symptoms worsen after 3 to 5 days	☎
Symptoms don't improve and still bother you after 10 days	☎
Wheezing or difficulty swallowing	☎
Sore throat, cough	▭
Congestion, general achiness	▭
Scratchy throat, runny/stuffy nose	▭

☎ Call the advice nurse ▭ Use self-care

For more about the symbols, see p. 3.

Fortunately, a cold will rarely require medical attention. Remember the following facts about colds:

- Because the common cold is a viral infection, there are no medicines that will cure it.

- Antibiotics are only effective for treating bacterial infections.

- Bacterial infections complicate only a small number of colds.

- Sinus congestion, colored nasal discharge, and headaches frequently accompany the common cold and do not always mean a serious infection.

- Symptoms start quickly. They worsen during the first 3 to 5 days and then slowly improve.

- A cold will usually go away naturally in 7 to 14 days, regardless of what you do.

- Some loss of appetite or difficulty sleeping is normal with colds, especially for children.

HYPERVENTILATION

Hyperventilation means breathing faster and more deeply than normal. Breathing too quickly causes the carbon dioxide levels in the blood to fall quickly. Hyperventilation is usually caused by anxiety, but injury or illness can also be the cause.

The person suffering from hyperventilation feels there is not enough air getting into the lungs and may complain of light-headedness. Feeling the need for more air, he or she breathes faster and makes the symptoms worse.

These symptoms may accompany hyperventilation:

• Rapid breathing

• Difficulty getting a deep, satisfying breath

• Light-headedness

• Numbness or tingling in the hands and feet and around the mouth

• Muscle twitching

• Fainting

Hyperventilation symptoms usually occur because too much carbon dioxide is given off during rapid breathing. Slowing breathing will restore the normal balance in the blood, and the symptoms should disappear.

SELF-CARE STEPS FOR HYPERVENTILATION

• Try to breathe more slowly and calmly. The anxiety that can cause hyperventilation can bring on greater anxiety, leading to a cycle that needs to be broken.

• If you are unable to calm down and slow your breathing, call the advice nurse.

• If you are prone to hyperventilation, learning deep-breathing exercises, such as those taught in yoga, may also be helpful. Because hyperventilation is caused by breathing too deeply and rapidly, it is recommended that you simply close your mouth and slow down the breathing rate. Hold your breath and silently count "one-one-thousand, two-one-thousand, three-one-thousand." Then take a shallow breath (mouth still closed) and repeat this. Within several moments, the symptoms should begin to disappear.

DECISION GUIDE FOR HYPERVENTILATION

SYMPTOMS/SIGNS	ACTION
First episode of hyperventilation	☎
Person has diabetes	☎
Hyperventilation following injury	☎
Hyperventilation with muscle twitching or tingling numbness in hands, feet, or around the mouth	☎
Hyperventilation with or without light-headedness	▭

 Call the advice nurse   Use self-care

For more about the symbols, see p. 3.

I have always prided myself on not drinking alcohol, but I drank about 20 cups of coffee and smoked two packs of cigarettes a day. One day I was sitting at work and my heart started to pound and then skip a beat. I thought I was having a heart attack. When I got to the emergency room, they did an EKG, which was normal. Then the medical provider asked about coffee and cigarettes, and said those were probably the cause. I stopped smoking immediately and cut way back on drinking coffee and I've never had another "heart attack" again.

Greg

PALPITATIONS

How many love songs speak of hearts skipping a beat? What sounds romantic can feel frightening, however.

Heart palpitations, the feeling that the heart has skipped a beat, usually are not dangerous and, in fact, everyone has them from time to time. However, a rapid heart rate or persistent palpitations should be discussed with your medical provider.

When the heart beats normally, the two smaller chambers contract together and then the two larger chambers contract together. This produces the familiar two-thump heartbeat sound. Heart palpitations, known in medical terms as arrhythmias, occur when the beating heart gets out of step. **Arrhythmias** vary from the feeling that the heart has skipped a beat to feeling that the heart is racing or fluttering.

Many arrhythmias are caused by common culprits: caffeine, nicotine, alcohol, stress, and worry. Relieving or ridding yourself of any or all of these can cut down on episodes of palpitations.

Keep in mind that serious heart conditions usually are marked by other symptoms too. If you are worried about irregular heartbeats or are having other symptoms with palpitations, such as pain, dizziness or feeling faint, call the advice nurse.

SELF-CARE STEPS FOR PALPITATIONS

- Stop smoking.
- Avoid caffeine and alcohol.
- When you exercise, be sure to warm up gradually, and allow yourself a cooldown period. This can help your heart return to its normal rate gradually.
- Practice stress- or anxiety-reducing techniques such as meditation, biofeedback, or yoga.

DECISION GUIDE FOR PALPITATIONS

SYMPTOMS/SIGNS	ACTION
Persistent heart palpitations or a rapid heart rate	
Palpitations and shortness of breath	
Palpitations and chest pain; dizziness or feeling faint; or sweating	

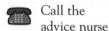 Call the advice nurse

For more about the symbols, see p. 3.

WHEEZING

If you hear a whistling sound that feels as if it's coming from your chest when you breathe, you could be wheezing.

Wheezing is caused by narrowing airways in the lungs. It's a sign that there is difficulty breathing. Wheezing can be caused by asthma (p. 241), bronchitis, smoking, allergies, pneumonia, sensitivities to chemicals or pollution, emphysema, lung cancer, heart failure, or even an inhaled object that is trapped in the airways.

The conditions that cause most cases of wheezing require medical attention. If you are under a medical provider's care for asthma, for example—and have developed an action plan with him or her—you don't have to run to the provider's office when you start to wheeze. Just follow your medical provider's recommendations. If you do not have asthma and develop wheezing, call the advice nurse.

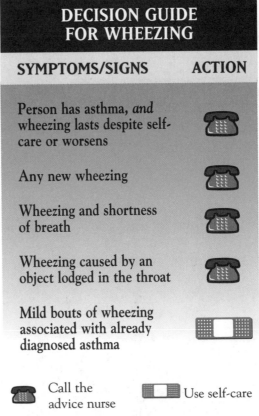

DECISION GUIDE FOR WHEEZING

SYMPTOMS/SIGNS	ACTION
Person has asthma, *and* wheezing lasts despite self-care or worsens	☎
Any new wheezing	☎
Wheezing and shortness of breath	☎
Wheezing caused by an object lodged in the throat	☎
Mild bouts of wheezing associated with already diagnosed asthma	🩹

☎ Call the advice nurse　　🩹 Use self-care

For more about the symbols, see p. 3.

SELF-CARE STEPS FOR WHEEZING

If you have been diagnosed as having asthma, follow the care plan given to you by your medical provider when you have a bout of wheezing. If you have not been diagnosed as having asthma, call the advice nurse.

MUSCLE AND JOINT PROBLEMS

Your muscular and skeletal systems have remarkable jobs. From everyday tasks like typing to dramatic athletic feats like windsurfing and gymnastics, your muscles and bones perform day after day and year after year. Although you may complain about the aches and pains that come with aging, you are lucky to have a musculoskeletal system that signals when you have pushed too hard. This section describes common problems of your muscles and joints and suggests ways to take care of nonurgent conditions at home.

Your medical provider can offer advice and treatment for most muscle and joint problems. If your condition is very hard to handle, your medical provider may involve other professionals who specialize in these problems.

Use the Decision Guides to see if your symptoms clearly need emergency medical services, require a call to the advice nurse, or can be treated using self-care. It is important to consider your own medical history and your current health when deciding what kind of care is right for you. If you have any conditions that do not seem to be healing normally, if the Self-Care Steps provided do not seem to help, or if you are uncertain about your symptoms, call the advice nurse. The advice nurse will evaluate your symptoms and recommend the next best steps for you to take.

ACHES AND PAINS IN MUSCLES AND JOINTS

Whether it's your shoulder, ankle, or some joint in between, pain in or around joints has similar causes and treatments throughout the body. Of course, a broken bone will cause pain and limit movement, but more often joint pain and limited mobility are caused by an injury to muscles, ligaments, or connective tissue. Knowing what happened before the pain started gives you an important clue to the problem. The following are common causes of muscle and joint pain.

Accidents

A fall, bump, blow, or sudden twist can cause bruising of soft tissues; bone fractures; joint dislocations; or torn muscles, tendons, or ligaments.

Repetitive Motions or Prolonged Overuse

All good things require moderation—including work and play. Too much of any activity—such as pitching too many games of softball, or working long hours typing at a computer—can cause inflammation and pain to the joint and surrounding tissues.

Overdoing It

If you've been indoors and inactive for months, a 25-mile bike ride or a day digging in the garden is apt to cause some muscle soreness. Injuries from overdoing it occur most often when people do strenuous activities without slowly building the strength and endurance needed. In addition, older people may be likely to injure themselves.

Muscle Imbalance

When muscles on one side of the body are much stronger than those on the other side (for example, biceps that are stronger than triceps), they put added stress on weaker muscles, often causing injury. For example, a weight lifter who overdevelops the chest and arm muscles, but neglects the muscles that support the upper back and shoulder blades, may wind up with a back or neck injury. The reason: the chest muscles overpower the back, causing constant tightness and muscle or joint pain.

SPECIAL CONCERNS FOR CHILDREN

Muscle and joint pains in children are treated much the same as they are in adults. Children and teenagers, however, should be given acetaminophen (Tylenol, Tempra, or a generic), never aspirin, to relieve pain. If the child can't move the joint, or pain increases with movement, call the advice nurse.

Until a child reaches maturity, the long bones in the body (arms and legs) have growth plates, called *epiphyses*. The epiphysis allows the bone to grow or lengthen. A fracture or dislocation can damage the epiphysis. This may slow or stop a bone's growth or make the bone grow crooked. Although it is common sense that any suspected broken bone should be evaluated by a medical provider, this is very important if the child complains of pain around a joint. A fracture to the epiphysis can occur without trauma, often through overuse (pitching too many fast balls or lifting heavy weights).

Broken bones and other injuries aside, it is common for children having growth spurts to have vague aches and pains for no apparent reason.

SELF-CARE STEPS FOR ACHES AND PAINS IN MUSCLES AND JOINTS

With a few exceptions, the **RICE** (Rest, Ice, Compress, Elevate) method explained below will reduce pain and help speed recovery of joint and muscle injuries.

Rest. For most injuries, rest the area until the pain stops. For simple sore muscles, however, gentle stretching will reduce stiffness more quickly. Hold the stretch for 30 to 60 seconds, then rest and repeat 5 to 10 times. Do this several times a day.

Ice. Ice is the most effective treatment for reducing inflammation, pain, and swelling of injured muscles, joints, and connective tissues—such as tendons, ligaments, and bursas. The cold helps keep blood and fluid from building up in the injured area, reducing pain and swelling. Apply ice as soon as possible after injury, even if you are going straight to the medical provider. To speed recovery and ease pain, raise the injured area and apply ice for 20 minutes (10 to 15 minutes in children) every 2 to 3 hours while awake. For best results, use crushed ice in a moist towel as an ice pack. You can also use a package of frozen vegetables such as corn, peas, or lima beans as a cold pack. Use an elastic bandage to hold the pack in place.

Compress. Between icings, wrap the injured area with an elastic (Ace type) bandage to help control swelling and provide support. Begin wrapping at the farthest point away from the body and wrap toward the heart. For example, to wrap an ankle you would begin at the toes and wrap to the mid-calf. Don't sleep with the wrap on, unless told to do so by a medical provider. And **don't wrap too tightly!** If the wrap begins to cause pain or numbness, or if toes are cool or white, remove the elastic bandage and wrap it more loosely.

Elevate. Raising the injured area above your heart will allow gravity to help reduce swelling by draining excess fluid. At night, place a pillow under the area to support and raise it.

In addition to RICE, there are several other things you can do to promote healing and relieve the pain of most muscle and joint injuries. These are the basics to remember, but check the topic on the following pages that addresses the joint where you are having pain.

If you need to, take anti-inflammatory drugs. Acetaminophen, aspirin, and ibuprofen often effectively treat muscle and joint injuries. Acetaminophen doesn't reduce inflammation. However, aspirin and other anti-inflammatories which can reduce inflammation are often more irritating to the stomach and bowel so that acetaminophen is better for patients with ulcers or other gastrointestinal problems. Also, aspirin should never be given to children or adolescents. When using aspirin, choose buffered aspirin or enteric-coated aspirin. All aspirin and other anti-inflammatory drugs should be taken with food. If these medications cause minor gastrointestinal upset after 7 to 10 days of use, call the advice nurse.

Slowly strengthen the injured area. Slow strengthening of the injured area after it has healed is advisable for keeping most injuries from occurring again. Your medical provider can recommend specific exercises, including range-of-motion exercises, muscle stretches, and specific weight training.

Heat before, ice after. Once the swelling has subsided—often it takes weeks—and you are working to strengthen the recovering area, you may apply heat before exercise to prepare the muscles, joint, and connective tissues for the workout. Apply ice soon after your workout to prevent inflammation and swelling.

I sprained my knee skiing last winter and had to use crutches. I was the most popular kid at school the day I showed up with those crutches. Everyone wanted to try them out. While my friends took turns on the crutches, I limped around on my sore knee. That night it started to swell up again pretty bad. I had to go back to the medical provider and have the water drained from the knee. That really hurt. So, I'd tell other kids with sprained knees not to let anyone else use your crutches. It's important not to put weight on a sprained knee.

Anna, age 9

I've fallen and hurt myself a number of times recently. I'm 76 and, at my age, I don't heal up as fast as I once did. After I sprained my wrist last spring, the doctor suggested I start exercising to build up my strength. Now I go for a walk every morning. At night while I'm watching TV, I use a resistance band—it's like a big rubber band—on my arms and legs. I really think it's helped. I don't feel quite so fragile anymore.

Latisha

DEFINITIONS OF COMMON MUSCLE AND JOINT PROBLEMS

Arthritis Inflammation, pain, swelling, stiffness and redness, or damage in joints. Arthritis may involve one joint or many joints, and has a number of causes.

Bruise Bleeding and damage to tissue underneath the skin, from a blow or fall. *Treatment:* apply ice right after injury.

Bursitis Swelling and inflammation of a bursa, causing pain and, occasionally, loss of motion. Bursas are fluid-filled sacs that lubricate and cushion joints. Bursitis can be caused by pressure (leaning on elbow), friction from overuse, or an injury. *Treatment:* RICE method (p. 73); see your medical provider if symptoms persist longer than 7 days.

Dislocation Separation of the bones in a joint, usually with tearing of the ligaments and capsule that support it. Dislocations can often accompany fractures. Deformity is usually visible, and movement is restricted. *Treatment:* leave the joint alone—*do not try to put it back!* However, try to support the limb in a comfortable position if possible. Apply ice and call the advice nurse.

Fracture A break in a bone, most often caused by a blow or fall. This may range in seriousness from a hairline fracture to a compound fracture (bones protrude through skin). Symptoms may include point tenderness over a bone, shooting pain, visible deformity, increased pain with movement, and, in severe cases, bone protruding through the skin. *Treatment:* if fracture is suspected, call the advice nurse; if spinal injury is suspected or the patient cannot walk, call 911.

Do not move the person. Until help arrives, apply ice to the area. If there is bleeding, apply pressure to stop the bleeding.

Ganglion A soft, fluid-filled cyst on the sheath of a tendon that may range from marble to golf-ball size. It is commonly found in the wrist, fingers, and foot; however, it may occur anywhere. Treatment is needed only if a ganglion is painful. Ganglions often disappear on their own.

Gout A disease that causes pain, swelling, redness, and extreme tenderness of a joint. An acute attack usually affects a single joint, most commonly in the big toe. Other joints such as those of the foot, ankle, knee, or wrist can also be affected. Pain worsens within the first 24 to 36 hours and may be so severe that the touch of a bedsheet is too much. Gout can be treated with prescription drugs.

Muscle cramp/spasm An involuntary shortening of a muscle, creating a painful spasm. Cramps can be caused by overuse, too much sweating, lactic acid buildup during or after exercise, or poor circulation (nighttime leg cramps). *Treatment:* stretch the muscle very slowly, apply ice, and drink plenty of fluids.

Muscle soreness/stiffness Usually results from overuse and is caused by microscopic muscle damage or lactic acid building up in the muscles. *Treatment:* drink plenty of water and move as much as is comfortable (such as walking or stretching). Stretch before and after exercise. Heat and massage can also be helpful.

DEFINITIONS OF COMMON MUSCLE AND JOINT PROBLEMS

Repetitive motion injuries These injuries can affect any tendon or muscle in the body. (Severe, long episodes may cause joint damage.) They are usually caused by too much of a particular motion—throwing, squeezing, lifting, pushing, or pulling. The injury may be a combination of tendinitis, bursitis, or trauma to specific tissues. *Treatment:* alternately apply cold and heat, take anti-inflammatory medications, engage in physical therapy and exercise. Sit, stand, or move in ways that avoid stress on affected joints and tendons.

Rotator cuff injuries The term "rotator cuff injuries" is often used as a catch-all to describe more than one problem, including tiny tears of the tendons supporting the shoulder (the rotator cuff) and impingement syndrome (compressing the tendons between bones, resulting in painful inflammation). The cause, result, and treatment, however, are similar. Repetitive overhead motions, such as throwing a softball, painting a ceiling, or swimming, often cause rotator cuff injuries. Symptoms include shoulder pain at night and pain when raising or lowering the arm between waist and shoulder height. If impingement occurs, pain may be worst when the arm is raised with the palm turned down—as when emptying a soda pop can. Tingling or numbness in the arm or fingers may also be felt.

Sprain Stretching or tearing a ligament beyond the normal range of motion. Ligaments connect bone to bone. Sprains may occur at any joint, but are most common in ankles, knees, wrists, and fingers. Symptoms include swelling, pain, and bruising. *Treatment:* RICE method (p. 73) for at least 72 hours, or until swelling begins to decrease.

Strain Stretching or tearing a muscle or tendon past its normal range of motion. Strains most often occur in the middle of the muscle. Symptoms include pain, swelling, muscle spasm, and limited movement. *Treatment:* ice, massage, and gently stretch the muscle three to five times a day.

Tendinitis Painful inflammation of the tendon. It is usually caused by overuse or an injury. Symptoms may include pain, tenderness, minor swelling, and sometimes limited motion. *Treatment:* RICE method (p. 73) and anti-inflammatory drugs.

ACUTE BACK PAIN

Also see Low Back Pain, p. 251.

Backaches are one of the most common reasons for a visit to a medical provider. Studies show that four out of every five people in the United States will suffer a bout of severe back pain at some time in their lives. Back pain is rarely the result of one incident. Rather, most back problems result from a lifetime of stress or strain to the back a little at a time.

Poor posture, improper lifting habits, prolonged standing, a stressful job, or declining physical fitness can all add up to a bad back. One episode of disabling back pain may simply be a cue that you have put more stress on your back than it can handle.

Weakened or strained muscles, over time, are responsible for most back pain. Only about 10 percent of back complaints are linked to pressure on the nerves in your back—this type of pain tends to spread more into your buttocks or legs.

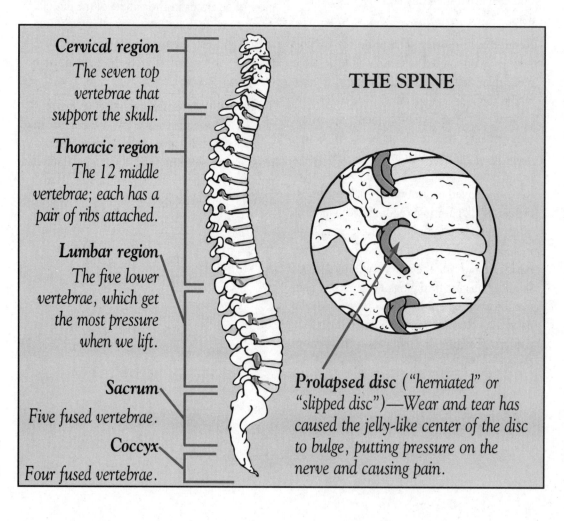

THE SPINE

Cervical region — *The seven top vertebrae that support the skull.*

Thoracic region — *The 12 middle vertebrae; each has a pair of ribs attached.*

Lumbar region — *The five lower vertebrae, which get the most pressure when we lift.*

Sacrum — *Five fused vertebrae.*

Coccyx — *Four fused vertebrae.*

Prolapsed disc *("herniated" or "slipped disc")—Wear and tear has caused the jelly-like center of the disc to bulge, putting pressure on the nerve and causing pain.*

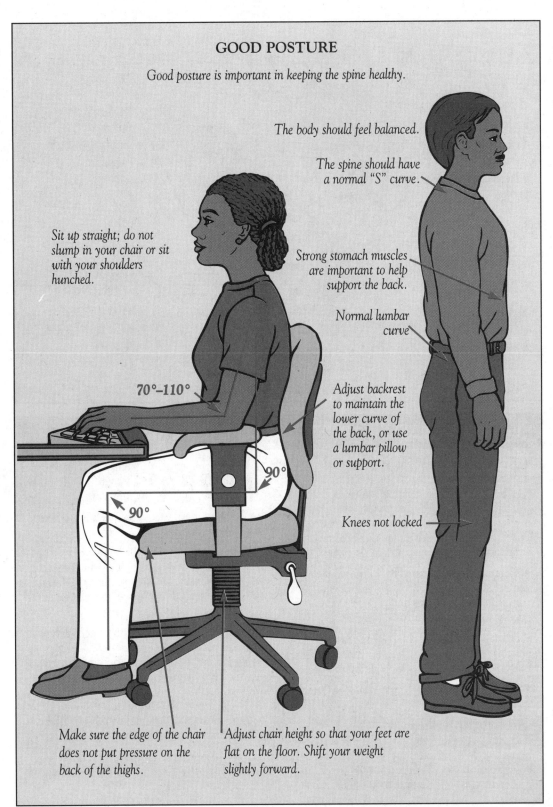

GOOD POSTURE

Good posture is important in keeping the spine healthy.

The body should feel balanced.

The spine should have a normal "S" curve.

Sit up straight; do not slump in your chair or sit with your shoulders hunched.

Strong stomach muscles are important to help support the back.

Normal lumbar curve

70°–110°

Adjust backrest to maintain the lower curve of the back, or use a lumbar pillow or support.

90°

90°

Knees not locked

Make sure the edge of the chair does not put pressure on the back of the thighs.

Adjust chair height so that your feet are flat on the floor. Shift your weight slightly forward.

I have found that for many cases of frequent backache a good swimming or water aerobics routine three times a week can help. Remember to start slowly and don't expect too much too soon. It can take 4 to 6 weeks to improve conditioning and reduce back pain.

Rehabilitation Specialist

Getting back to work or your usual daily activity within a few days is an important part of healing. You can start with either "light" duties or limited activities. It probably will be a little uncomfortable, but limited activity prevents your back from becoming weak and stiff.

Rob, back pain patient

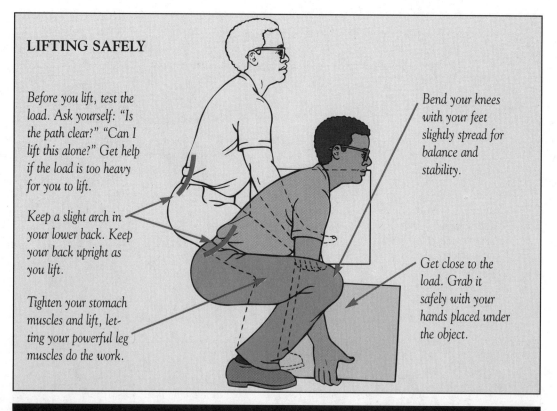

LIFTING SAFELY

Before you lift, test the load. Ask yourself: "Is the path clear?" "Can I lift this alone?" Get help if the load is too heavy for you to lift.

Keep a slight arch in your lower back. Keep your back upright as you lift.

Tighten your stomach muscles and lift, letting your powerful leg muscles do the work.

Bend your knees with your feet slightly spread for balance and stability.

Get close to the load. Grab it safely with your hands placed under the object.

SELF-CARE STEPS FOR BACK PAIN

• The most important health care treatment is *the care that you give to yourself.* If you fail to take an active role in treating your back, a bad cycle can develop. To protect yourself from pain, you may tend to become less active. But if you are inactive, your muscles become weaker and more susceptible to strains or sprains.

• Carefully add activities back into your day as you begin to recover from the worst of your back pain. Gradual stretches and regular walking are good ways to get back into action.

• Learn safe back exercises like modified sit-ups and low back stretches, and do them regularly (see Exercises to Keep Your Back Fit, p.252).

• Take time to relax. Tension will only make your back feel worse.

Quick Relief Method

For acute back pain, you can try these steps for 2 hours, but do not exceed the recommended daily dosages for any of the medications listed. Also, this method is suitable only for adults.

1. Take 2 ibuprofen (Advil) OR 1 naproxen (Aleve) OR 2 extra-strength aspirin. (Do not take on an empty stomach.)

2. In addition, take 2 extra-strength acetaminophen (Tylenol).

3. Apply a heating pad or hot moist towel compress to your lower back for 20 minutes, then switch to an ice compress or massage for the next 20 minutes. Continue to alternate heat and ice for the next 2 hours.

4. Lie on your back on a firm surface such as a carpeted floor with feet on a chair or couch. Your legs should be bent at 90° at the hips and knees as if you were sitting in a chair. Roll to one side with your legs still bent when you need to apply ice. The heating pad or warm towel should be as flat as possible. Slide it under your back and bottom while your legs are on the chair.

5. Every 15 minutes, draw one knee up to your chest and hold it there for 15 seconds. Repeat with the other knee.

DECISION GUIDE FOR ACUTE BACK PAIN

SYMPTOMS/SIGNS	ACTION
Weakness or numbness of a lower limb	
Paralysis, confusion, or shock	
Back pain and temperature of a level you believe to be a fever	
Back pain and nausea, vomiting, or diarrhea	
Back pain and painful or frequent urination, menstrual bleeding, or stomachache	
Pain traveling down leg or arm	
Pain is worse rather than better after 3 days	
Pain from tension, "posture" pain, soreness from exercise	
"Usual" back or neck soreness	

Note: Worker's Compensation regulations require that any injury occurring at work be reported.

 Call the advice nurse    Use self-care

For more about the symbols, see p. 3.

ACUTE NECK PAIN

The neck, or cervical spine, is the most flexible part of the spine, providing the greatest range of motion. But, because it is not well protected by muscles, it's also easy to injure. Daily stress, poor posture, trauma, and wear and tear from overuse and aging are the most common sources of neck pain.

Severe trauma to the neck may cause a fracture, creating risk for permanent paralysis. For possible neck or other spinal injuries from a severe blow or other trauma, **keep the injured person still**. *Do not move the person* without a back board or cervical collar *and* the help and direction of a trained paramedic or other medical professional.

A Bad Night's Rest

How you sleep at night can affect your neck during the day. A soft mattress, pillows that force your neck into awkward angles, and uncomfortable sleeping positions may be to blame if you awaken with a "crick in the neck." But the tossing and turning of a bad night's rest may be less to blame than awakening suddenly from a good sound sleep. A sudden jerk of the neck upon awakening can leave neck muscles tight and sore.

Body Mechanics

Poor sitting and standing posture—slumped shoulders, a "drooping" head, slouching or "rounding" of the lower back—can cause neck pain. But bad body mechanics are more than poor posture. Repeated tasks, such as holding the phone with your shoulder or always carrying a

MUSCLES OF THE BACK OF THE HEAD AND NECK

Splenius capitis muscle

Sternocleido-mastoid muscle

Levator scapulae muscle

Trapezius muscle

Deltoid muscle

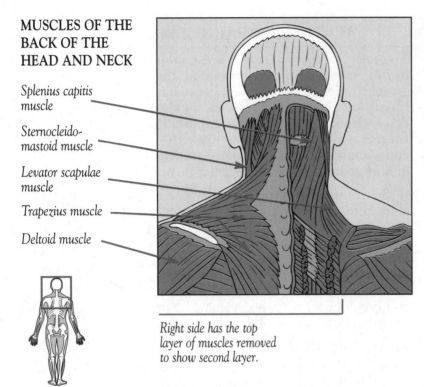

Right side has the top layer of muscles removed to show second layer.

heavy briefcase or shoulder bag on the same side of the body, can also cause muscle stiffness or imbalance. Workstations, too, may force your body into less than the best positions.

Stress

The neck and upper back muscles are often among the first to become tense when a person is under emotional stress. Whenever these muscles remain tight for a long time, they may ache, become sore, and even cause headaches.

Neck Sprains and Strains

The term "whiplash" is often used to refer to neck sprains and strains that result when the neck is forced suddenly forward, backward, or both, such as from a rear-end car collision. But contact sports, a fall, or a sudden twist can cause similar injuries. Pain from neck sprains and strains may spread into the shoulders, upper back, and arms, and sometimes as far as the legs. Pain may remain for 6 weeks or longer, but generally improves with normal use.

Neck pain can often be relieved or prevented with a few adjustments to the way we work and rest. Even if the pain is caused by an injury or a worsening condition, self-care can often provide relief.

SELF-CARE STEPS FOR NECK PAIN

• If you wake up often with a sore neck, consider sleeping in a different position, getting a new mattress and box spring, or putting a $^3/_4$-inch plywood board between the mattress and box spring for extra support.

• If you sleep on your side, choose a pillow that allows your head to rest comfortably centered between your shoulders. If you sleep on your back, choose a pillow that doesn't push your chin toward your chest. A special cervical-support pillow or a rolled towel pinned around your neck can also help you position your spine correctly. Avoid sleeping on your stomach.

• Learn to relax. If daily stress makes your neck and upper back muscles tense, take time out to relax.

• If your neck or upper back muscles feel tight and sore, especially from stress, ask a friend to massage the area for a few minutes.

• The spine naturally curves in at the neck, out at the upper back, and in again at the lower back. An easy way to improve your posture is to focus on keeping the natural curve at the lower back. When you do this, the rest of the spine tends to pull into place, straightening your shoulders and head as well. Be sure, however, that your effort to "straighten up" doesn't cause your neck or abdomen to "stick out."

• Use a telephone headset if you spend a lot of time on the phone. Keep your briefcase or purse as light as possible and routinely switch carrying sides. When either is packed full, try to distribute the weight evenly on each side of your body by splitting the contents into two bags or briefcases. Hold reading materials and place computer screens at eye level; don't bend over your work. Type with your elbows, hips, and knees at 90-degree angles, and make sure you have good low-back support.

• Ice a sore neck 10 to 15 minutes several times a day to relieve pain and inflammation. A bag of frozen peas or corn makes a great cold pack for the neck. Switching between heat and ice may also work.

• A warm shower or heating pad on top of a moist warm towel can help loosen sore, tight muscles. Apply heat for 20 minutes, three times a day starting no sooner than 2 days after injury. But ice may be better for relieving pain even long after an injury, especially if muscle spasms are present. Follow with gentle stretching.

• Take anti-inflammatory drugs for pain. If pain persists, your medical provider may prescribe other drugs.

• Take a load off. When pain is at its worst, rest. Lie flat on your back for an hour or so with a fairly flat pillow supporting your head. Extended bed rest, however, can make neck problems worse by allowing muscles to weaken from lack of use.

• Stretch! Working on the problem is especially important for the neck. Reduce stiffness and soreness by gaining motion and strength with the stretches shown below.

NECK STRETCHES

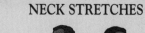

Turn right, hold two counts.
Turn left, hold two counts.

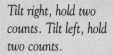

Tilt right, hold two counts. Tilt left, hold two counts.

Chin down, hold two counts. Return to starting position.

• After exercise, cool down in a healthy posture. One of the best—and easiest—times to assume a healthy posture is when your muscles and joints are loose after exercise.

I work a lot on a computer. Long hours at the computer often left me with a headache and pain in the neck. When our office moved last month, I got a new adjustable computer station and chair. A consultant who was setting up my workstation suggested I raise the computer screen higher so it would be at my eye level. I rarely get neck pain and headaches at work anymore. What a difference!

Mark

DECISION GUIDE FOR ACUTE NECK PAIN

SYMPTOMS/SIGNS	ACTION
Pain after a sudden twist or blow, or the head being thrown forward or backward	☎
Burning, shooting pain; shoulder weakness; or loss of feeling in shoulder after a trauma that caused neck and shoulder to twist in opposite directions at the same time	☎
Stiff, sore neck with fever and headache	☎
Any severe trauma or blow to the head or neck	☎
Neck pain and temperature of a level you believe to be a fever	☎
Pain is the same or worse after 7 to 10 days of self-care	☎
Stiff, sore neck upon awakening	▭
Muscle tension and pain, especially while working or under stress	▭

☎ Call the advice nurse   ▭ Use self-care

For more about the symbols, see p. 3.

ANKLE PAIN

The ankle is one of the most commonly injured joints of the body. Strains and sprains reign in ankle injuries, but tendinitis, bursitis, and fractures also happen.

The ankle is the juncture of three bones: the tibia and fibula of the lower leg and the talus of the foot (the ankle bone). Held together by ligaments and tendons, the ankle allows the foot a wide range of motion. Because of the ankle's crucial role in walking and standing, ankle injuries should be taken seriously and treated properly.

Strains, Sprains, and Fractures

Twisting your ankle may cause stretching or tearing of the ligaments and tendons (for definitions of strains, sprains, and fractures, see p. 74). This most often occurs on the outside of the ankle. Mild strains or sprains may cause mild to moderate pain and little or no swelling. The ankle can support weight, but usually a limp is apparent. Moderate sprains hurt more when you move, and swelling and tenderness increase. Walking is hard and often crutches are needed for a few days.

A sprain is generally severe when the ligament and tendons are stretched or completely torn (ruptured). Severe sprains are accompanied by severe pain, swelling and tenderness, limited motion, bruising, and inability to walk or bear weight on the ankle. Moderate and severe sprains also may cause bruising in the foot and toes, and up the side of the leg.

With a strain, sprain, or fracture, you may hear or feel a snap, pop, or crack at the time of injury. The RICE method (p. 73) is the right first step for all three. Unless the ankle is obviously deformed, very painful, or unable to bear any weight, a sprained ankle can be treated safely at home for the first 24 hours using the RICE method and avoiding weight on the sprain. With a mild or moderate sprain, swelling should stop within 24 hours and the ankle should begin to improve (although not be healed) within 48 hours. If it doesn't, call the advice nurse.

Achilles Tendinitis and Bursitis

Tendinitis and bursitis at the back of the ankle are very much alike. The treatment,

causes, and symptoms of the two are similar. The Achilles tendon is a large strong band that attaches the calf muscle to the heel. Underneath the Achilles tendon are bursas that may also become inflamed.

Symptoms of **Achilles tendinitis** include pain in the calf and ankle, which is worse when you wake up in the morning and generally better as the ankle is "warmed up" with use. Occasionally, with an improper warm-up or sudden move-

---

SELF-CARE STEPS FOR ANKLE PAIN

As with other joint injuries, the first step in treatment for most ankle injuries—including sprains, strains, and Achilles tendinitis and bursitis—is the RICE method and anti-inflammatory drugs (p. 73). But there are some other things you can do as well to treat sprains and other injuries:

Sprains

• Stay off the ankle as much as possible until the swelling stops, usually about 24 to 48 hours.

• Use crutches if bearing weight is painful.

• If swelling lasts longer than 3 days, alternately soak the ankle in cold water (45° to 60° F) for 1 minute and then in warm water (100° to 105° F) for 2 or 3 minutes. Do this for 15 to 20 minutes total, and stop if swelling increases. Print the alphabet in the air with your big toe to help increase range of motion.

RANGE OF MOTION EXERCISE

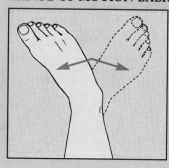

Keeping your leg still, bend your ankle back and forth from left to right ten times. Repeat this exercise several times a day.

• As the swelling and pain decrease, begin gentle stretching and strengthening exercises to regain range of motion.

Other injuries

Strains Follow the RICE method (p. 73) and avoid bearing weight on the ankle for 24 to 48 hours. If pain and swelling are worse after 24 hours, call the advice nurse. If you still can't bear weight on the ankle after 48 hours, see your medical provider. As the swelling and pain decrease, begin gentle stretching and strengthening exercises to regain range of motion (see illustration on this page).

Tendinitis and bursitis Decrease activity for 1 to 2 weeks or until fairly pain free. Apply heat to the area before stretching, and ice when you have finished. If there is no improvement in 10 to 14 days, call the advice nurse.

Gout Call the advice nurse if you think you might have gout.

Swelling If your ankles swell after you've been sitting or standing for a long time, raise your legs. Increase activity and movement to prevent swelling. If swelling continues longer than 3 days or if there is pain without injury, call the advice nurse.

OTTAWA ANKLE RULES

The following motions are known as the Ottawa Ankle rules. They can be used to look for a possible injury to a bone in your foot or ankle. Call the advice nurse if you notice a sharp pain as your fingers move over bony areas that is different from any tenderness you might feel in the softer muscle areas.

Sit in a chair with your knees bent at a 90 degree angle and your feet flat on the floor. Bend down and, with your index and middle fingers, apply light pressure over the following areas.

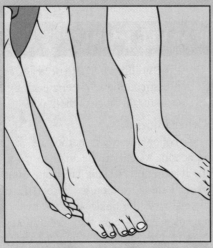

1. *Move fingers over the bone that runs along the outside of your foot from your little toe back toward your heel.*

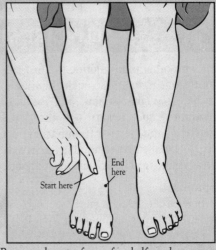

2. *Press on the top of your foot halfway between your toes and your ankle. Then, pressing gently, move your fingers toward the sole on the inside of your foot.*

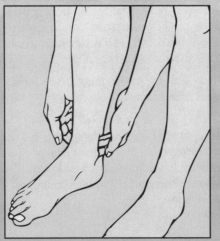

3. *Using both index fingers, press on the backside of your ankle bone on both sides.*

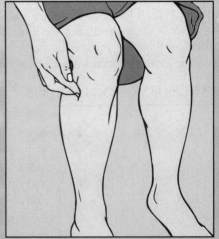

4. *Press on the bone on the outside of your leg just below your knee.*

DECISION GUIDE FOR ANKLE PAIN

SYMPTOMS/SIGNS	ACTION
Pain at back of ankle—begins slowly and may be worse when you wake up (Achilles tendinitis)	☎
No improvement of tendinitis symptoms after 10 to 14 days	☎
Unable to bear any weight at all	☎
Pain and swelling increasing 24 hours after injury	☎
Red/warm/swollen ankles; fever; feeling ill or having recently been ill with a sore throat or skin infection	☎
Chronic swelling in ankles, feet or lower legs; difficulty breathing	☎
Swelling in only one ankle or leg with pain, no injury	☎
Pain on inner side of ankle; ankle twisted inward when injury occurred	☎
Swelling, pain, and possible bruising from sudden twist or force	▭

☎ Call the advice nurse   ▭ Use self-care

For more about the symbols, see p. 3.

ment, the Achilles tendon can tear or even rupture. Any deformity in the calf should be seen by a a medical provider right away. **Bursitis** usually causes a soft, fluid-filled lump at the back of the ankle, along with pain similar to that of tendinitis.

Common causes of tendinitis and bursitis in the ankle include tight calf muscles, overuse, sudden stress from a quick movement, and repeated motion, such as running. Shoes are often the culprit. Switching from high heels or cowboy boots to flat shoes, or wearing shoes that fit poorly or provide inadequate support and cushioning can also inflame tendons and bursas in the ankle.

Gout

Sudden pain, swelling, redness, and extreme tenderness in a joint can be signs of an acute attack of gout. Most often gout begins in the big toe, but may move up the leg to other joints, including the ankle and knee. If you have these symptoms of gout (see definition, p. 74), call the advice nurse. Gout can be treated effectively.

Swelling without Injury

Sitting or standing for long periods without moving may cause the ankles and feet to swell. This type of swelling usually goes away overnight or lasts only a few days. Occasionally, swollen ankles can be a sign of something more serious. If your ankles remain swollen for more than 3 days or if just one leg is affected, call the advice nurse.

ELBOW PAIN

The elbow lets the hand turn from palm up to palm down, position itself to write, turn a screwdriver or doorknob…and the list goes on.

The elbow is the junction of three bones: the humerus in the upper arm and the ulna and radius in the lower arm. Tendons and muscles provide mobility and more support, and bursas within the joint cushion and lubricate the elbow's movement. The bony point at the back of the elbow is the end of the ulna, and two smaller bony points on either side are called *epicondyles*.

Pain in the elbow can occur from overuse, a fall or blow to the joint, or a force that causes the elbow to bend backward. Some common elbow injuries are discussed below.

Tendinitis

Elbow tendinitis is called by many names—tennis elbow, golfer's elbow, pitcher's elbow—but can be caused by any number of repeated motions. The action isn't as important as the repetition.

Tendinitis pain usually is concentrated at the inside or outside of the elbow and may spread up or down the arm, depending on which tendon is inflamed. Often the pain occurs only with certain movements, such as lifting objects in certain ways, rotating your hand, or clenching or squeezing something in your fist. Treatment is the same, no matter which tendon is involved (see Self-Care Steps below).

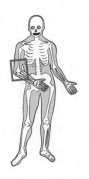

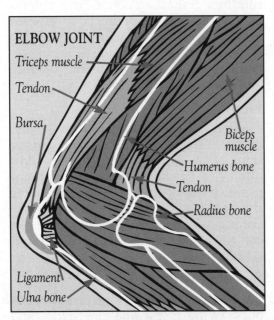

ELBOW JOINT

Triceps muscle

Tendon

Bursa

Biceps muscle

Humerus bone

Tendon

Radius bone

Ligament

Ulna bone

SELF-CARE STEPS FOR ELBOW PAIN

• Tendinitis, bursitis, and hyperextended elbow in adults can usually be treated effectively using the RICE method and anti-inflammatory drugs (p. 73) until the pain and swelling decrease.

• It is very important to rest from the activity that caused the pain in the first place. But this might not be possible if the injury is from a task that's a normal part of a job (for example, hammering for carpenters). If this is the case, call the advice nurse.

• Gentle stretching and strengthening exercises are also an important part of recovery and preventing future injury. Stretches, along with arm curls using light weights or squeezing a rubber ball in the palm of your hand, are examples of exercises you can do to regain strength and range of motion after the pain is better.

Bursitis

Inflammation of a bursa causes a soft, fluid-filled lump at the point of the elbow. Bursitis can be quite painful, especially at the tip of the elbow. With self-care, acute cases will usually heal within 7 to 10 days. Call the advice nurse if the bursa is red or hot, the elbow looks infected, or pain and swelling do not improve by this time.

Hyperextended Elbow

This occurs when the elbow is "bent backward" by force, such as from a fall or a backhand tennis swing that goes awry. The result is pain and swelling in the joint capsule and soft tissues at the front of the elbow. A splint or sling to support the elbow may be needed until the pain stops. With self-care (described on p. 86), recovery can be expected within 3 to 6 weeks.

DECISION GUIDE FOR ELBOW PAIN

SYMPTOMS/SIGNS	ACTION
Numbness or tingling in 4th and 5th fingers	☎
Loss of strength in hand or arm	☎
Elbow cannot be bent or straightened	☎
Joint or bursa is red, swollen, or hot; fever present (possible infection)	☎
Elbow deformity after fall	☎
Severe pain in upper arm (biceps) after sudden or violent motion	☎
Pain in elbow, limited to only certain movements of elbow and hand, especially after overuse	🩹
Pain, swelling, or soft lump on tip of elbow without fever, redness, or pain	🩹
Bruise from a fall or blow	🩹

☎ Call the advice nurse   🩹 Use self-care

For more about the symbols, see p. 3.

My husband and I had planned a wonderful rafting trip with friends. I don't normally work out at all, but I didn't think rowing a raft on a fairly fast-running river would be very strenuous. I was wrong. About 2 hours into the expedition, I could feel a "clicking" on the inner side of my right elbow. By the time we pulled out of the water, I could barely row. That night in our tent, a sharp pain began in my elbow. It hurt so bad, I could barely sleep. I iced down the elbow and took some aspirin. In the morning, the pain wasn't so bad, but another day of rowing was out of the question. A friend happened to have an elastic bandage; wrapping the elbow helped. After returning home, I called the medical provider's office. They said it was probably tendinitis and recommended some exercises and stretches to help strengthen the area and prevent future injury.

Joanne

FOOT PAIN

The main source of most foot pain involves improper foot function or bio-mechanics. Shoes rarely cause foot deformities, but may irritate them. A properly fitting shoe, with good arch support, cushioning, and a "toe box" that doesn't pinch and squeeze the toes or ball of the foot will prevent irritation to bony joints and the skin over them that can cause problems and pain.

Flat feet or high arches can contribute to painful problems in the feet, knees, and even hips. When the arch is too high or low, other structures in the foot and leg have to work longer and harder than intended. The added stress, weight, and poor motion can cause fatigue, pain, and inflammation. Arch supports (orthotics) and exercises to stretch and strengthen the arch and lower leg help relieve many problems related to weak arches. But for many people, having flat feet or high arches never causes a problem.

Heel Pain

Two closely related conditions—heel spurs and plantar fasciitis—are common sources of pain in the heel and arch of the foot. They involve the heel bone and the *plantar fascia*, a strong band of connective tissue at the bottom of the foot that runs from the heel to the base of the toes. Its job is to help maintain or hold the arch together and serve as a shock absorber during activity.

Overstretching of this band of tissue can result in strain and later inflammation where it's attached to the heel bone. **Plantar fasciitis** is marked by a dull ache in the arch or pain in the heel. The pain is worst when you wake or after resting. Walking may hurt at first, but once the plantar fascia is "warmed up," the pain may decrease.

Plantar fasciitis most often occurs when activity suddenly increases, or is due to shoes with poor support. Switching from high heels or cowboy boots to flat shoes or athletic shoes can irritate the fascia, causing pain. Gaining 10 to 20 pounds can have the same effect. Working out or standing and walking on hard surfaces, such as concrete, or wearing shoes that do not have good arch support can also lead to the problem.

Repeatedly overstretching the plantar fascia can cause heel spurs. A **heel spur** is bone growth on the heel bone where it connects to the plantar fascia. As the plantar fascia is pulled and stretched, it pulls the lining of the heel bone away from the main bone, causing a bony growth, or spur, to develop. The pain stems from the irritation of the plantar fascia pulling on the bone. The spur does not necessarily require removal to relieve heel pain.

Heel pain and plantar fasciitis often have similar symptoms and are sometimes considered together as **heel spur syndrome**. In some cases, however, heel spurs may cause a deep tenderness in the bottom of the heel when weight is placed on the foot. Self-care (see p. 91) and rest will sometimes relieve heel spurs and plantar fasciitis. If symptoms continue despite these measures or if pain is severe, call the advice nurse.

Stress Fractures

Sometimes it's not the connective tissues in the foot that give way or get inflamed, but the bones themselves. Stress fractures occur most often in the second metatarsal. The metatarsals are the long bones that connect to the toes.

High-impact activities such as running, basketball, or high-impact aerobics pose particular risk for stress fractures of the foot. Postmenopausal women with lower bone density, women with absent or infrequent periods, or anyone on long-term steroid or hormone therapy may be more likely to have stress fractures.

Stress fractures most often appear several weeks into a new or more intense training schedule or from landing wrong after jumping. At first, pain may be mild enough that it can be ignored. After time, however, the mild pain gives way to sudden, intense pain.

Treating stress fractures in the foot mostly involves time—usually at least 1 month—to allow the bone to heal. With the exception of fractures in the fifth metatarsal, a cast is usually not needed. A wooden shoe or postoperative shoe is usually worn to allow the fracture to heal. A stress fracture in the fifth metatarsal can be serious because it often resists healing. Fractures may need a cast, and crutches may have to be used for 6 weeks to several months. In some cases, surgery may be needed.

Corns

These yellowish calluslike growths develop on tops of the toes in spots where shoes rub. If the rubbing continues, corns can become red, inflamed, and painful. The best way to prevent corns is to wear shoes with a toe box—the area surrounding the toes and ball of the foot—large enough to comfortably fit your foot without rubbing.

I work in a department store, standing all day long on carpet-covered concrete. By the end of the day, my feet are swollen and ache. My back often hurts, too. I usually wear pumps with fairly low heels—about an inch high. But still, my feet are killing me at the end of each day. A friend suggested I find a pair of dress shoes with more cushion in the sole. I have to wear dress shoes, so comfortable athletic shoes are out. I finally found a pair that didn't pinch my toes and had a cushioned sole and only a small heel. The salesperson recommended adding arch-support inserts. With the new shoes and putting my feet up during breaks, I'm finally making it through the day without hurting!

Margaret

Bunions

A bunion is a swelling on the side of the foot that is usually a symptom that the foot isn't working properly, often because of a flat-foot condition. Instability and muscle imbalance cause the big toe to slant in toward the other toes. The joint where the big toe connects to the foot (the end of the first metatarsal) pokes out on the inner side of the foot. This is caused by poor alignment and is not a growth of bone. The bunion may also become inflamed and sore, especially if rubbed by a shoe. A similar problem, called a "tailor's bunion," may develop on the opposite side of the foot, where the little toe meets the fifth metatarsal.

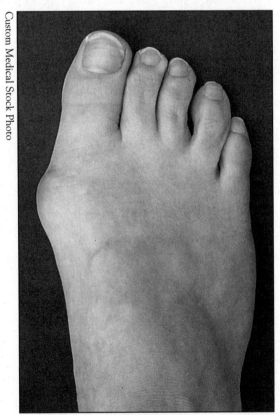

Custom Medical Stock Photo

A bunion on the inner side of the foot.

Hammertoe

Hammertoe is a deformity in which the toe buckles, causing the middle joint of the affected toe to poke above the other toes. The deformity may also cause the toe to become bent at the middle joint so that it turns in toward the toe next to it. Tight shoes can rub and put pressure on the raised portion of the hammertoe, often making a corn form. Hammertoes may cause no problems at all, or they can be a source of pain, especially if the person wears tight or ill-fitting shoes.

Plantar Warts

Plantar warts, like warts in other areas of the body, are caused by a virus. Weight bearing causes plantar warts to grow inward. The result is a painful lump on the bottom of the foot that feels like you are walking on a pebble. Children and teens are more likely than adults to get plantar warts. Plantar warts are often difficult to treat, but a slow approach is best (see Self-Care Steps, p. 91). If plantar warts interfere with walking, call the advice nurse.

SELF-CARE STEPS FOR FOOT PAIN

Good shoes can be important in preventing and relieving foot pain. Shoes should support the arch and cushion the heel, ball, and outside of the foot. They shouldn't pinch the foot or toes or be so loose that your feet slide around in them. A good heel height is generally between $1/2$ and $1^1/_2$ inches. For shoes that don't already offer enough arch support or cushioning, commercial arch-support and cushion inserts may be worth buying.

With the exception of plantar warts or trauma to the foot, checking the shoes you've been wearing is the first step in caring for foot pain. Anti-inflammatory drugs (aspirin, ibuprofen, or naproxen) will help relieve pain and inflammation. Other treatments for specific conditions are discussed below.

For heel spurs and plantar fasciitis
• Rest the foot, avoiding high-impact activities for 3 to 6 weeks. Switch to low-impact activities, such as walking, biking, or swimming. Walking is particularly good.

• Apply ice to the heel two to three times daily.

• Support the arches of your feet to protect them from further stretching and tearing. Place arch supports even in your slippers and put them on first thing when getting out of bed.

For stress fractures
• Call the advice nurse if pain continues or worsens after a week or two of nonimpact activity and anti-inflammatory drugs.

• Avoid high-impact activities. Switch to weight-bearing, low-impact or nonimpact activities, such as walking or low-impact aerobics. Weight bearing strengthens bones and prevents bone loss. Resume your regular workout or other activities slowly after pain gets better and the fracture heals.

For corns
• Soak feet in a solution of Epsom salts and water for 15 minutes. Dry carefully and apply a moisturizer. Rub the corn with a clean nail file or pumice stone, using a side-to-side motion. Repeat daily until the corn is gone.

• Use a nonmedicated corn pad to relieve pressure on the area.

For hammertoes
• Wear shoes with a toe box large enough to accommodate the hammertoe.

• Treat accompanying corns as described above.

For bunions
• Choose shoes with a larger toe box (squared or rounded toe).

• Put a piece of foam or cotton between the affected toes to see if it eases the pressure.

• Place padding around the bunion to relieve pressure and rubbing from shoes. Moleskin and bunion pads are available at most drugstores.

• Try using an arch support to stop the jamming of the long bone and the big toe.

• Call the advice nurse if pain lasts, interferes with walking, or is not relieved with self-care.

For plantar warts
• Soak foot for 10 minutes in a solution of 2 tablespoons mild household detergent (such as dish soap) and $1/2$ gallon warm water. Cut a piece of 40 percent salicylic-acid plaster (available at drugstores) the size of the wart and apply it to the wart. Cover with tape or a bandage. Remove the plaster in 2 days. Brush the wart with a toothbrush soaked in soap and water. Repeat this procedure for 2 weeks until the wart is gone.

• If warts remain despite self-care, or if they interfere with walking, call the advice nurse.

• Do not try to *cut* warts out!

DECISION GUIDE FOR FOOT PAIN

SYMPTOMS/SIGNS	ACTION
Unable to move foot or bear weight after a trauma, such as a blow or fall	
Pain in heel or arch, especially upon awakening; tender points on bottom of foot between heel and ball (see heel spurs or plantar fasciitis, p. 88)	
Corns, plantar warts, bunions, or hammertoes	
Pain, burning, tingling, or numbness in the toes, between the toes, and at the ball of the foot; swelling at the top of the foot; symptoms get worse with pressure	
Heel spurs or plantar fasciitis not relieved with self-care within 3 to 6 weeks	
Suspected stress fracture	
Foot pain from overuse or injury; can bear weight	

 Call the advice nurse    Use self-care

For more about the symbols, see p. 3.

HAND AND WRIST PAIN

Together, the wrist and hand are composed of 29 bones: 19 in the hand and fingers, 8 in the wrist, and 2 in the forearm. The wrist, hand, and fingers are capable of a great variety of movements. But the forearm muscles are actually responsible for most of the movement and strength of the hand and fingers.

Because the wrist and hand have little protection, they are perhaps more likely to fracture than other bones in the body. Falls and blows are common causes of wrist and hand injuries. But, as with other joints, overuse and repeated motions can take their toll on the hand and wrist, causing a variety of conditions, such as tendinitis and carpal tunnel syndrome. The injuries listed below are by no means the only conditions that can cause pain or limit the function of the hand and wrist, but they are some of the more common ones.

Fractures and Sprains

Fractures and sprains of the wrist, hand, and fingers can be hard to pinpoint without an X-ray. Unless deformity, a change in feeling, or lack of motion is noticeable, you may start with self-care. If pain or stiffness lasts more than 24 hours after injury, it should be seen. Children in obvious overnight discomfort should be seen right away.

When a wrist is fractured, the break often occurs at the end of the radius, one of the long bones of the forearm. These fractures require careful attention. Another fracture near the wrist—a navicular (a small wrist bone located at the base of the thumb) fracture—can cause long-term problems, is difficult to diagnose, and takes a long time to heal.

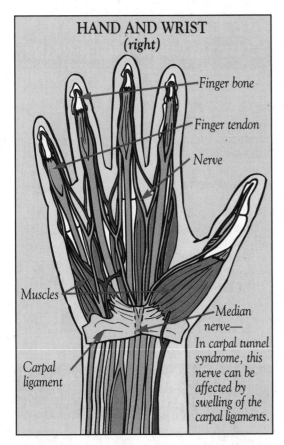

HAND AND WRIST
(right)

Finger bone

Finger tendon

Nerve

Muscles

Median nerve—

In carpal tunnel syndrome, this nerve can be affected by swelling of the carpal ligaments.

Carpal ligament

Because the bone is so small and almost all of its surface touches other bones, an improperly healed fracture can cause the navicular to rub and scrape in places it shouldn't. The result is pain and loss of range of motion in the wrist.

If you fall on your outstretched hand, bending your wrist back, and the pain does not get better within a day, call the advice nurse.

Tendinitis

It is common for tendons in the wrist, hand, and fingers to become irritated from overuse or repeated motions, causing pain, swelling, and stiffness.

Tendinitis pain in the wrist may spread down to the fingers or up to the elbow. Tendinitis in the fingers may affect one or more fingers at the same time. Pain may be constant or felt only with certain movements. The area around the tendon may be tender. You may even notice a cracking sound or odd feeling when you bend or flex the finger or wrist.

Carpal Tunnel Syndrome (CTS)

A condition caused by pressure on a large nerve in the wrist as it passes through a "tunnel" formed by tendons, CTS causes pain that may spread into the hand and forearm. There may be numbness and tingling in the fingers, especially your thumb, index, and middle finger, and loss of strength in the hand. You may find yourself dropping things often or even being awakened at night by tingling and numbness in your hand.

Mallet Finger

You reach to catch a ball and instead of landing in your palm, it smacks right into the end of your finger. The result: a mallet finger. Inside the finger, a tendon is partly torn. From the outside, you may see very little, but the finger cannot be fully straightened. With time, however, mallet fingers usually heal on their own.

Skier's Thumb

This often happens during a fall while skiing. The pole catches on the snow or ground and pulls the thumb away from the fingers. But any forceful motion that pulls the thumb in the wrong direction can cause "skier's thumb," a tear in the ligament connecting the thumb to the metacarpal bone of the hand.

DECISION GUIDE FOR WRIST PAIN

SYMPTOMS/SIGNS	ACTION
Numbness or tingling in fingers during day or awakened by these symptoms at night	
Fever or rapid swelling in joint, accompanied by pain	
Pain that shoots up the wrist	
Pain spreading up from wrist to elbow/shoulder/neck	
Wrist pain and neck stiffness	
Dropping objects or difficulty holding objects	
Clicking, popping, grinding	
Visible deformity after a fall	
Pain after falling on outstretched hand	
Tendinitis symptoms (p. 93)	
Injury not affecting movement	

 Call the advice nurse

 Use self-care

For more about the symbols, see p. 3.

DECISION GUIDE FOR HAND & FINGER PAIN

SYMPTOMS/SIGNS	ACTION
Symptoms not improved after 4 to 8 hours of self-care	
Mallet finger (p. 93)	
Tender spot on shaft of finger bones (not at joint)	
Pain, swelling, and bruising after thumb is bent backward	
Injury not affecting movement	

SELF-CARE STEPS FOR HAND AND WRIST PAIN

- Apply ice immediately.
- Always remove rings before exercising or doing manual labor. If you are wearing rings and hurt your hand, remove them immediately before swelling has a chance to begin.

REAR VIEW OF HIP & THIGH

FRONT VIEW OF HIP & THIGH

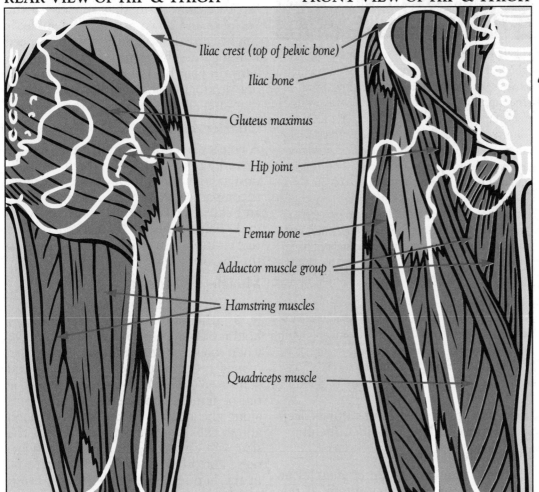

Iliac crest (top of pelvic bone)

Iliac bone

Gluteus maximus

Hip joint

Femur bone

Adductor muscle group

Hamstring muscles

Quadriceps muscle

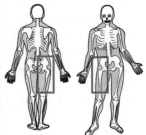

HIP AND THIGH PAIN

The hip is one of the most stable joints in the body. A "ball-and-socket" joint, the hip is surrounded by large muscles and a deep socket. Because of its stability, few problems occur with the hip joint. Most often, pain in the hip and thigh involves injury to muscles, tendons, or bursas, usually from a fall, a blow, or overuse of some kind. Some common hip injuries are discussed below.

Hip Pointer

A hip pointer is a bruise or tear in the muscle that connects to the top of the ilium, the crest of the pelvis just below the waist. Symptoms include local pain, tenderness, and possibly swelling. Climbing stairs may be difficult, and it may hurt to walk. A hip pointer can be caused by a blow, a fall, or a quick twist or turn of the body. Sometimes the pain increases several hours after the injury.

Groin Pull

This is a pull of the muscles that bring your leg back to the body (adductors). Groin pulls are fairly common among those who play sports such as hockey, tennis, or basketball. A groin pull can

I spent most of Saturday pulling weeds from my flower and vegetable gardens. I even dug up a good number of dandelions in the yard. By Sunday night, though, I was paying the price of doing too much in one day. All that squatting on Saturday left the front of my thighs so stiff and sore I could barely walk down the stairs. I tried applying ice to the area and doing gentle stretches to relieve the tightness. Aspirin also seemed to help. By Tuesday, my legs were pretty much back to normal. The next time I pull an all-day stint in the garden, I plan to stretch out well before and afterward, as well as several times throughout the day, and drink plenty of fluids.

Terry

SPECIAL CONCERNS FOR CHILDREN

Children can have most of the same hip and thigh problems as adults—most of which involve the muscles and connective tissues of the hip, thigh, and buttocks. But several problems unique to children may affect the bones directly. And because children are still growing, these problems often require medical attention to prevent long-term problems. Any time a child or teenager has a limp that lasts more than a few days, call the advice nurse. For any child or teenager involved in athletics, proper stretching (smooth, slow stretches, not bouncing) and slow strengthening of muscles are important to prevent injuries in the hips and legs, as well as other parts of the body.

Synovitis

Synovitis is an inflammation of any joint. In children, synovitis of the hip occurs most commonly between the ages of 6 and 10. Care by a medical provider is often required.

cause pain, tenderness, and stiffness deep in the groin, making activity difficult.

Pulled Hamstring

The hamstring is a group of muscles at the back of the thigh that attach at the pelvis and just below the knee. Pulls or tears may occur from a sudden forceful move, such as sprinting to steal a base. Hamstring injuries most often occur in the center of the muscle, but the hamstring can also tear from the pelvic bone, just under the buttocks. Hamstring pulls and tears cause pain and sometimes bruising or a lot of swelling.

Bursitis

The hip actually contains 13 different bursas. But most often, bursitis in the hip involves the "hip socket." It causes tenderness, pain, and swelling on the outer part of the hip where some of the large buttock muscles attach. Bursitis in the hip can cause pain that spreads to the buttocks and down as far as the ankle. It can be caused by activities (such as speed walking, aerobic dance, or carrying a baby on your hip) or conditions (such as one leg being shorter than the other) that alter the normal tilt of the pelvis.

Charley Horse

A charley horse is a painful muscle cramp caused by bruising of the thigh. In addition to cramping, charley horses are often accompanied by swelling, pain, stiffness, and skin discoloration (from the bruising). Follow the RICE method (p. 73) right after any significant blow to the thigh.

Muscle Tightness

Any time you tighten a muscle repeatedly, as when running or hammering, or hold it in one position for a long time, as when squatting or working at a computer, it may become stiff. Often stiffness and pain aren't felt until the next day. The tensor fasciae latae muscle, which runs along the outside of the upper leg and allows the leg to move outward to the side, is a common site for muscle tightness. But other muscles, including those in the buttocks and in the inside, front, and back of the thigh, can also become tight. Usually, muscle tightness lessens with a warm bath, stretching, and drinking plenty of water.

Chronic Hip Pain

Many other conditions can cause hip and thigh pain. Some, like arthritis or chronic bursitis, involve the hip directly. But low back problems, hernias, and inflammation of the urinary tract, reproductive system, or intestine can also cause hip pain—sometimes with little or no symptoms in the area of the body with the real problem. Whenever hip or thigh pain lasts more than 7 to 10 days, call the advice nurse.

SELF-CARE STEPS FOR HIP AND THIGH PAIN

Simple muscle tightness is probably the most common injury in the hips and thighs. The RICE method and anti-inflammatory drugs (p. 73), and gentle stretching of the tight and painful muscles will help speed recovery. Stretching before and after an activity and slowly strengthening muscles before demanding major efforts from them are effective ways to prevent muscle tightness—and most other hip and thigh injuries—in the first place. Below are specific things you can do to speed recovery of other hip and thigh injuries.

Hamstring stretch—*Lie on the floor on your back with your left leg bent. Grab the back of your right knee. Slowly straighten your leg. Feel the stretch on the back of your thigh. Hold for a count of five. Switch to your left leg and repeat.*

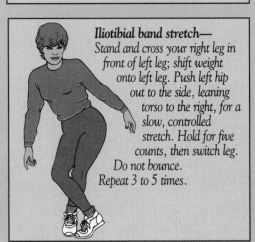

Iliotibial band stretch—Stand and cross your right leg in front of left leg; shift weight onto left leg. Push left hip out to the side, leaning torso to the right, for a slow, controlled stretch. Hold for five counts, then switch leg. Do not bounce. Repeat 3 to 5 times.

Quadriceps stretch—*Stand leaning against a wall. Grab your left foot with your left hand. Gently pull backward, feeling a stretch in the front of your thigh. Hold for a count of five. Be sure your other leg is slightly bent at the knee. Switch to your right leg and hand.*

For a hip pointer and groin or hamstring pulls or tears

The RICE method and anti-inflammatory drugs (p. 73) usually reduce pain. Depending on the damage to the muscle tissue, you may need crutches for a few days.

For bursitis

Use the RICE method and anti-inflammatory drugs (p. 73). Avoid the activity that started the inflammation.

For a charley horse

Apply ice to the entire muscle (or as much of it as you possibly can) right after the injury to slow blood flow and swelling. Rest the area; don't work through the pain. Use the RICE method and anti-inflammatory drugs (p. 73). If not better in 7 to 10 days, call the advice nurse.

For chronic hip pain

Because excess body weight can stress the hip joint, losing weight can often help relieve hip and thigh pain from chronic conditions. Walking is a good way to lose pounds and strengthen hip and thigh muscles. But any time hip or thigh pain lasts more than 7 to 10 days, call the advice nurse.

DECISION GUIDE
FOR HIP AND THIGH PAIN

SYMPTOMS/SIGNS	ACTION
Pulled or torn muscle causing tenderness to touch; stiffness; pain; difficulty walking, running, or climbing stairs	☎
Pain on outside of hip, possibly down to the knee	☎
Swelling, pain, or stiffness after a blow to the thigh	☎
Dull pain in hip and groin while walking or climbing stairs	☎
Severe pain in buttocks with exercise; pain stops when activity stops	☎
Pain interrupts sleep	☎
Severe pain after a fall or blow	☎
Symptoms do not improve within 7 to 10 days	☎
Overuse or injury pain that lasts less than 7 days	🩹

☎ Call the advice nurse

🩹 Use self-care

For more about the symbols, see p. 3.

KNEE PAIN

The knees are a common spot for injuries in athletes and nonathletes alike. They bear a great deal of the stress from high-impact activities such as running, aerobic dance, skiing, and other sports. Even everyday activities such as squatting, stooping, kneeling, lifting, and climbing stairs can take their toll. In addition to wear, tear, and sudden twists, the knees are open targets for blows, especially during contact sports.

The knee is composed of four bones: the femur (thigh bone), the tibia and fibula of the lower leg, and the patella (kneecap). The ends of the femur and tibia meet at the knee to form the joint. They are held together with four ligaments. The medial collateral ligament runs along the inner side of the knee and the lateral collateral ligament on the outside. Two cruciate ligaments run diagonally within the knee.

Cartilage provides a protective, lubricating "cover" over the bone surfaces of the joint. Two discs of cartilage, called *menisci*, attach to the cartilage of the knee and fit into the joint to form shock-absorbing cushions. The cartilage prevents the tibia and femur from rubbing against one another. The tendons of the hamstring and quadriceps support and help hold the knee in place. The patella is located in the tendon of the quadriceps.

Most knee injuries involve a blow, sudden twist, or a hard landing after a jump. Complex injuries are not unusual. A single strong blow in just the right place may tear cartilage and sprain several ligaments. Except for overuse injuries such as runner's knee and mild sprains, knee injuries should be evaluated by a medical provider to find out how bad the injury is and exactly what structures are affected. Common injuries are described below.

Sprains

A blow or sudden twist of the knee can sprain ligaments on either side of the knee, causing swelling (usually within an hour), pain, and difficulty walking. The sprained side may be tender to the touch. Even mild knee sprains often take 2 to 3 weeks to fully heal.

A strong blow to the inner or outer side of the knee will sprain the ligament on the opposite side as the knee is forced to bend sideways. If pain is felt on the side where the blow occurred, it's probably a bruise and not a sprain.

Anterior Cruciate Ligament (ACL) Injuries

ACL injuries are the second most common sports injury, after ankle sprains. If the force from a blow, twist, or hard landing is strong

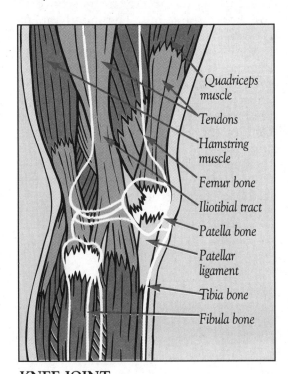

KNEE JOINT
Three-quarter view of front right knee

Labels: *Quadriceps muscle*, *Tendons*, *Hamstring muscle*, *Femur bone*, *Iliotibial tract*, *Patella bone*, *Patellar ligament*, *Tibia bone*, *Fibula bone*

enough, the anterior cruciate ligament within the knee can be stretched or torn. ACL injuries are common in contact sports, skiing, or basketball or as a result of a trip or fall. You may hear or feel a loud pop when the injury occurs. ACL injuries often bring sudden pain, knee instability, rapid swelling, and limited movement. But in some cases, symptoms may take as long as 6 to 12 hours to appear.

Torn Cartilage

The same traumas that can result in sprains can also tear the menisci. Often, cartilage tears occur with sprains. This is especially true of ACL injuries. Repeated squatting or kneeling can also stress cartilage, increasing the risk of injury. Swelling may be immediate or appear within 24 hours of injury. Continuing pain and a clicking or locking with knee movement are other symptoms of torn cartilage.

Once the cartilage is torn, the knee may buckle or lock without warning, putting surrounding ligaments and tendons at risk of injury. Wearing a brace during activity can help protect the knee from further injury, but surgery may be needed to remove pieces of torn cartilage. Unlike bone, tendons, and ligaments, cartilage does not knit back together once it is torn.

Dislocations

With a strong enough blow or twist, either the kneecap or the femur and tibia may dislocate. Dislocations of the knee or kneecap cause very bad pain and visible deformity. Both conditions are serious and require prompt medical attention.

The kneecap normally rides in a groove at the end of the femur, where it is held in place with tendons attached to the quadriceps muscle in the front of the thigh and lower leg. A blow, quick pivot, or twist can knock the kneecap out of its groove, usually to the outer side of the knee. A dislocated kneecap may pop back into place on its own, but you should still see a medical provider to check for fractures. If the kneecap is broken, surgery may be needed to wire the bone together so it can heal.

Runner's Knee (Chondromalacia Patellae)

The most frequent cause of knee pain and the most common overuse injury in the knee is runner's knee. This condition can be brought on by any number of activities that place stress on the knee. Wearing shoes that provide inadequate support may contribute to it.

Runner's knee develops because the kneecap fits incorrectly in its groove at the end of the femur. The misalignment is often caused by the foot rolling too far inward. If not properly centered, the kneecap rubs against the femur, causing wear and tear on the cartilage behind the kneecap. Aching and swelling may be present around the kneecap or at the back of the knee, especially during and after activity. Squatting or sitting with the knees bent for a long time can also be painful. Grinding or popping may be felt as the knee bends and straightens.

Jumper's Knee (Patellar Tendinitis)

This condition is an inflammation of the quadriceps tendon at the top of the kneecap or the patellar tendon, attached at the bottom. Jumping is a common cause of inflammation and tearing.

Housemaid's Knee (Prepatellar Bursitis)

This is fairly common in people who work on their knees. Carpet layers, roofers, and people who install flooring are candidates for prepatellar bursitis, which is also called housemaid's knee or milkmaid's knee. Symptoms include a squishy, swollen area in front of the kneecap, pain, and stiffness. In more severe cases, swelling may extend above and to the sides of the kneecap. An inflamed bursa may break internally on its own. If this happens, the body absorbs the excess fluid and the swelling and inflammation usually stop. The best prevention for housemaid's knee is wearing knee pads whenever working on your knees for any length of time.

Iliotibial Band Syndrome

The iliotibial band consists of a muscle that begins at the top rim of the pelvis (the portion of the hip felt just below the waist) and a tendon that fits into the outside of the knee. Exercise can cause the band to tighten, irritating the knee and sometimes the point of the hip. The pain usually begins 10 to 20 minutes into a run or other exercise routine and stops when the activity stops. Iliotibial band syndrome often grows worse, with pain increasing and starting sooner in a workout. Stretching and ice are the keys to relieving the syndrome (see Self-Care Steps, on next page).

I'd made a resolution this year to run a marathon. I began training, running 45 minutes 4 days a week. By the end of the first month, my right knee was swollen, hurt, and I couldn't run. Even sitting at my desk at work made my knee hurt. When I called my medical provider's office, they suggested the RICE method, anti-inflammatory drugs, and 30-degree leg extensions to strengthen my inner thigh muscles. After the inflammation went down, I took a more moderate approach to training. I did the leg extensions regularly and slowly worked my way up toward my mileage goals. I bought shoes that better supported my feet, and I apply ice after each run. I won't make the marathon this year, but next year I expect to be in good shape!

David

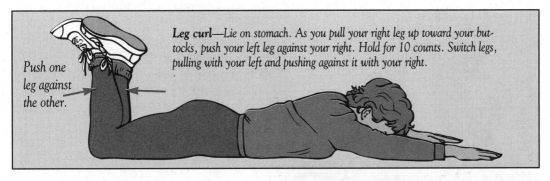

Push one leg against the other.

Leg curl—Lie on stomach. As you pull your right leg up toward your buttocks, push your left leg against your right. Hold for 10 counts. Switch legs, pulling with your left and pushing against it with your right.

SPECIAL CONCERNS OF CHILDREN

As with adults, knee injuries are common in young athletes. Wearing knee pads and supportive shoes can help prevent such injuries. But when they do occur, call the advice nurse.

SELF-CARE STEPS FOR KNEE PAIN

Overuse injuries, such as runner's knee, tendinitis, and bursitis, can usually be treated safely at home with the RICE method, anti-inflammatory drugs, and exercise to strengthen the area after the pain is gone (see p. 73).

For mild sprains

• Follow the RICE method (p. 73). Rest the knee as long as it aches. After the first 72 hours, soak your knee in a warm whirlpool or bath. Use crutches if needed.

• After the pain is better, work to strengthen the muscles around your knee. Leg curls (p. 101), leg extensions (below), and riding a stationary bike are good strengthening exercises. If you choose a stationary bike, set the seat high enough so that your knee doesn't bend much and set the controls so that there is no drag.

• Call the advice nurse if symptoms do not improve within 3 to 4 days.

For severe sprains, ACL injuries, and cartilage tears

• Follow the RICE method (p. 73) and take anti-inflammatory drugs for pain and swelling. Use crutches if needed. Call the advice nurse within 24 hours of injury.

For runner's knee, tendinitis and bursitis

• Follow the RICE method and use anti-inflammatory drugs. (p. 73) Check your shoes to make sure they provide proper support.

• After the pain is better, exercise to strengthen the area. Recommended exercises are illustrated on p. 101 and below.

For iliotibial band syndrome

• Stretching is the key to relieving this problem. Stretch the iliotibial band (see illustration p. 97), holding the stretch for 20 to 30 seconds and repeating three to six times. Do this three to five times a day until you no longer feel pain with running. To prevent it from happening again, do this stretch before and after each run.

• If symptoms are not better within 10 to 14 days with the stretching routine, call the advice nurse.

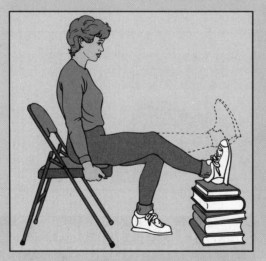

Leg extension—Sit with knees bent at a 60-degree angle; straighten leg; hold for count of five, then slowly bend leg to rest on stool or pile of books. Switch legs. You can add leg weights for added resistance.

DECISION GUIDE FOR KNEE PAIN

SYMPTOMS/SIGNS	ACTION
Severe blow or injury to knee; severe swelling; unable to move knee; visible deformity of knee	
Tendon below kneecap inflamed; pain going up stairs or jumping	
Soft, squishy swelling beginning in front of knee; pain; stiffness (see Prepatellar Bursitis, p. 101)	
Pain around or under kneecap; pain increases when you are climbing stairs or sitting for long periods	
Bursitis symptoms do not improve within 7 to 10 days; or signs of infection appear (local heat, redness, increased swelling, pain, and tenderness)	
Pain after sudden twist or blow to side of knee; swelling; cannot bear weight	
Pain after sudden twist or blow to side of knee; rapid swelling; limited movement	
Pain after sudden twist or blow to side of knee; swelling; can bear weight, but may limp	

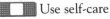 Call the advice nurse

Use self-care

For more about the symbols, see p. 3.

LOWER-LEG PAIN

The lower leg is made up of two bones, the tibia and the fibula. As with other parts of the leg, pain in the lower leg can be caused by overuse, overexertion, or trauma from a fall or blow. In addition to orthopedic problems, the lower leg can also be affected by heart and circulatory diseases, such as congestive heart failure, or blood clots and inflammation in the veins of the legs. The main symptom of such diseases is swelling in the legs and feet from extra fluid (edema).

Swelling (Edema) in the Lower Leg

Occasional swelling in the leg is common. It can occur from sitting or standing for long periods, water retention related to a woman's period or during pregnancy, allergies, varicose veins, or even sitting in the sun too long. In most cases, it goes away on its own overnight. Chronic swelling, however, can be a sign of the following conditions that may require medical care.

Phlebitis

Phlebitis is an inflammation of a vein, sometimes accompanied by a blood clot. The inflammation can cause aching, swelling, and redness in the lower portion of one leg. A blood clot in one of the veins of the leg can further increase swelling by blocking the flow of blood back to the heart. With nowhere else to go, the blood seeps out of the vein into the surrounding tissues, causing swelling. **If you suspect phlebitis, call the advice nurse right away.**

Intermittent Claudication

Intermittent claudication is pain caused by narrowing of the arteries (atherosclerosis) that creates a buildup of fluid in the leg and keeps the lower leg muscles from getting enough oxygen. The condition usually occurs in older adults and heavy smokers. Activity may cause pain, as the working muscles fail to get the oxygen they need. The pain is relieved shortly after exercise or activity is stopped. If you have these symptoms, call the advice nurse.

Other Causes of Lower-Leg Pain

Of course, overuse and trauma can also cause pain in the lower leg. The following conditions are among the most common.

Shin Splints

A shin splint causes aching at the front or inner side of the lower leg. Generally there is no swelling, redness, or bruising. The pain may begin suddenly or build slowly. A shin splint is an overuse injury that causes inflammation of the shin muscles, sometimes pulling muscle away from the bone. Tiny tears in the muscle may also contribute to the pain.

The most common causes of shin splints include:

- Muscle imbalance (calf muscle is much stronger than the shin muscles)
- Not enough shock absorption during high-impact exercise (from wearing worn-out shoes or shoes without enough padding)

- Running on the balls of the feet, without allowing the heel to touch the ground

- Flat feet

- Doing too much activity too fast (starting out jogging 5 miles instead of 2, or hiking in boots you're not used to)

- A tight Achilles tendon (the tendon at the back of the heel and ankle)

Shin splints are a common injury among runners and other athletes, store clerks, warehouse and factory workers, and others who are on their feet all day on hard concrete floors in shoes (especially high heels or cowboy boots) that don't provide good support.

Stress Fractures

Stress fractures can result from overuse, a blow, or twisting the lower leg. Stress fractures are common in high-impact activities. Stress fractures are hard to detect on X-rays until about 10 to 14 days after the fracture begins. You may notice a sudden spreading pain in your shin during or after exercise. In most cases, people with stress fractures can pinpoint exactly where the pain is coming from by pressing on the spot. Although a cast is not needed, stress fractures should be checked with X-rays until fully healed, usually about 6 weeks. During this time, rest the leg by avoiding high-impact activities. Generally, low-impact activities, such as walking, bicycling, or swimming, are safe to do while a stress fracture heals.

SPECIAL CONCERNS FOR CHILDREN

Growing pains are not a myth, but a real problem in children between the ages of 6 and 12. The pains usually occur in the evening, often in the calves and thighs. Acetaminophen or ibuprofen, along with a heating pad set on "low" or soaking in a warm bath, will provide relief. Do not give aspirin to children or adolescents. Call the advice nurse if the pain is always in the same spot; if there is swelling, redness, tenderness to the touch, or fever; or if your child is limping.

SELF-CARE STEPS FOR LOWER-LEG PAIN

- As with most other injuries in the extremities, the RICE method and anti-inflammatory medications (p. 73) provide the core of treatment for shin splints, stress fractures, and contusions. For chronic swelling in both legs without pain, try raising your legs and call the advice nurse.

- For shin splints, rest the leg for 3 to 6 days, then do only low-impact activities (bicycling, walking, swimming) to keep up strength and prevent recurrence. After aching has gotten better, return slowly to your usual activities. You can also wrap the ankle and shin for support.

Achilles tendon stretches and exercises to strengthen the front of the leg may also be helpful. An ice massage four times a day is beneficial: freeze water in a paper cup; tear away the cup to expose the ice, and massage the ice over the painful area for 10 or 15 minutes.

- Wear shoes with good support and cushioning. Even if the outside of an athletic shoe looks fine, the cushioning in the sole may have lost its resiliency with wear and you may need a new pair. Also check to see if the heel counter (the part that supports your heel) is broken down and the bottoms are worn evenly.

I've been jogging three times a week for the past several months. I usually jog along the paved paths in the city parks. Recently, I noticed a sharp pain in the middle of my shin every time I ran. By the next day, the pain was usually gone. So I would run again on my usual schedule. Each time I ran, the pain got worse. I tried icing it after each run and took some over-the-counter Aleve. But the problem kept getting worse. I finally saw my medical provider, who ordered X-rays and said I had a stress fracture exactly where I was feeling the pain—in the middle of my shin. The medical provider recommended the RICE method and said to switch to biking or swimming to stay in shape while the fracture healed. In about six weeks I was able to gradually return to my running schedule. The provider said the fracture probably started from worn out, improperly fitted running shoes. I spent the extra money to invest in a comfortable pair that fits my running style.

Cary

DECISION GUIDE FOR LOWER-LEG PAIN

SYMPTOMS/SIGNS	ACTION
Shin splint does not get better within 2 to 3 weeks	☎
Gradual increase in shin or ankle pain; pain increases during or after activity	☎
Pain along the front or inner edge of the shin bone	☎
Children: pain in legs, calves, or thighs at the end of the day or at night (see Special Concerns for Children, p. 105)	☎
Painful and sudden swelling and redness in only one leg (see phlebitis, p. 104)	☎
Swelling and pain after a blow to the front of the leg	☎
Numbness or tingling in foot after a blow to the shin	☎
Pain from overuse or blow; can bear weight	▭
Chronic swelling, without pain	▭
Blow to shin area, bruising, no swelling	▭

☎ Call the advice nurse   ▭ Use self-care

For more about the symbols, see p. 3.

SHOULDER PAIN

The shoulder is one of the most vulnerable joints in the body. Made for movement in all directions, the bones forming the shoulder joint give little in the way of stability. The shoulder is the junction of three bones: the upper-arm bone (humerus), the collarbone (clavicle), and the shoulder blade (scapula). But the smaller rotator cuff muscles, along with ligaments and other muscles and tissues, provide support and allow the shoulder a wide range of movement. Like other joints in the body, the shoulder can be injured by trauma (such as a fall or a blow) and overuse or repeated motions that add up over time.

Overuse Injuries

Three common overuse injuries include tendinitis, bursitis, and rotator cuff injuries (see Definitions of Common Muscle and Joint Problems, pgs. 74–75, for descriptions and treatments).

Trauma

A sudden twist, fall, or blow can lead to a sprain, shoulder dislocation (the upper arm bone comes "out of socket"), a partial dislocation, or broken bone. With any of these conditions, you may hear or feel popping, snapping, or tearing when the injury occurs. You may be unable to move your shoulder and, except for a sprain, there may be visible deformity of the shoulder. In most cases a sprain can be treated safely at home using the RICE method (p. 73).

Another possible injury caused by falls or blows to the shoulder is an **acromioclavicular (AC) joint separation**. The AC joint is held together by ligaments, which connect the collarbone to a narrow part of the shoulder blade that extends to the front of the shoulder. AC separations can range from bruising the joint to "stretching" or completely tearing the ligaments. With AC separations, a painful lump may form at the end of the collarbone, near the shoulder.

Muscle Imbalance

General muscle aches and tightness around the shoulder, upper back, or neck are often caused by muscle imbalance, which occurs when one side of the body is much stronger than the other side. Stretching and ice applications can help relieve the pain. But to keep it from happening again, weight training to strengthen the weaker side of the body is important.

I scraped and painted my entire garage in one weekend with no problems. Three days later, I noticed I had missed several spots on the eaves of the garage. It took less than an hour to get them done, but that night I had an awful pain in my shoulder. I tried icing the shoulder and took some aspirin. I got tired of holding the ice pack, so I wrapped it in place with an elastic bandage. When I called the medical provider's office in the morning, the nurse said I had used the RICE method—exactly what I should have done. He said to keep doing it until the pain got better—which it did a few days later.

Jack

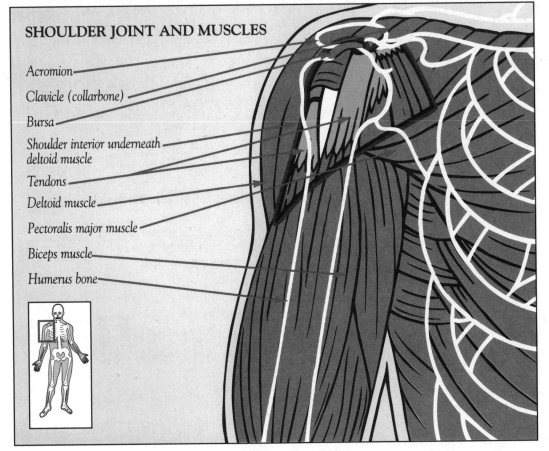

SHOULDER JOINT AND MUSCLES

Acromion
Clavicle (collarbone)
Bursa
Shoulder interior underneath deltoid muscle
Tendons
Deltoid muscle
Pectoralis major muscle
Biceps muscle
Humerus bone

SELF-CARE STEPS FOR SHOULDER PAIN

Overuse and muscle imbalance injuries can usually be treated with self-care. The RICE method and anti-inflammatory drugs, (p. 73) are the basics of self-care for shoulder injuries. Also, to keep it from happening again, you should work to strengthen the muscles around the joint. Your medical provider can suggest appropriate exercises. Finally, limit use of the shoulder until symptoms improve.

DECISION GUIDE FOR SHOULDER PAIN

SYMPTOMS/SIGNS	ACTION
Overuse injury still present or worse after 7 to 8 days, despite self-care	
Unable to raise arm	
Trauma with sudden pain; a pop, snap, or cracking sound or feeling; inability to move shoulder; a deformity or lump	
Sudden pain in shoulder; no injury; and able to move arm without increasing pain	
New numbness or tingling in arms, hands, or fingers	
New pain in other shoulder	
Shoulder pain after activity, limited to only certain movements	

 Call the advice nurse    Use self-care

For more about the symbols, see p. 3.

SPASMS/CRAMPS

There's nothing to propel you out of bed with a shout in the middle of the night like a muscle cramp. Cramps occur when the muscle suddenly contracts. Why they often happen in the middle of the night, however, is one of life's little mysteries.

Both activity and inactivity can lead to cramps and spasms. Muscles that have been overused, such as in exercise, may cramp. Similarly, muscles that have been underused, such as by sitting in the same position too long, also may cramp.

There are several theories about why muscles cramp. One theory is that cramps are the result of dehydration. Another theory is that cramps result from low levels of calcium and/or potassium. Because these are just theories, and evidence of the effectiveness of treatment may vary, you may find that nothing works to relieve your cramps.

Most muscle cramps aren't signs of a serious problem. Still, dealing with them promptly may help provide relief from pain—and there's no ignoring the pain from a muscle cramp.

SELF-CARE STEPS FOR SPASMS/CRAMPS

- Stretch out the cramped muscle. For a leg cramp, sit with your leg flat on the floor and pull your toes toward you. For a foot cramp, walk on it.

- You can easily locate the muscle that's cramping. Gently but firmly massage the cramp.

- Another pain management technique that works for some people is pinching the upper lip. Tightly squeeze the skin of your upper lip, just below the nose, between your thumb and index finger.

- Take acetaminophen or ibuprofen for pain that continues after the cramp.

PREVENTIVE STEPS

- Drink plenty of liquids before, during, and after exercise. Although water is best, any other drinks (except caffeinated ones, which cause dehydration) are fine. Drink an hour before exercising, and then every 12 to 15 minutes during exercise.

- Be sure to warm up before and cool down after exercising.

- Changes in diet are sometimes recommended for controlling cramps. Try to add more calcium- and potassium-rich foods to your diet. Eat low-fat dairy products to increase calcium; foods such as dried apricots, whole-grain cereal, dried lentils, dried peaches, bananas, citrus fruits, and fresh vegetables are good sources of potassium. Even if these changes do not help your cramps, it won't hurt to get more variety into your diet.

DECISION GUIDE FOR SPASMS/CRAMPS

SYMPTOMS/SIGNS	ACTION
Heaviness and pain deep in the leg or calf muscle or swelling, redness, or unusual warmth	
Neck or back spasm plus numbness, tingling, or weakness	
Prevention steps don't relieve episodes of muscle cramps or spasms after several weeks	
Occasional cramps that come and go	

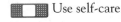 Call the advice nurse   Use self-care

For more about the symbols, see p. 3.

I always scoffed at my inactive brother who complained about his back. I was a runner and general exercise junkie, and I was treating my body right, by golly. Imagine my surprise when I became nearly incapacitated with back and leg muscle spasms after running a marathon. The pain was terrible. My trainer suggested changes in diet and more liquids, and that helped.

Ron

SKIN AND HAIR PROBLEMS

Your skin offers the most visible indication of your overall health. This section describes common problems of hair and skin, and suggests ways to take care of nonurgent conditions at home.

Your medical provider can offer advice and treatment for many skin and hair problems. If your condition is especially difficult to handle, your medical provider may involve other professionals who specialize in the care of skin.

Use the Decision Guides to see if your symptoms clearly need emergency medical services, require a call to the advice nurse, or can be treated using self-care. It is important to consider your own medical history and your current health when deciding what kind of care is right for you. If you have any conditions that do not seem to be healing normally, if the Self-Care Steps provided do not seem to help, or if you are uncertain about your symptoms, call the advice nurse. The advice nurse will evaluate your symptoms and recommend the next best steps for you to take.

ACNE

Who among us has not looked in the mirror and seen the blemish we were sure would ruin our day, if not our life? Three out of four teenagers have some acne, and some adults continue to have acne into their twenties, thirties, and forties.

When hair follicles in the skin become plugged with a combination of sebum (fat) and cellular material, a pimple results (See color photo, p. 279).

In teenagers, acne is linked to hormonal activity and often occurs on the face, back, chest, and upper arms. Adult acne shows up mainly on the face. An especially problematic form of adult acne, called **rosacea**, affects the skin of the nose, forehead, and cheeks. Acne rosacea usually responds well to medical treatment.

The good news is that in most cases, acne eventually goes away. The bad news is, it doesn't go away overnight. A regular skin care regimen can help avoid outbreaks.

I'm 34 years old and I'm sick and tired of having pimples. This has been going on since I was 17. I can't seem to point to any one thing that makes my acne flare up, but antibiotics and Retin-A help contain it.
Betsy

Occasionally, a medical provider may recommend a topical medicine, oral antibiotics, or both. Lotions, creams, or gels containing vitamin A acid (tretinoin—commonly called Retin-A) can help stop pimples from forming by preventing dead skin cells from sticking to the wall of the hair follicle. Antibiotics work by keeping bacteria from forming and reducing inflammation. Rare cases of serious acne can be treated with a pill containing vitamin A called isotretinoin (Accutane). All of these medications have side effects, however, and should not be taken by pregnant women. Women of childbearing age should only use Accutane after having a full discussion with their medical providers.

Proper treatment of acne makes scarring unusual. However, if scarring does occur, the skin's appearance can be improved through cosmetic surgery.

Although acne is not life threatening, its effects on self-esteem and self-confidence should not be downplayed.

HOW ACNE DEVELOPS

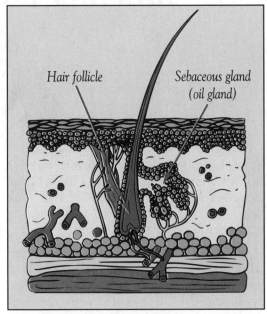

Normal hair follicle and skin structure

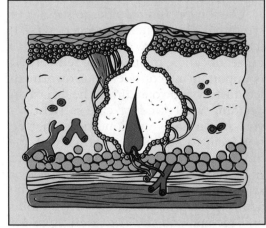

Whiteheads *form when pores become clogged with oily secretions and hair follicles break down.*

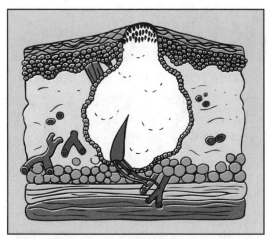

Blackheads *form when the clogged pore is invaded by bacteria and pus. Blackheads should not be squeezed because this can cause further spreading of the bacteria.*

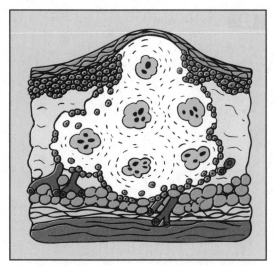

Acne or pimples *form when the hair follicle walls rupture. Acne can then spread. Squeezing the pimple can cause the infection to spread further.*

SELF-CARE STEPS FOR ACNE

- Wash your face once or twice daily with the cleanser of your choice.

- Use an "acne" cream or lotion. Start with over-the-counter lotions that contain benzoyl peroxide, sulfur, resorcinol, or salicylic acid as the main ingredient.

- Use an oil-free moisturizer labeled "non-comedogenic." This means that the product has been tested and found not to cause pimples.

- Don't open your pimples unless your health care provider has given you instructions on how to do it correctly.

DECISION GUIDE FOR ACNE

SYMPTOMS/SIGNS	ACTION
No improvement or worsens after 6 to 8 weeks of self-care	☎
Lowered self-esteem because of appearance	☎
Tendency to scar	☎
Mild acne	🩹

☎ Call the advice nurse   🩹 Use self-care

For more about the symbols, see p. 3.

ATHLETE'S FOOT

You don't have to be an athlete to get athlete's foot, a common fungal skin infection that thrives in hot, moist conditions.

Caused by the same fungus as ringworm and jock itch, athlete's foot usually shows up between the toes. Symptoms can include red scaling and peeling or dead skin. The affected area may itch and develop a musty odor.

Although annoying, athlete's foot usually responds to prompt treatment. Left unchecked, however, it can spread to the toenails, causing nails to thicken and discolor.

SELF-CARE STEPS FOR ATHLETE'S FOOT

- Wash feet often and dry thoroughly, especially between toes.

- A hair dryer, set on the coolest setting, can dry skin fast and well.

- After drying, apply an antifungal product such as clotrimazole (Lotrimin) or tolnaftate (Tinactin).

Note: Powders help keep the area dry, which adds to comfort and may prevent spread of infection. Lotions and creams can attack the infection more directly.

DECISION GUIDE FOR ATHLETE'S FOOT

SYMPTOMS/SIGNS	ACTION
Self-care doesn't noticeably improve the problem in 2 weeks	
Toenails thickened and pitted due to the fungus	
Athlete's foot responds promptly to self-care	

 Call the advice nurse

 Use self-care

For more about the symbols, see p. 3.

BLISTERS

Blisters are usually caused by repeated rubbing or friction on tender skin until fluid collects under the outer layer of skin. Blisters often form on hands unaccustomed to physical labor and feet exposed to ill-fitting shoes. However, blisters can also be caused by burns, allergic reaction, and chemical irritation.

Blisters can also signal other health problems. Blisters that appear on the genitals can be herpes simplex virus type 2 (see AIDS and Other Sexually Transmitted Diseases, p. 211). Blisters that form a ring on the scalp or body can be ringworm (p. 127). If you have unusual blisters, call the advice nurse.

To keep common blisters from developing, wear work gloves when doing physical labor. Extra socks, a bandage, or petroleum jelly on a foot likely to blister can reduce friction and prevent a blister.

Hiking precautions include good shoes and thin inner socks. Carry an extra pair of socks in case feet get wet. Use moleskin for any areas of skin that feel hot, one of the first signs of a blister.

SELF-CARE STEPS FOR BLISTERS

• Friction blisters are best left unbroken if skin irritation can be avoided until the fluid disappears.

• For blisters on the feet use "second skin," an over-the-counter product, to help when walking.

• If the blister breaks open, treat it like an open wound. Wash it with soap and warm water. Apply an antibacterial ointment and cover with a clean bandage. Watch for signs of infection, which may include redness, pain, swelling of lymph nodes, or fever. Call the advice nurse if the wound becomes infected.

DECISION GUIDE FOR BLISTERS

SYMPTOMS/SIGNS	ACTION
Blisters, with new fever	☎
Unusual blister appears without a known cause	☎
Signs of infection (fever, increased redness, pain, or swelling of lymph nodes) develop	☎
Minor blister	🩹

 Call the advice nurse

 Use self-care

For more about the symbols, see p. 3.

I think of myself as a tough guy with a high pain threshold, but when I got a boil on my buttocks, I thought I'd go through the roof every time I sat down. It got so my co-workers noticed me eyeing the chairs in the conference room, trying to decide which might be most comfortable. When my boil finally went away, I was the happiest man alive.

Andy

BOILS

When skin bacteria, called *staphylococci*, invade a hair follicle, a boil results. Skin tissue swells, and a tender and red, pus-filled lump emerges (see color photo p. 279). The pus contains white blood cells fighting the infection. Until the boil opens and the pus is released, the boil will be painful and tender to the touch.

Boils usually range from the size of a pea to that of a walnut or larger. Although boils may be found anywhere on the body, they most commonly occur in areas where there is hair and chafing, such as the neck, armpits, genitals, breasts, face, and buttocks.

Boils can be contagious. Scratching can spread the infection to other areas of the body. Keep the boil area clean and always wash hands after touching it.

Carbuncles are extremely large boils or a series of boils, usually deeper and more painful than regular boils. Call the advice nurse if you suspect you have a carbuncle.

SELF-CARE STEPS FOR BOILS

• Apply warm, saltwater compresses (mix 1 teaspoon salt with 1 quart of warm water) to relieve pain and bring the boil to a head.

• Keep the area clean to prevent the spread of bacteria.

• Take a pain reliever to reduce pain and inflammation.

• When the boil comes to a head, you may try to open it using a sterilized needle. Carefully wipe away the pus.

Note: Do not squeeze the boil or attempt to drain it before it clearly comes to a head. Squeezing it before this happens may succeed only in driving the infection deeper into the skin.

• Wash gently and cover with thick, absorbent gauze.

DECISION GUIDE FOR BOILS

SYMPTOMS/SIGNS	ACTION
Boil not coming to a head or improving after 5 days of self-care	
Temperature of a level you believe to be a fever; red streaks leading away from the boil	
Boil above the lips, on the nose, or in the ear	
Person also has diabetes, is HIV+, or has problems fighting infections	
Boil responding well to self-care	

 Call the advice nurse    Use self-care

For more about the symbols, see p. 3.

DANDRUFF

The stigma attached to dandruff is far worse than the condition warrants. Everyone can get dandruff. The skin all over your body, including your scalp, sheds dead cells all the time. Dead skin cells on the scalp may stick together and become visible white flakes.

Dandruff is not contagious and is a very common problem. It affects about 20 percent of adults in the United States, men and women alike. It is, however, fairly easy to control.

SELF-CARE STEPS FOR DANDRUFF

• Gently brush hair before each washing.

• Wash hair every day, which may be enough to keep mild dandruff under control.

• Use antidandruff shampoos if the scalp is red and scales are obvious.

• Follow shampoo directions: most say to lather and let it sit for at least 5 minutes before rinsing.

• If a dandruff shampoo seems to lose its effectiveness after several weeks, try another.

• Try not to scratch or brush the scalp hard. Too much scratching may cause more dandruff.

DECISION GUIDE FOR DANDRUFF

SYMPTOMS/SIGNS	ACTION
No improvement after several weeks of self-care	
Constant irritation or itchiness	
Thick scales, yellowish crusts, or red patches	
Responds to self-care	

 Call the advice nurse

 Use self-care

For more about the symbols, see p. 3.

ECZEMA

If you're scratching patches of reddened skin that look flaky or scaly, the medical provider may say you have eczema or "dermatitis." Both terms mean an inflammation of the skin. There are several different types of eczema or dermatitis.

Atopic dermatitis usually develops in childhood and may last into adulthood, although an adult can develop atopic dermatitis without a previous history of it. Some people with atopic dermatitis have a greater chance of having hay fever or asthma than other people.

In babies, atopic dermatitis takes the form of a rash around the mouth and cheeks. In older children, rashes may appear behind the knees, in the creases of the elbows, and on the neck. In atopic dermatitis, the skin is extremely itchy and usually dry (see color photo, p. 280).

Contact dermatitis results from an allergy or exposure to an irritant (see Rashes, p. 126). When the skin touches something to which it is allergic or that it finds irritating, it becomes itchy and red (see color photo p. 280). Common types of contact dermatitis include diaper rash and poison ivy. Allergic reactions can be caused by hair dyes, jewelry containing nickel, and some rubber compounds. Irritant contact dermatitis may be caused by repeated use of soaps, solvents, and detergents.

Itch-scratch-itch cycle dermatitis develops when an itchy area is scratched or rubbed repeatedly. The skin becomes harder and annoyingly itchy. Scratching makes this worse. It may be hard to break the itch-scratch-itch cycle.

Seborrheic dermatitis is red, flaky, slightly itchy skin on an adult's scalp and face (for infants, see Cradle Cap, p. 137, color photo, p. 280). The area from the side of the nose to the corner of the mouth may be affected, as well as the scalp and eyebrows.

SELF-CARE STEPS FOR ECZEMA

- Wash the skin gently in cool or warm water, not hot, and don't bathe too often if you tend to have dry skin.

- Use mild unscented soaps or cleansers and moisturize skin with bath oil after each bath or shower.

- Keep nails short to reduce damage to the skin by scratching.

- Dress lightly and wear soft, nonscratchy clothes.

- Apply a cold compress for temporary relief of itching.

- Apply over-the-counter 1 percent hydrocortisone creams to relieve itching.

- Protect the skin from contact with harsh chemicals and substances to which you are allergic; use latex gloves and wear protective clothing, if possible.

DECISION GUIDE FOR ECZEMA

SYMPTOMS/SIGNS	ACTION
Sores are crusting or weeping or itching is very bad	
Rash appears infected	
Self-care is not providing relief after 2 weeks	
Dermatitis responds promptly to self-care	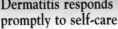

 Call the advice nurse

Use self-care

For more about the symbols, see p. 3.

HAIR LOSS

Everyone loses between 50 and 100 hairs per day. The average lifespan of hair is 3 to 4 years. Ninety percent of the hairs on your head are actively growing. The other 10 percent are resting, a stage that lasts between 2 and 6 months, after which the hairs fall out.

Losing more than 50 to 100 hairs a day has a variety of causes. Hereditary balding is the most common cause of hair loss. Despite common myth, hereditary balding can be inherited from either the mother's or father's side. Hereditary balding affects both men and women, although in different ways. Men's hairlines recede and eventually join bald spots on the top and back of the head. Some women notice a slow or episodic thinning on the front of the head. The earlier the thinning starts, the worse it's likely to be.

Some prescription drugs can cause hair loss. (Certain blood pressure medicines, anticoagulants, antidepressants, and antiarthritic and antigout drugs can cause reversible hair loss.) Radiation and chemotherapy used to treat cancer can cause people to lose up to 90 percent of their hair. Birth control pills can cause increased hair loss while they are taken and for several months after the pills are discontinued.

Rising and dipping hormone levels can be hair loss culprits in women. Many women may lose hair after childbirth, and a few have hair loss during menopause (p. 154) or during post-menopausal hormone therapy.

Crash diets have been implicated in hair loss, and ringworm (p. 127), a fungal infection, can cause scaly bald spots.

Hairstyle traction baldness can occur in those who wear tight braids or ponytails.

My dad has a receding hairline, my older brother has a receding hairline, my younger brother has a receding hairline. Even my mother's hair is thinning. In my family, losing one's hair is part of our heritage. You look at family pictures and everyone has a glint off the top of their heads— or they're wearing hats.

Brad

SELF-CARE STEPS FOR HAIR LOSS

Although there's no cure for hereditary baldness, there are some remedies if your appearance bothers you:

• Use toupees, wigs, or hairpieces to cover thinning or bald areas.

• Do what the hairdressers do: color or perm your hair, but avoid overbleaching, which causes hair breakage; use a hair dryer for more volume; wash daily with a gentle shampoo; use mousse.

• If you suspect your hairstyle is causing your hair to fall out, avoid curlers, braiding, ponytails—anything that puts traction on the hair.

• Surgery is available to transplant hair to your head from other parts of your body. Discuss options with your medical provider.

When the baby was about 4 months old, I was combing my hair one day and a lot of it came out in my hand. My hair got really nice and thick when I was pregnant and even though I was prepared for hair loss after I had the baby, I still was shocked when it happened.

Sandy

DECISION GUIDE FOR HAIR LOSS

SYMPTOMS/SIGNS	ACTION
Sudden hair loss with scabs or scales on scalp, pain, soreness, or tenderness	☎
Bald spots suddenly appear, rather than slow symmetrical thinning	☎
Suspicion that a drug may be causing hair loss	☎
Bald spots and scaly spots, pus, or scabs (see Ringworm, p. 127)	☎
Gradual hair thinning or loss	▭
Occurs 2 to 3 months after surgery, major illness, or childbirth	▭

 Call the advice nurse

 Use self-care

For more about the symbols, see p. 3.

HIVES

Hives occur when something prompts cells to release histamine, a chemical found in cells under the skin. The histamine causes nearby blood vessels to dilate (open up). Fluid leaks out and collects under the skin in a raised, flushed, itchy bump called a wheal or hive. Some wheals look like mosquito bites. Wheals often come in groups and may be as small as $1/4$ inch or as large as 2 or 3 inches across (see color photo p. 286).

Some people know that certain foods or drugs give them hives. For most others, the causes may not be obvious.

"Acute" hives (hives that are usually a reaction to a removable stimulus such as a drug) can last for hours or days. Chronic hives (often of unknown cause) can last for weeks or months.

Foods that can cause hives in some people are peanuts (and other nuts), eggs, beans, chocolate, strawberries (and other berries), tomatoes, seasonings (mustard, ketchup, mayonnaise, spices), fresh fruits (especially citrus fruits), corn, fish (both freshwater fish and shellfish), milk, wheat, and cheese.

Drugs that have been known to cause hives in some people include penicillin, sulfa antibiotics, and codeine.

Some extensive hives outbreaks can be very serious, such as when hives form on the lips and in the throat, interfering with breathing and swallowing. This condition is very rare, however.

SELF-CARE STEPS FOR HIVES

• Take an oral antihistamine such as Benadryl. This may also make you drowsy, so follow package directions carefully.

• Topical anti-itch treatments can be used but generally are of little help.

• Rub ice directly over hives or take a cool shower for temporary relief from itching.

• Soak in a lukewarm or cool bath with 1 cup of baking soda or an oatmeal product such as Aveeno.

• If hives develop after a bee sting or other insect bite, call the advice nurse.

DECISION GUIDE FOR HIVES

SYMPTOMS/SIGNS	ACTION
Extreme difficulty breathing with hives having developed within the last 30 to 60 minutes	
No response to self-care after 10 days	
Hives develop shortly after you begin taking a new drug	
Hives cause very bad discomfort	
Big hive develops at bite site or after bee or other insect sting	
Widespread hives over body	
Difficulty breathing	
Extensive hives with swelling around the face and in the throat and mouth	
Hives respond well to self-care	

 Emergency, call 911

 Call the advice nurse   Use self-care

For more about the symbols, see p. 3.

I don't know what causes my hives, which makes it hard to avoid the problem. Sometimes I'll go for weeks without any problems, and sometimes it's every day for weeks at a time. I suspect I'm overly sensitive to changes in routine and temperature.

Sally

INFECTED WOUNDS

All wounds—from paper cuts to gunshot wounds—share a danger of infection. Bacterial infection usually occurs within 24 hours but can take up to 3 to 4 days to develop. A prolonged increase in pain, redness, or swelling around a wound is cause for concern.

If a wound results from a dirty object, a tetanus shot may be needed to prevent this disease. Once the series of basic tetanus immunizations is completed, a tetanus booster shot is needed every 10 years and more often if a wound is at high risk for tetanus. The advice nurse can help determine if a tetanus booster is needed.

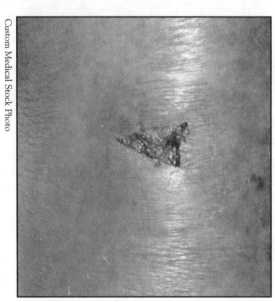

Custom Medical Stock Photo

An infected wound

SELF-CARE STEPS FOR WOUNDS

 • Carefully wash the wound with soap and warm water immediately. Remove all dirt and debris. Washing a wound early will reduce the number of germs in and around a wound, so the body's natural defenses can stop infection.

• After cleaning, leave the wound open to the air unless it will get dirty easily or oozes blood. If necessary, cover the wound with a dressing or bandage. Change the bandage daily, checking for signs of infection. An antibiotic ointment can be used around the wound to keep the bandage from sticking to the wound.

DECISION GUIDE FOR INFECTED WOUNDS

SYMPTOMS/SIGNS	ACTION
Increased pain at the wound site	
Redness or swelling around the wound	
Swollen lymph nodes (see Swollen Glands, p. 54)	
Temperature of a level you believe to be a fever	
Red streaks spreading from the wound site toward the center of the body	
Pus draining from the wound	

 Call the advice nurse

For more about the symbols, see p. 3.

JOCK ITCH

Jock itch is one of the most descriptive names for an ailment. Jock itch is a fungal skin infection in the groin that mainly affects men but occasionally can affect women as well.

Jock itch thrives in the warm, moist area of the groin. Fortunately, in most cases, self-care will clear up the red, raised, itchy areas on the skin in 1 to 2 weeks.

SELF-CARE STEPS FOR JOCK ITCH

• Wash the groin daily with a mild unscented soap; rinse and dry thoroughly.

• After drying, try an over-the-counter antifungal cream (such as Lotrimin), then powder with talc or baby powder to reduce moisture and friction.

• When the rash clears, keep the area as dry as possible and, as a preventive measure, apply an antifungal powder daily to prevent flare-ups.

• Call the advice nurse if self-care does not improve the problem or infection worsens within 2 weeks.

DECISION GUIDE FOR JOCK ITCH

SYMPTOMS/SIGNS	ACTION
Self-care does not clear up the problem	
Fungal infection becomes worse rather than better after 2 weeks of self-care	

Call the advice nurse

For more about the symbols, see p. 3.

POISON IVY/POISON OAK/POISON SUMAC

A simple walk through the woods shouldn't make you miserable. If you touch poison ivy, poison oak, or poison sumac, however, you may get an allergic reaction to these plants (see Allergic Reactions, p. 179).

The poison trio contain an almost invisible clear-to-slightly-yellow oil called *urushiol*, which comes from any cut or crushed part of the leaves, stem, or vine crawling on the ground. When the oil touches skin, it penetrates within minutes. In 12 to 48 hours, a red, itchy rash and tiny, weeping blisters may appear (see color photo p. 281). The oil can be carried on paws or fur of cats and dogs, on shoes or clothing, or on garden tools.

Poison ivy usually grows east of the Rocky Mountains as a vine or shrub. Its leaves are in clusters of three, and it has yellowish-white berries. It grows very easily and is widespread both inside and outside "city limits."

Poison oak grows west of the Rockies as a shrub, small tree, or, less often, a vine. It has greenish-white berries and has leaves in clusters of three, similar to those of poison ivy.

Poison sumac is usually found in swampy, boggy areas in the South and northern wetlands. It's a tall shrub with 7 to 13 pointed, small leaves per branch and cream-colored berries.

Your best defense against the poison trio is twofold: learn to identify them by sight, and watch what you are handling when gardening or cleaning up around the yard.

The most common exposures to poison ivy occur when pulling weeds or "cleaning up" at the cabin, gardening around the edges of the lawn, and gathering or exploring in wooded areas.

SELF-CARE STEPS FOR POISON IVY/POISON OAK/POISON SUMAC

• Wear rubber gloves if you're allergic and have to work near infested areas.

• Wash suspected areas of contact with soap and water as quickly as you can. Also, take off and wash any clothes that have come in contact with the plant.

• If water isn't available, wipe affected areas with rubbing alcohol.

• Use soap and water to rinse off pets, clothes, shoes, and camping or gardening gear after contact with infested areas.

• Calamine lotion may relieve initial itching and help dry the rash.

• Over-the-counter antihistamine pills may help relieve itching and help avoid an allergic reaction.

• A soak in lukewarm water mixed with oatmeal or baking powder may soothe irritated skin and dry oozing blisters.

Poison ivy is a climbing vine or shrub with clusters of three shiny pointed leaves, greenish flowers, and white berries.

Poison oak is a shrub-like relative of poison ivy that has leaves growing on a single stem.

Poison sumac, also called poison dogwood, is a tall shrub found in swamps and wetlands. It has greenish flowers and cream-colored berries.

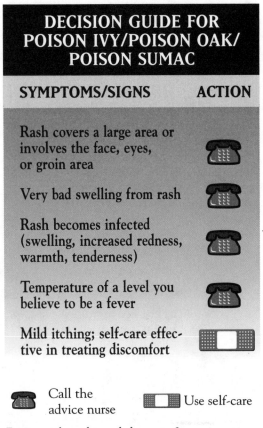

DECISION GUIDE FOR POISON IVY/POISON OAK/ POISON SUMAC

SYMPTOMS/SIGNS	ACTION
Rash covers a large area or involves the face, eyes, or groin area	☎
Very bad swelling from rash	☎
Rash becomes infected (swelling, increased redness, warmth, tenderness)	☎
Temperature of a level you believe to be a fever	☎
Mild itching; self-care effective in treating discomfort	▭

☎ Call the advice nurse

▭ Use self-care

For more about the symbols, see p. 3.

RASHES

Most of us have had skin rashes at one time or another. Symptoms can include red swollen patches, raised red dots, itching, burning, and blisters that may weep or ooze. The rash usually develops when the skin comes into contact with an irritating chemical. Poison ivy (p. 124), cosmetics, deodorants, soaps, metals, and dozens of other natural and artificial substances can cause contact dermatitis (see Allergic Reactions, p. 179).

SELF-CARE STEPS FOR RASHES

 The first step in treating a rash is to find out what may have caused it. **Ask yourself these questions:**

• Have I started a new drug?

• Have I changed soaps, shampoos, deodorants, cosmetics, or hair dyes lately?

• Does the rash appear on a part of the body where clothes are worn?

• Have I worn any new jewelry or used new hand cream or nail polish?

• Have I been near plants such as poison oak, poison ivy, or poison sumac?

If you suspect any of these substances may have caused the rash, try to avoid them.

Second, follow these self-care steps to treat the rash:

• Gently wash the affected area with mild soap and water.

• Relieve itching by using calamine lotion or over-the-counter hydrocortisone cream.

• Watch the rash for 24 hours to see if it spreads or changes.

DECISION GUIDE FOR RASHES

SYMPTOMS/SIGNS	ACTION
Temperature of a level you believe to be a fever	
Lasts longer than 2 weeks	
Rash in groin area that is bright red, raw, or sore-looking; has blisters or crusty patches	
Red streaks leading toward the center of the body	
Reddened, sunburned-looking skin that feels like sandpaper	
Swollen joints, chills, dizziness, nausea	
Burning eyes and nose, weeping blisters	
Swollen glands in groin	
Expanding circular rash	
Tolerable pain or itching	

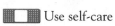 Call the advice nurse   Use self-care

For more about the symbols, see p. 3.

RINGWORM (FUNGAL INFECTION)

Ringworm is an outdated term for a fungal skin infection. The name "ringworm"—going back to the early fifteenth century—comes from the idea that the skin infection was caused by a burrowing worm. Fungal skin infections, like athlete's foot and jock itch, are caused by tiny fungal organisms that can be seen only under microscopes. Fungal infection is no longer believed to be a sign of poor hygiene or squalid living conditions.

The fungal infection starts as a small spot, then spreads or radiates out in a ringlike pattern (see color photo p. 282). It can infect most surfaces of the body, including the nails. On the scalp, it may show up as areas of hair loss.

Fungal infections are contagious. Some kinds can be spread to humans by cats and dogs.

DECISION GUIDE FOR RINGWORM (FUNGAL INFECTION)

SYMPTOMS/SIGNS	ACTION
What appears to be a fungal infection of the scalp, face, or fingernails	
More than one affected area or the infection is spreading	
Fungal infections on the feet and groin (see Athlete's Foot, p. 114, and Jock Itch, p. 123)	
Improvement within 1 to 2 weeks with self-care remedies	

 Call the advice nurse   Use self-care

For more about the symbols, see p. 3.

SELF-CARE STEPS FOR RINGWORM (FUNGAL INFECTION)

• Over-the-counter antifungal creams work well for fungal infections on the feet. However, groin and body lesions do not respond as well to these creams. Try Tinactin or Monistat on small patches, especially for areas other than the feet. Apply twice a day for at least 2 weeks.

• Keep moist areas dry. Use powder after bathing. Try drying the affected area with a hair dryer set on cool.

• Thoroughly clean combs and hats.

• If your pets develop scaly, hairless skin lesions, have the animals checked for fungal infection by a veterinarian.

I couldn't figure out what was causing Jessica's itching. I thought it might be chicken pox, so I took her to the medical provider. I was mortified to discover she had scabies—which meant her brother probably had it, too. Luckily, the treatment was quick and effective.

Judy

SCABIES

For unknown reasons, the incidence of scabies is on the rise. Like head lice, scabies can occur in any family, in any neighborhood. It is no longer believed to be a sign of poor hygiene or squalid living conditions.

The tiny mites that cause scabies are passed easily from one person to another. The mites burrow into the skin, where the females lay eggs that hatch in about 5 days. The cycle then begins anew (see color photo p. 282).

Scabies causes very tiny bumps that itch a lot, especially at night. The itching doesn't begin until several weeks after the mites have taken up residence in the skin (see color photo p. 282).

Scabies most often appears in the finger webs and around the wrists, but itchy areas may occur anywhere. It often affects the male genital area. The burrowing of these mites leaves very tiny grooves and tunnels on the skin that may look somewhat like white splinters.

When someone in the household has scabies, the entire household should be treated at the same time.

SELF-CARE STEPS FOR SCABIES

• Call the advice nurse to discuss the problem. If the symptoms clearly are from scabies—or if you know you were in contact with someone infested by scabies—the advice nurse will tell you what steps you will need to take.

• Wash all bedding and clothing used before or during treatment.

DECISION GUIDE FOR SCABIES

SYMPTOMS/SIGNS	ACTION
Very itchy white or gray lines or red patches appear on the body	☎
Criss-crossing, itchy lines or tunnels in the skin	☎
Fairly certain that the rash and itching are caused by scabies	☎
Constant itching and rash of an unknown cause	☎

☎ Call the advice nurse

For more about the symbols, see p. 3.

SUNBURN

Sunburn results from overexposure to ultraviolet (UV) radiation from the sun. In a first-degree burn, symptoms include redness, sensitivity, and pain. If you have a sunburn, stay out of the sun until the skin recovers. Long exposure can lead to the swelling and blistering of a second-degree burn.

Sunburn can be prevented by avoiding too much sun, particularly between 10 a.m. and 2 p.m. and in midsummer. Sunscreens and sun-blocking lotions protect by filtering out the UV rays that cause sunburn. The higher the sun protection factor (SPF), the greater the protection against sunburn. A sunscreen of at least SPF 15 is recommended even during winter months. You should apply sunscreen daily to all exposed skin areas before going outside. This is especially important for children.

Sunburn is uncomfortable, usually for 24 to 48 hours. Frequent overexposure to the sun can cause long-term damage to the skin.

Some drugs can make you more sun-sensitive, causing you to burn with little exposure to the sun. Before starting a drug, ask your medical provider or pharmacist about the possible reactions to sunlight. Drugs that react to sunlight include tetracycline and sulfa antibiotics.

We always thought you had to get red first to get a really good tan, so we'd spend hours in the sun the first day we went out. Oh, we suffered for days afterward, but we thought we were suffering for beauty. Little did we know those dark tans we craved would come back to haunt us 30 years later.

Kathy

SELF-CARE STEPS FOR SUNBURN

• The best treatment for sunburn is to soak the affected area in cold water (**not ice water**) or apply cold compresses for 15 minutes. This will reduce swelling and provide quick pain relief. Do not apply greasy lotions such as baby oil or ointment to sunburned areas. They can make the burn worse by sealing in the heat.

• If sunburn affects large areas of your body, soak in a cool bath. A half cup of cornstarch, oatmeal, or baking soda in the bath will help reduce inflammation and soothe sunburned skin.

• Drink plenty of fluids to prevent dehydration when you have a sunburn.

• Adults who do not have stomach problems or a history of allergy to aspirin products can take aspirin to reduce inflammation. Acetaminophen (Tylenol, Tempra, or a generic) or ibuprofen (Advil, Nuprin, or a generic) can also be used to relieve discomfort. Do not give aspirin to children or adolescents.

• For the most protection from sunburn, apply sunscreen 45 minutes before exposure to sunlight. Reapply sunscreen often during extended exposure. Apply to dry skin after swimming or strenuous activities that cause heavy perspiration.

• The sun's rays are more intense at higher altitudes, nearer the equator, and on the water and in the snow. Zinc oxide products block all the sun's rays and are good for the nose and lips.

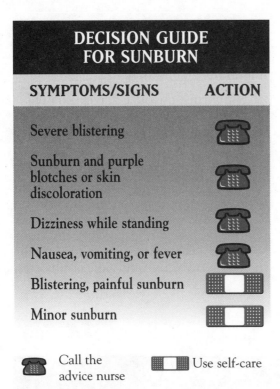

DECISION GUIDE FOR SUNBURN

SYMPTOMS/SIGNS	ACTION
Severe blistering	☎
Sunburn and purple blotches or skin discoloration	☎
Dizziness while standing	☎
Nausea, vomiting, or fever	☎
Blistering, painful sunburn	🩹
Minor sunburn	🩹

☎ Call the advice nurse

🩹 Use self-care

For more about the symbols, see p. 3.

SPECIAL COMPLAINTS OF CHILDREN

As any parent knows, caring for a young child's health problems can be one of the most agonizing aspects of parenthood. Distinguishing mild childhood illnesses from more serious concerns can be challenging. So, too, is easing the discomfort of small patients.

This section describes common health problems of children and suggests ways to take care of nonurgent conditions at home. Your child's medical provider can offer advice and treatment for most common problems of children. If your child's condition is especially hard to handle, his or her provider may involve other professionals who specialize in children's health problems.

Use the Decision Guides to see if your child's symptoms clearly need emergency medical services, require a call to the advice nurse, or can be treated using self-care. It is important to consider your child's medical history and current health when deciding what kind of care is right. If your child has any conditions that do not seem to be healing normally, if the Self-Care Steps provided do not seem to help, or if you are uncertain about your child's symptoms, call the advice nurse. The advice nurse will evaluate the symptoms and recommend the next best steps to take.

ALLERGIC REACTIONS (CHILDREN)

Any time a substance—whether it's food, medicine, or pollen—causes unpleasant symptoms, it is correct to say a "reaction" to that substance is occurring. Rarely, however, can these reactions be classified as an actual allergy. Many common reactions such as stinging eyes from irritants in the air, vomiting from certain antibiotics, or heartburn from some foods are not brought on by allergies. A "true allergy" is a highly specific response by the body's immune system (such as hives, wheezing, or a drop in blood pressure) to a particular chemical found in whatever substance has entered the body.

If your child develops a new symptom you believe was caused by breathing, swallowing, or touching something, simply describe the symptoms that concern you and tell what you think triggered them when you call the advice nurse. The nurse may ask if the child is allergic to any medications. Answer yes only if a medical provider has diagnosed the child as having a true allergy to a particular medication.

Medications

While almost any drug can cause an allergic reaction in a child, most medications do not cause any problems. If a reaction does occur, it is likely to be a mild rash such as hives. It is important to distinguish between an allergic reaction to a medication and a drug side effect. For example, many antibiotics can cause stomach upset if not taken with food. Nausea and vomiting, however, are not typical symptoms of allergic reactions.

Penicillin and related drugs are responsible for many of the mild allergic reactions seen in children. However, sensitivity to most drugs is not easy to detect. If you suspect that your child is having an allergic reaction to a medication, call the advice nurse.

New Foods

When an infant or toddler suffers an allergic reaction to a new food, it can be very scary for both the child and the parent. Responses to new foods can range from a simple rash to minor sniffles and cough to abdominal cramps and vomiting. In rare cases, a food allergy can cause a severe condition called anaphylaxis characterized by rapid swelling of parts or all of the body and difficulty breathing.

The culprits in 90 percent of food allergies are proteins found in cow's milk, egg whites, peanuts, soybeans, and wheat. Other foods that can cause problems include berries, shellfish, corn, and beans. Although chocolate was thought to be a common food allergy in children, researchers now realize that it is seldom to blame.

SELF-CARE STEPS FOR ALLERGIC REACTIONS TO MEDICATION

The best way to care for an allergic reaction to a drug is to treat the symptoms. Since the most common form of reaction is a rash, take the following measures to relieve the child's discomfort.

• Give the child over-the-counter antihistamine medicine (such as Benadryl) to reduce swelling and itch. Follow package directions to determine the proper dosage based on the child's age and weight.

• Add $1/2$ cup baking soda, or an oatmeal bath product (such as Aveeno) to a cool bath to help relieve itching.

SELF-CARE STEPS FOR ALLERGIC REACTIONS TO NEW FOODS

• If the child has been diagnosed by a medical provider as having an allergy to a particular food, remove that food from the child's diet.

• If you suspect a particular food is causing an allergic reaction, try removing that food from the child's diet for 2 weeks. Symptoms will reappear when you add the food back into the diet if the child has an allergy to that food.

• Suspected food allergies should be confirmed with a medical provider.

Watch for the following symptoms if you think your child might have a food allergy:

- abdominal pain, diarrhea, nausea, vomiting

- rash or hives (see color photo, p. 286)

- nasal congestion

- swelling of the lips, eyes, face, tongue, or throat

DECISION GUIDE FOR ALLERGIC REACTIONS TO NEW FOODS

SYMPTOMS/SIGNS	ACTION
Difficulty in breathing worsening rapidly	
Swelling of the face, hands, eyes, or lips	
Nausea, vomiting, diarrhea, abdominal pain	
Hives or other skin rash from a known food allergy	

 Emergency, call 911   Call the advice nurse

 Use self-care   *For more about the symbols, see p. 3.*

DECISION GUIDE FOR ALLERGIC REACTIONS TO MEDICATIONS

SYMPTOMS/SIGNS	ACTION
Difficulty in breathing worsening rapidly	
Swelling of the face, hands, eyes, or lips	
Nausea, vomiting, diarrhea, abdominal pain	
Hives or other skin rash	 &

BIRTHMARKS

Birthmarks—skin markings that appear at birth or shortly thereafter—often cause parents concern, however they are not a sign that the baby is sick. Most birthmarks disappear or become less obvious before the child is 2 years old. Although the vast majority of birthmarks require no treatment, there are a variety of medical procedures that can be used to remove birthmarks that do not go away as the child gets older.

Milia

These small white bumps on a newborn's face resemble whiteheads. They are harmless and disappear without treatment (see color photo p. 285).

Stork Bites

Also called "salmon patches," these flat, light pink spots appear on up to 50 percent of newborn babies. They are found most frequently on the eyelids, upper lip, between the eyebrows, or on the back of the neck. These marks become more prominent during bouts of crying or when the baby's body temperature changes. Stork bites on the face usually fade over time, while ones found on the back of the neck may last but become less noticeable as the child's hair grows (see color photo p. 283).

Hemangiomas

These harmless, bright red raised marks are really a cluster of blood vessels close to the surface of the skin. It is not known what causes them. Strawberry hemangiomas, which usually appear on the face, scalp, back, or chest, are more common in girls. They are seldom present at birth, appearing sometime within the first 2 months of the child's life, and usually do not require treatment (see color photo p. 283).

Port Wine Stains

These flat hemangiomas consisting of dilated blood vessels are permanent marks. They occur primarily on the face. There are a number of treatments available to lighten or permanently remove this type of birthmark (see color photo p. 283).

Mongolian Spots

These harmless gray-blue marks are common to children of African-American, Hispanic, Asian, or Native American ancestry. They most frequently appear on the back or buttocks and fade before the child is 7 years old (see color photo p. 283).

 Call the advice nurse

For more about the symbols, see p. 3.

DECISION GUIDE FOR BIRTHMARKS

SYMPTOMS/SIGNS	ACTION
Signs of infection (redness, swelling, or pus) develop on or around the birthmark with or without a fever	
Bleeding from the birthmark	

SELF-CARE STEPS FOR BIRTHMARKS

- Keep the birthmark area clean and dry; no other care is necessary.

- Avoid using harsh soaps. Excessive cleaning will not cause the birthmark to fade sooner.

- If the birthmark is permanent and you are considering having it removed, call your medical provider.

- Call the advice nurse if you notice changes in the appearance of the birthmark such as bleeding or discharge from the area.

CHICKEN POX

Chicken pox is normally a mild disease of childhood. (It affects 4 million American children each year.) Adults who have never had the disease can get chicken pox, although only 4 percent of adults have not had the disease.

The early symptoms of chicken pox are cold symptoms, fever, abdominal pain, headache, and a general feeling of illness. These can come with the rash or before it by a day or two. The fever may be higher the first few days after the rash appears (see color photo p. 279).

The rash appears as small, itchy, red bumps and spots on the face, scalp, shoulders, chest, and back. It is also normal for it to appear inside the mouth, on the eyelids, and in the genital area. Some people may have just a few bumps, while others are covered with them.

The early bumps are usually flat, red marks with a central clear blister. The blisters quickly break open and become dry crusts or scabs, which fall off within 2 weeks (see color photo p. 279). New sores will continue to appear for the first 4 to 5 days, so all stages of the rash may be present at the same time.

Chicken pox is usually spread by breathing in droplets coughed, sneezed, or breathed out by an infected person. Between exposure to the disease and the appearance of symptoms, there is an incubation period of 10 to 21 days. Usually a person develops the symptoms 14 to 16 days after exposure.

SELF-CARE STEPS FOR CHICKEN POX

Relieve the itching

Scratching the scabs off chicken pox sores can lead to more itching and/or infection. These steps will help reduce the urge to scratch:

• Give your child cool baths every 3 to 4 hours.

• Add Aveeno oatmeal (follow directions) or baking soda (about a half cup) to tub water to reduce itchiness.

• Give acetaminophen (Tylenol, Tempra, or a generic) if symptoms are very bothersome. Do not give aspirin to children or adolescents.

• Keep your child's fingernails trimmed short.

• Have your child wear clean, cotton gloves to reduce the danger of scratching. (For infants, mittens are easier to put on.)

• Apply calamine lotion and/or hydrocortisone products to itchy areas.

Manage other symptoms

• Drink plenty of cold fluids.

• To reduce fever, give acetaminophen. Do not give aspirin to children or adolescents.

• For mouth ulcers, feed your child a soft, bland diet. Avoid salty foods and citrus fruits and juices.

• For painful or itchy pox in the genital area, apply petroleum-based A&D ointment or an over-the-counter local anesthetic.

• If a sore seems to be infected (is warm, red, or tender), wash with antibacterial soap and apply antibacterial ointment.

• Keep your child cool and quiet, however, he or she does not need to stay in bed.

• You may send your child back to school or day care when fever has disappeared and all sores are crusted over.

The worst part about chicken pox is the itching. The other bad part is that I can't see my friends or go anywhere because people who haven't had it before could catch it. The best part is that I've probably given it to my brother already and he doesn't even know it.

Kristine, age 8

A child can spread the disease to others before he or she even has any symptoms of chicken pox. The contagious period begins about 2 days before the rash appears and continues until new sores stop appearing. Once all the sores have turned to scabs, the contagious period is over.

If your child has been exposed to chicken pox, there is nothing you can do during the incubation period to prevent the disease in household members who aren't already immune to it.

Chicken pox may leave permanent scars, especially in teenagers and young adults. Temporary marks may remain for 6 months to a year before fading away.

A vaccine for chicken pox is used in several other countries, and has been approved for general use in the United States. It is recommended for children over 12 months of age who have not had chicken pox (see Chicken Pox Vaccine, p. 203).

PREVENTIVE STEPS

• Have your child avoid contact with others during the contagious period—until all sores have turned to scabs. That means anyone with chicken pox should not be at work, school, or day care while contagious. If other people may have been exposed to the disease, be sure to call and tell them to watch out for spots about 2 weeks from the date of exposure.

• It's nearly impossible to prevent the spread of chicken pox within a household. Some studies find that nine times out of ten, siblings of a chicken pox patient will get the disease.

DECISION GUIDE FOR CHICKEN POX

SYMPTOMS/SIGNS	ACTION
Blistery, red rash and confusion, delirium, forgetfulness, or other mental changes	
Child is hard to awaken, very tired	
Stiff neck and very bad headache, difficulty breathing	
Lymph nodes become larger or more painful to the touch	
Itching does not respond to treatment, lasts longer than 2 weeks	
Pain with urination	
Suspicion that several sores are infected (swelling, increased redness and pus draining from sore)	
Sore in or near the eye, causing redness, drainage, pain, or changes in eyesight	
Normal chicken pox symptoms, including rash, fever, and itching	

 Call the advice nurse ▭▭ Use self-care

For more about the symbols, see p. 3.

CRADLE CAP

New mothers dislike cradle cap more than their infants do. Cradle cap is oily, yellowish scales or crusts that appear on babies' heads—most often on the scalp but occasionally behind the ears or on eyebrows. (see color photo p. 280).

Common in children less than 1 year old, cradle cap may be a mild form of dermatitis. Cradle cap doesn't cause the baby any discomfort, but a new mother may be unhappy with the baby's appearance. Fortunately, cradle cap is easy to treat at home.

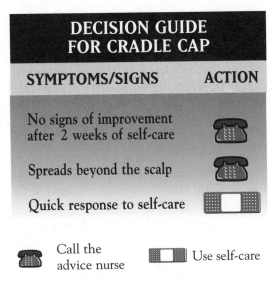

DECISION GUIDE FOR CRADLE CAP

SYMPTOMS/SIGNS	ACTION
No signs of improvement after 2 weeks of self-care	☎
Spreads beyond the scalp	☎
Quick response to self-care	🩹

☎ Call the advice nurse 🩹 Use self-care

For more about the symbols, see p. 3.

SELF-CARE STEPS FOR CRADLE CAP

• Soften the crusty scales with baby or mineral oil and leave on the baby's head for about 30 minutes.

• Use a soft brush to loosen the scales after soaking in oil. A clean, soft toothbrush works well.

• Gently rub difficult areas with a washcloth or gauze dipped in oil to remove scales.

• Shampoo the baby's head thoroughly to remove the oil. Excess oil remaining on the scalp can actually worsen the cradle cap.

• Don't use dandruff shampoos on your infant.

CROUP

Croup is a viral infection that causes inflammation and swelling of the vocal cords in young children. In some children, croup is a recurring problem. Episodes of croup are outgrown as the airway passages grow larger. After the age of 5 it is uncommon.

Croup is marked by a distinctive seal-like barking cough, hoarseness, and difficult breathing. Croup can last as long as 3 to 5 days and may be accompanied by a cold or fever.

Croup without fever (spasmodic), the most common and mildest type of croup, comes on suddenly, usually during the night. The child may have seemed perfectly healthy during the day or have the mildest cold but suddenly wakes up with a violent fit of croupy coughing.

Croup with fever (laryngotracheo-bronchitis) is a more serious form of croup, which inflames the area around the vocal cords down to the large bronchi (airways). It is usually accompanied by a chest cold and often a fever. The croupy cough and tight breathing may start slowly or suddenly at any time of the day

SELF-CARE STEPS FOR CROUP

 • Put moisture into the air to make it easier to breathe. The simplest method is to take the child into the bathroom, close the door, turn on the hot water faucet of the shower, and sit with the child upright on your lap on the bathroom floor for 15 to 20 minutes, inhaling steam. Other options are a brief walk outdoors or a cool-mist humidifier in the child's bedroom.

• Give plenty of clear fluids, such as water or diluted juice, to help loosen the cough.

• Use acetaminophen (Tylenol, Tempra, or a generic). Never give aspirin to children or adolescents.

• Elevate the head of your child's bed.

• Remember, a child with croup is often frightened and crying, so try to reassure your child with a hug or distract him or her with a book or favorite game.

Note: cough medicines and antibiotics are not effective in treating croup.

DECISION GUIDE FOR CROUP

SYMPTOMS/SIGNS	ACTION
Child cannot relax enough to sleep after 20 minutes of steam inhalation	
Child has had croup symptoms for more than 3 nights	
Child is coughing and breathing with increasing difficulty	
Child drools and has great difficulty swallowing	
Child cannot bend his or her neck forward	
Child has blue or dusky lips or skin	
Child cannot swallow saliva	
Child wakes with a croupy cough but no fever, perhaps makes high-pitched noises when inhaling	

 Call the advice nurse   Use self-care

For more about the symbols, see p. 3.

or night. If your child does not respond promptly to simple home measures, call the advice nurse.

Most children with croup can be cared for at home. Three key elements in treatment are moist air, keeping the child sitting up or propped up, and encouraging plenty of fluids.

CRYING IN INFANTS

For a newborn baby, crying is the only means available to communicate. An infant may cry for several reasons: hunger, gas, a wet diaper, or just prior to a bowel movement. Babies cry, too, when they are tired or sick.

SELF-CARE STEPS FOR CRYING IN INFANTS

• Try the obvious methods of relief first, such as picking the infant up, changing the diaper, or burping him or her. Some medical providers believe that holding the baby over your heart will help to stop crying.

• Try offering a pacifier, walking with the baby or rocking in a chair, or taking the infant for a ride in the car.

• If you believe all the baby's needs are met and the crying still doesn't stop, it may be necessary to let the child cry until he or she gets tired and falls asleep. Put the baby down in another room, close the door, and check on him or her in an hour.

• Note whether the crying seems to fit into the baby's normal pattern. If it seems unusual, the baby may be sick.

• Call the advice nurse if the baby continues to cry without stop for more than 4 hours without any obvious cause, or if you find yourself losing patience and are worried that you may harm the baby.

There is no easy way to determine what is excessive crying. Crying for 20 or 30 minutes a few times a day may be a typical pattern for one infant but unusual for another. The amount of crying can also vary from one day to the next for the same baby. As a caregiver, it is important for you to be aware of the reasons that your baby cries and what is normal for him or her. A sudden, dramatic change in a child's crying pattern may be a sign of illness.

Colic

Colic, defined as a difficulty in digesting breast milk or formula, is marked by a bloated stomach and long crying spells lasting up to 2 or 3 hours. It most commonly occurs in the late afternoon or evening hours. Caring for an infant with colic can be a frustrating and exhausting experience. The good news is that most cases of colic go away by the time the baby is 4 months old.

DECISION GUIDE FOR CRYING IN INFANTS

SYMPTOMS/SIGNS	ACTION
Continuous crying for longer than 4 hours that is not typical for the child	
Suspicion that the baby is ill	
Sudden change in length of time baby cries	
Fussiness not typical for the child that continues for more than 3 straight days with no obvious cause	
Concern that you or someone else may harm the baby	
Reason for crying is obvious	

 Call the advice nurse

Use self-care

For more about the symbols, see p. 3.

SELF-CARE STEPS FOR COLIC

• Bouts of colic usually occur after feedings. If you feel confident that the child has eaten enough, avoid feeding the baby again since that may aggravate the condition. Try offering a pacifier instead.

• Hold the baby upright to ease the discomfort. If you want to lie the baby down, try placing him or her stomach-down across your lap and rub the baby's back.

• Sometimes a car ride can soothe a baby into sleep.

DIAPER RASH

Even with the best care, babies can develop the occasional case of diaper rash. This uncomfortable red irritation (see color photo p. 280) on the skin of the buttocks and genital area is caused by the area coming in contact with urine and stool in the baby's diaper. Diaper rash will often go away by itself without treatment.

SELF-CARE STEPS FOR DIAPER RASH

• Change the baby's diapers frequently. If you use plastic pants with cloth diapers, go without the plastic pants for a few days to allow the skin to breathe.

• Clean the baby's skin thoroughly (with warm water and mild soap) at each diaper change. Apply petroleum jelly several times a day to clean, dry skin to protect it from irritation.

• If the diaper rash is very bad, allow the child to go without diapers as much as possible for a couple of days. Exposing the skin to air will make the child more comfortable and speed healing.

DECISION GUIDE FOR DIAPER RASH

SYMPTOMS/SIGNS	ACTION
Signs of infection (increased redness, or discharge from the rash) with or without fever	
Diaper rash that doesn't improve after 3 days of self-care	
Repeated bouts of diaper rash	
Diaper rash without other symptoms	

 Call the advice nurse   Use self-care

For more about the symbols, see p. 3.

IMPETIGO

As children, our parents often told us not to scratch sores or insect bites. There's a good reason for this. Impetigo is a contagious bacterial infection most often seen at the site of broken skin. Red sores start to ooze a straw- or honey-colored liquid, which, when partially dried, becomes a crust or scab (see color photo p. 282). Touching or picking the sores can spread bacteria to other parts of the body—or other people.

Impetigo in infants starts with a small blister containing yellowish or white pus surrounded by reddened skin. The blister breaks easily, leaving a small raw spot that may not crust over as with older children. Impetigo in infants is most often found in moist areas, such as the diaper edge, groin, or armpit.

With quick and careful home treatment, impetigo can be brought under control in several days.

SELF-CARE STEPS FOR IMPETIGO

- Gently and frequently clean sores with antibacterial soap and water or hydrogen peroxide.

- Apply an antibiotic ointment using a Q-tip.

- Don't cover with a Band-Aid unless the sore is in an area where the scab may rub off. To keep children from scratching, cover with a dry gauze pad and keep the tape as far from the sore as possible.

- Wash your hands well with antibacterial soap and water after cleaning sores and applying ointment.

- Make sure everyone in the household uses separate towels, washcloths, and bath water.

DECISION GUIDE FOR IMPETIGO

SYMPTOMS/SIGNS	ACTION
Self-care does not control or clear up the problem in 5 days	
Infant has small, pus-filled blisters that break easily and leave a raw spot behind	
Large blisters develop	
Blisters show other signs of infection (warmth, increased redness, or increased tenderness)	
Urine turns red or cola-colored, and a headache occurs	
Mild impetigo	

 Call the advice nurse   Use self-care

For more about the symbols, see p. 3.

I was concerned when Adrianne got impetigo. She had a cold and had gotten a sore between her nose and upper lip. She said it itched and kept rubbing it. Soon it was really red, and then it started to weep a gold liquid. I called the medical provider and followed her directions faithfully. I was so relieved to see Adrianne get better after a couple of days.

Carole

I was very surprised one day when a note came home from my daughter's day care that head lice was going around. To be on the safe side, the day care asked all of us to wash our children's heads with special head lice shampoo, and wash their bedding and pillows in hot water. I don't think my daughter had head lice, but I do think quick action kept it from spreading.

Jennifer

LICE

We all itch from time to time, but if your child is infested with head lice, you'll know. Lice make you itch constantly. Lice can be spread by shared bedding, hats, or even combs, but having lice is no longer believed to be a sign of poor hygiene or squalid living conditions.

Lice feed on human blood. As they burrow into the skin, their saliva causes intense itching. Adult lice are the size of a pinpoint. Their eggs, which they cement to hair shafts with a gluelike substance, are easier to spot (see color photo p. 281). The eggs, called nits, are white and shaped like footballs or cattails. A female louse can lay up to six eggs a day, and between 50 and 100 in her lifetime. Left untreated, lice are annoying and easily spread.

More than 6 million cases of head lice are reported annually among school-age children, and the infestation can easily spread to other family members. When diagnosed, head lice should be treated promptly and steps taken to prevent their spread to others.

A case of head lice is often mistaken for dandruff (p. 117). Symptoms include itching, white nits on hair shafts that aren't dislodged with regular shampooing, and red bite marks along the nape of the neck and around the ears.

SELF-CARE STEPS FOR LICE

• To kill lice, you must use a shampoo just for that purpose. Several are sold over-the-counter. Follow the directions on the box, including leaving the shampoo on the affected area for several minutes. This gives the medicine time to work.

• After shampooing, use a rinse made of equal parts white vinegar and water. This will help remove stubborn nits.

• Combing hair with a fine-toothed comb also will help remove nits after shampooing.

• Wash everything that has touched the affected area. Bedding and clothing must be washed in hot water for at least 10 minutes and machine dried at the hottest setting for at least 20 minutes. Vacuum furry toys, carpets, drapes, mattresses, and upholstery, including fabric-covered car seats and headrests. Soak all combs, brushes, and hair accessories in hot water or alcohol for at least 10 minutes.

📞 Call the advice nurse

🩹 Use self-care

For more about the symbols, see p. 3.

DECISION GUIDE FOR LICE

SYMPTOMS/SIGNS	ACTION
Signs of infection on skin or scalp (redness, swelling, or tenderness)	
Head lice without other symptoms	

TEETHING

For many babies, the only symptoms they experience when teething are increased drooling and an urge to chew on all objects within reach. For others, the process of the teeth cutting through the gums is very uncomfortable, causing crankiness and sleep problems.

Contrary to popular belief, teething doesn't usually cause fever and diarrhea. If your baby develops these symptoms, it is wise to look for other causes.

SELF-CARE STEPS FOR TEETHING

- Place several teething rings in the refrigerator. An icy cold teething ring may soothe sore gums.

- Give the baby acetaminophen (Tylenol, Tempra, or a generic) to relieve pain. Aspirin should never be given to children or adolescents.

- If the baby is old enough, offer slices of frozen fruits such as bananas and apples to chew.

DECISION GUIDE FOR TEETHING

SYMPTOMS/SIGNS	ACTION
Symptoms of illness such as diarrhea or fever in addition to symptoms of teething	
Self-care steps do not relieve discomfort after 7 days	
Teething without symptoms of illness such as fever or diarrhea	

 Call the advice nurse   Use self-care

For more about the symbols, see p. 3.

UMBILICAL CORD PROBLEMS

The umbilical cord that connected the baby to the placenta during the 9 months in the womb is cut at the time of birth. The newborn is left with a small stump which dries up and falls off within a couple of weeks. Keeping the cord stump clean will promote healing and avoid complications. Call the advice nurse if you have any questions about the appearance of the stump.

SELF-CARE STEPS FOR UMBILICAL CORD PROBLEMS

- Wash the umbilical cord stump 2 or 3 times a day with soap and water. Dry thoroughly.

- In the morning and evening, swab the stump and the stump area with a cotton ball dipped in rubbing alcohol.

- Call the advice nurse if you notice any signs of infection (fever, swelling, redness, or discharge from the cord site).

DECISION GUIDE FOR UMBILICAL CORD PROBLEMS

SYMPTOMS/SIGNS	ACTION
Cord has not fallen off more than 4 weeks after birth	
Signs of infection (fever, swelling, redness, or discharge from the cord site)	
Bleeding from the cord stump	

 Call the advice nurse

For more about the symbols, see p. 3.

SPECIAL COMPLAINTS OF MEN

Although current news has focused on the special health concerns of women, men have some unique problems as well. For example, annual death rates for men with prostate cancer are similar to the rates of breast cancer deaths in women. There may be more of a stigma in talking about men's health issues, but progress in treating men's health problems will be difficult until men are encouraged to deal with their health concerns openly.

This section describes common problems realted to men's health and suggests ways to take care of nonurgent conditions at home. Your medical provider can offer advice and treatment for most gender-related problems you may encounter. If your condition is especially hard to treat successfully, your medical provider may involve others who specialize in diagnosing and treating men's problems.

Use the Decision Guides to see if your symptoms clearly need emergency medical services, require a call to the advice nurse, or can be treated using self-care. It is important to consider your own medical history and your current health when deciding what kind of care is right for you. If you have any conditions that do not seem to be healing normally, if the Self-Care Steps provided do not seem to help, or if you are uncertain about your symptoms, call the advice nurse. The advice nurse will evaluate your symptoms and recommend the next best steps for you to take.

HERNIAS

Although hernias can occur in men and women, they are far more common in men.

Inguinal Hernias

An inguinal (groin) hernia occurs when the lining of the abdominal cavity weakens, allowing part of the intestine to balloon out. These hernias are more common in older adults as a result of strained or weak abdominal muscles but can happen at any age. In infants, hernias are in the muscle layer.

One of the chief causes of hernias is too much abdominal pressure caused by heavy lifting or straining during bowel movements. Correct lifting (using your legs and keeping the back straight) can reduce your risk of hernia. Also, avoiding constipation

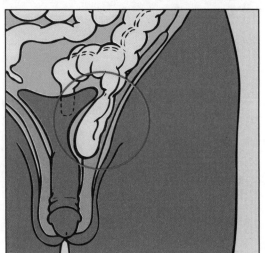

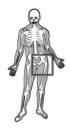

In the above inguinal hernia, the intestine has bulged through the passage where the testicle descends into the scrotum.

or treating it promptly if it does occur can reduce straining during bowel movements.

Hernia symptoms and pain may start slowly or you may one day feel that something isn't quite right. Symptoms include:

- Aches and pain in the abdomen that start and stop
- A feeling of pressure or weakness in the groin
- Visible bulges slightly above or within the scrotum
- Pain and tenderness in the lower abdomen and scrotum

SELF-CARE STEPS FOR INGUINAL HERNIAS

- Avoid activities such as heavy lifting that cause straining and more abdominal pressure.
- Use correct lifting techniques.
- Don't strain during bowel movements.

DECISION GUIDE FOR HERNIAS

SYMPTOMS/SIGNS	ACTION
New, rapidly increasing pain in groin	
Aches and pain in abdomen that start and stop	
Pressure or weakness in groin area	
Visible bulges above or within scrotum	
Pain and tenderness in lower abdomen or scrotum	
New heartburn, indigestion, or hiccuping following meals	

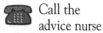 Call the advice nurse

For more about the symbols, see p. 3.

Hiatal Hernias

A hernia at the spot where the esophagus passes through the diaphragm to the stomach is called a hiatal hernia or hernia of the diaphragm. This hernia is caused by a weak spot in the diaphragm muscle that allows the stomach to push up through the diaphragm.

These hernias are usually not painful by themselves. However, food or acid may pass back into the esophagus. This can cause heartburn, indigestion, chest pains, hiccuping, or belching following meals.

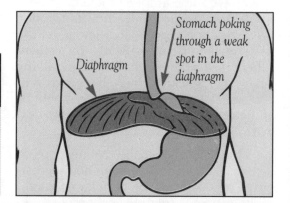

Diaphragm

Stomach poking through a weak spot in the diaphragm

SELF-CARE STEPS FOR HIATAL HERNIAS

 • Treatments for hiatal hernias include taking antacids, avoiding irritating foods, and raising the head of the bed several inches to help prevent stomach contents from flowing back into the esophagus.

- Other treatments that can offer relief include avoiding going to sleep or lying down shortly after eating, and eating small, frequent meals. Medical providers may also recommend prescriptions or over-the-counter medications to help control heartburn, which can contribute to hiatal hernia. Surgery to tighten the hiatal opening is a last resort if other measures fail to provide relief.

TESTICULAR PAIN

Suddenly painful testes signal medical conditions that are potentially very serious. Since this type of pain can have several causes, call the advice nurse right away if you feel persistent, sharp pain, or swelling in the testes. Prompt medical attention can prevent the unnecessary loss of the testicle.

Lumps within the scrotum are usually benign, and are often a cyst or other inflammation. However, a scrotal lump, whether or not it is painful, should always be checked by your medical provider to be sure that it is not a tumor.

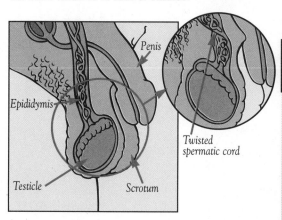

Testicular torsion occurs when a testicle gets a twist in the spermatic cord from which it is suspended within the scrotum. This unusual condition can occur on its own—even while the person sleeps—or after strenuous activity at any age. It can strangle the blood supply to the testicle and, without immediate treatment, can cause permanent damage.

Sudden pain, severe enough to cause vomiting and nausea, is the main symptom of testicular torsion. Your medical provider may be able to carefully shift the testicle back into its normal position. Sometimes, however, surgery to securely anchor it in place will need to be performed within several hours.

Epididymitis is the inflammation of the long, coiled tube (epididymis) that carries sperm from the testicle. It is often caused by a bacterial or chlamydial infection traveling from the urinary duct to the sperm duct. Epididymitis is usually treated with antibiotics.

Orchitis is an infection of the testicle that often occurs at the same time as epididymitis. Orchitis can also be a viral infection connected to the mumps. Although this condition is rare, it can cause infertility and irreversible damage to the testes.

If you feel sudden pain in your testes or find a scrotal lump, call the advice nurse.

SELF-CARE STEPS FOR TESTICULAR PAIN

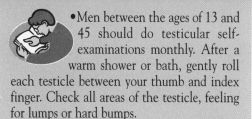

• Men between the ages of 13 and 45 should do testicular self-examinations monthly. After a warm shower or bath, gently roll each testicle between your thumb and index finger. Check all areas of the testicle, feeling for lumps or hard bumps.

DECISION GUIDE FOR TESTICULAR PAIN

SYMPTOMS/SIGNS	ACTION
Scrotal lump	
Sudden, painful swelling in testes	

Call the advice nurse

For more about the symbols, see p. 3.

SPECIAL COMPLAINTS OF WOMEN

Until recently, research on women's health concerns has been largely neglected. Many of the major studies in understanding disease processes have been conducted on men only.

This section describes common problems related to women's health and suggests ways to take care of nonurgent conditions at home. Your medical provider can offer advice and treatment for most gender-related problems. If your condition is especially hard to handle, your medical provider may involve other professionals who specialize in women's health.

Use the Decision Guides to see if your symptoms clearly need emergency medical services, require a call to the advice nurse, or can be treated using self-care. It is important to consider your own medical history and your current health when deciding what kind of care is right for you. If you have any conditions that do not seem to be healing normally, if the Self-Care Steps provided do not seem to help, or if you are uncertain about your symptoms, call the advice nurse. The advice nurse will evaluate your symptoms and recommend the next best steps for you to take.

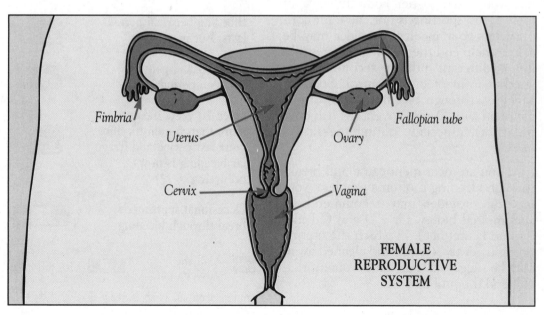

Fimbria

Uterus

Cervix

Fallopian tube

Ovary

Vagina

**FEMALE
REPRODUCTIVE
SYSTEM**

I'm 46 years old and have rarely had problems with my menstrual cycle. It's always been fairly regular, with about 28 days from the start of one period to the next. But in the last 6 months I've had bleeding in the middle of the month about four times. The first two times it was just spotting for 2 days—enough to need a panti-liner, but not much more. Still, I was concerned. I decided to start a diary to record the days I had bleeding, how heavy or light the flow was, and what other things were happening at that time.

The third month, the bleeding lasted as long and the flow was as heavy as my periods usually are. After the bleeding stopped, I went to see my medical provider. I showed her the diary. After examining me, she said I was probably nearing menopause and that irregular periods and spotting are common among premenopausal women.

Not knowing when spotting or a full-fledged period might start is still a nuisance. But I feel better knowing that nothing is wrong.

Virginia

BLEEDING BETWEEN PERIODS

Bleeding between periods can be inconvenient and annoying. In most cases, however, it is nothing to worry about. In fact, most women have spotting, breakthrough bleeding, or irregular periods at some point in their lives. But, because bleeding between periods can also be a sign of more serious problems, it merits a call to the advice nurse if it happens more than 2 months in a row.

Spotting (light bleeding) or breakthrough bleeding (heavier bleeding) between periods usually lasts 1 or 2 days. About 10 percent of women regularly have spotting around the time of ovulation. Bleeding between periods is also common when hormones are fluctuating (rising and falling) the most—during the first few years of menstruation and again as women approach menopause.

Spotting is very common in women with intrauterine devices (IUDs). It may also occur if the hormone levels in the birth control pills a woman is taking are not well-suited to her body. In most of these cases, spotting is not cause for concern, but your medical provider may be able to help end the problem by prescribing a different pill or recommending another form of birth control. Spotting and breakthrough bleeding are also very common with Depo-Provera (a birth control shot), especially during the first 3 months.

If you are near menopause and breakthrough bleeding is often a problem, your medical provider may recommend an endometrial biopsy. Or a D and C (dilation and curettage), in which the uterine lining is gently scraped and cleaned away, may be suggested. For some women, that will end the problem.

If you are having spotting or breakthrough bleeding that is accompanied by unusual pain, lasts 3 days or more, is very heavy, or happens more than 2 months in a row, you should call the advice nurse. Also, if pregnancy is a possibility and you are spotting, you should call the advice nurse.

DECISION GUIDE FOR BLEEDING BETWEEN PERIODS

SYMPTOMS/SIGNS	ACTION
Very heavy bleeding (for example, bleeding enough to soak a pad or tampon an hour for 2 to 3 hours in a row)	☎
Spotting or breakthrough bleeding occurring 2 or more months in a row	☎
Menstrual pattern doesn't return to normal by the third month	☎
Bleeding between periods lasts 3 or more days	☎
Bleeding and pain between periods	☎
Over 40 years old and more than 6 months since your last period and irregular bleeding is now occurring	☎
Occasional spotting or breakthrough bleeding	▭

☎ Call the advice nurse   ▭ Use self-care

For more about the symbols, see p. 3.

SELF-CARE STEPS FOR BLEEDING BETWEEN PERIODS

• After a while, many women take their menstrual cycles in stride. Many find it difficult to remember the exact date of the first day of their last period, let alone dates a few months earlier. That's why it's important to keep a menstrual diary if you begin having bleeding that is unusual for you. Keep a written record of the dates of your periods and any bleeding between periods. Also note how long the bleeding lasted and how heavy the flow was. This diary can help your medical provider find the possible cause and decide whether the between-period bleeding is anything to be concerned about.

• Wear a pad or tampon to protect your clothing while you are bleeding, just as you would during a regular period.

• Avoid aspirin while you are bleeding. It may increase the flow.

• Relax. In many instances, spotting and breakthrough bleeding are nothing to worry about.

BREASTFEEDING PROBLEMS

Also see Breastfeeding/Bottlefeeding, p. 190.

Breast milk has several advantages for newborn babies: It contains all the essential nutrients in their ideal proportions and provides natural protection against infection. Very few new mothers are physically unable to breastfeed. Some of the most common problems—pain, engorged breasts, or a low milk supply—can be overcome with persistence and support from your medical provider and family.

Engorgement (overly full, hard breasts) occurs when the milk first comes in. It may also make the breasts feel sore in between feedings. Mild swelling and tenderness is normal for 24 to 48 hours. More severe engorgement can be caused by not feeding correctly or often enough.

Nipple pain is often caused by the baby latching on to the nipple incorrectly.

PREVENTIVE STEPS

• Hold the baby close to your breast (nose and chin should lightly touch your breast) to reduce tugging.

• Encourage letdown before feedings by gently massaging the breasts from the fleshy part down to the nipple.

• Try to get the baby to open wide and take a portion of the areola (the darkened area around the nipple), not just the tip of the nipple.

• Make sure the baby eats at least eight times in 24 hours.

• Vary the baby's nursing positions.

• Wear a supportive bra.

After reading about the benefits of breastfeeding, I was determined to make it work for my baby and me. Instead, I was frustrated and in pain. My nipples were sore and cracked and my left breast became inflamed. I felt like I had the flu and could barely get out of bed, much less feed my baby.

Kim

If a breast infection (a localized "abscess" or generalized "mastitis") is diagnosed, an antibiotic will be prescribed. Breastfeeding can continue normally without danger from the infection or the antibiotic. It usually becomes less painful and more enjoyable with time.

Family Practitioner

DECISION GUIDE FOR BREASTFEEDING PROBLEMS

SYMPTOMS/SIGNS	ACTION
Part or all of one breast becomes inflamed, or painful lump in one breast	
Temperature of a level you believe to be a fever	
Nipple pain lasts beyond 1 week; cracked or bleeding nipples	
Engorgement lasts longer than 48 hours	
Unable to get baby to nurse at least six times in 24 hours	
Nipple tenderness at latch-on does not get better after the first minute when the baby begins to swallow	
Normal engorgement, short-term nipple pain	

 Call the advice nurse    Use self-care

For more about the symbols, see p. 3.

SELF-CARE STEPS FOR BREASTFEEDING PROBLEMS

For engorgement
• Apply warm compresses to breasts for a few minutes to help the milk start to flow (called letdown).

• Do gentle breast massage.

• Encourage frequent feedings (every 2 to 3 hours).

• Use cold compresses after feedings for up to 10 minutes for comfort and to reduce swelling.

• Acetaminophen (Tylenol, Tempra, or a generic) may be used for pain relief; follow the manufacturer's instructions.

For sore nipples
• Do gentle breast massage to assist letdown.

• Begin feedings on the least tender nipple.

• Encourage frequent feedings limited to 10 to 15 minutes per breast.

• Apply a drop or two of expressed breast milk to the nipples after feedings to ease nipple discomfort.

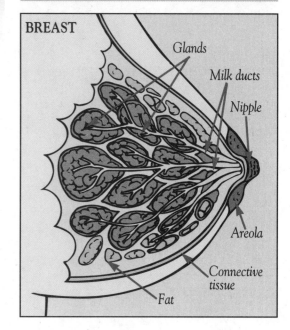

BREAST

Glands

Milk ducts

Nipple

Areola

Connective tissue

Fat

DIFFICULT PERIODS

Menstrual periods are different from woman to woman. For some, they may last only 3 days, and for others, they are as long as 7 days. The flow may be light or heavy, and cycles from the start of one period to the start of the next can be anywhere from 21 to 40 days. Over the years, a woman's menstrual pattern is likely to change. In the early years, it may be irregular and heavy. As time goes by, it may come like clockwork. The amount of flow may change over time as well.

All these variations are normal. For most women, menstruation comes and goes each month with ease. But for others—or at various times in a woman's childbearing years—periods can be complicated by pain (**dysmenorrhea**) or premenstrual symptoms.

Menstrual cramps are most common between the ages of 15 and 24 years and among women who have not given birth. Pain can be mild or so severe that it sends the woman to bed for 1 to 3 days. Very bad cramps may be accompanied by diarrhea, nausea, and headache.

Researchers in the 1970s and 1980s discovered higher than average levels of **prostaglandin**—fatty acids in the body that act much like hormones—in the menstrual fluid of women who suffered from cramps. Prostaglandins serve many functions in the body, but too much can cause pain from uterine irritability or contractions. This source of menstrual pain is often common to women of the same family.

Other reasons for painful periods may be **fibroids** (noncancerous growths) in the uterus, infection, or **endometriosis** (uterine lining growing outside of the uterus). If your periods become more painful or begin to last longer than they used to, you should call the advice nurse. Intrauterine contraceptive devices (IUDs) may also cause pain during menstruation.

Premenstrual Syndrome

Some women feel irritable or depressed, retain fluid or have bloating, and have headaches beginning a few days before their periods. Usually these premenstrual symptoms go away as soon as the menstrual flow begins. About 5 percent of women have more severe symptoms of premenstrual syndrome (PMS), including a monthly cycle of anxiety, depression, and sometimes changes in behavior.

SELF-CARE STEPS FOR DIFFICULT PERIODS

For painful periods
• Use aspirin or ibuprofen. Aspirin usually relieves mild to moderate menstrual pain. Ibuprofen (Advil, Motrin, or a generic) is often effective when the pain is worse. If you do not get enough relief from these over-the-counter drugs, your medical provider may be able to prescribe a higher dose of ibuprofen or a prescription nonsteroidal anti-inflammatory drug. Begin taking the drug at the first sign of symptoms, whether menstrual bleeding has actually begun or not.

• Apply heat. A heating pad or hot-water bottle placed on the lower abdomen will ease the pain. Taking a warm bath may also help.

• Raise your hips. If you find yourself in bed because of cramps, try lying on your back with your hips elevated above the level of your shoulders. Put your feet up on the footboard of the bed or the arm of the couch and place pillows under your hips. Firm massaging of the lower back may also help.

For premenstrual symptoms or syndrome
• Avoid salt and caffeine, and drink plenty of fluids to relieve water retention and bloating.

• Exercise regularly and eat a well-balanced diet, low in sugar and high in protein and fiber.

• Daily vitamin B_6 supplements (50 milligrams a day) may help relieve premenstrual symptoms.

My periods were never easy. Other women barely seemed to notice theirs, but I was having such bloating before and awful cramps during my periods that I'd come to dread them. My first semester at college, I missed 1 or 2 days of class each month because of menstrual cramps. The nurse on campus told me to start taking ibuprofen or aspirin the day before I expected my period, to head off the cramps. It worked! I still had some pain, but it wasn't nearly as bad. I was able to attend classes. She also said to avoid salt and increase the amount of fluids I drink to relieve the bloating and fluid retention. Knowing what to do has made a big difference. I don't dread my periods like I used to!

Karen

DECISION GUIDE FOR DIFFICULT PERIODS

SYMPTOMS/SIGNS	ACTION
Very heavy bleeding (enough to soak a pad or tampon an hour for 2 to 3 hours in a row)	☎
Severe depression, anxiety, or other premenstrual symptoms that are not relieved with self-care	☎
Pain during period is worse than it used to be	☎
Painful periods or cramps that can be relieved	▭
Mild to moderate premenstrual symptoms	▭
More than your usual amount of menstrual flow	▭

☎ Call the advice nurse

▭ Use self-care

For more about the symbols, see p. 3.

MENOPAUSE

The years leading up to menopause, when ovulation and menstruation stop, are different from woman to woman. Some women menstruate regularly until their periods suddenly stop. Others may see changes in the amount of menstrual flow or the length of time between periods. Still others have missed periods or bleeding between periods. Although irregular periods are often a normal part of the years leading up to menopause, irregular vaginal bleeding can also be a warning sign of other health problems. If your periods become irregular or you have bleeding between periods, keep a menstrual diary and check with your medical provider or call the advice nurse. (See also Missed Periods, p. 157, and Bleeding between Periods, p. 150.)

As many as 80 percent of women have hot flashes as they near menopause. Some women may have them before periods stop. **Hot flashes**—a flushed feeling that usually begins around the chest and spreads to the neck, face, and arms—usually last 3 to 4 minutes and can occur as often as once an hour. Often hot flashes are followed by sweating and then chills. They can happen any time of day—or night—and may last for up to 5 years, as the woman's body adjusts to the ovaries' much lower production of the hormones estrogen and progesterone. Hot flashes rarely last longer than 5 years.

Increasingly, researchers have come to believe that a lack of adequate sleep as a result of nighttime hot flashes is to blame for much of the moodiness and other psychological symptoms linked with menopause. Scientific studies have yet to prove a relationship between lower estrogen levels and depression, moodiness, irritability, fatigue, or other psychological symptoms commonly felt during menopause. Lack of adequate sleep, however, can cause any number of these symptoms, making nighttime hot flashes a likely culprit. Other life issues happening along with menopause may also add to depression or other symptoms. Some examples are career issues, children leaving home, caring for aging parents, or, possibly, struggling with what it means to be growing older and experiencing bodily changes that come with aging.

Reduced estrogen levels in the body do, however, contribute to vaginal dryness and urinary problems, both of which can continue to be problems well beyond menopause. With much less estrogen in the body, the vaginal walls lose elasticity, become thinner, and secrete less fluid. A drier, less elastic vagina can mean discomfort or pain during or after intercourse. Surprisingly, avoiding intercourse can make the problem worse, while continued sexual activity improves blood circulation and suppleness of the vagina, thus reducing or stopping discomfort during intercourse.

Hormone replacement therapy (HRT) can relieve vaginal dryness, reduce or end hot flashes, help bladder symptoms, prevent osteoporosis, and may reduce cardiovascular disease risk. In the 1960s, estrogen was often given alone, and some women later developed a low-grade endometrial (uterine) cancer. When both estrogen and progesterone are given as HRT, however, the risk of endometrial cancer is actually less than if the woman is taking no estrogen at all. For this reason, combined estrogen and progesterone is recommended for women who have not had a hysterectomy. Estrogen alone is recommended for those who have had a hysterectomy.

Many women and medical providers worry that estrogen replacement therapy may increase the risk of breast cancer. The largest and most carefully done studies, however, show no absolute evidence that this is true. Furthermore, estrogen has been shown to lower the risk of cardiovascular disease and osteoporosis. Most experts today agree

I knew I was going through "the change" when I started waking at night with hot flashes. I've always had trouble getting back to sleep once awakened. But I found that lowering the thermostat and putting a few layers of thin blankets on the bed helped. That way I could easily uncover to cool off or cover up to warm up without getting out of bed or waking up fully. When I started exercising regularly and stopped drinking so much coffee, the hot flashes seemed to let up a bit and I slept better all the way around.

Thelma

SELF-CARE STEPS FOR MENOPAUSE SYMPTOMS

- Dress in layers and wear loose clothing.

- Set the thermostat at 68° F or lower.

- Drink plenty of water. Six to eight glasses a day is about right.

- Exercise regularly. Thirty minutes of moderate, weight-bearing exercise (such as walking) 3 days a week can help reduce hot flashes and guard against osteoporosis by building stronger bones. Non-weight-bearing exercise, such as swimming or bicycling, will also help with hot flashes and benefit your heart, but is not helpful in preventing osteoporosis.

- Avoid caffeine and alcohol, which can intensify hot flashes and cause insomnia.

- Use a water-soluble lubricant (K-Y Jelly, Astroglide, Replens, Surgilube) to relieve vaginal dryness. Don't use petroleum jelly products, such as Vaseline.

- Allow yourself time to become aroused before having intercourse. Menopause does not cause you to lose your sex drive. By savoring the moment, intercourse can be even more enjoyable, and less uncomfortable if you suffer from vaginal dryness.

- Eat a balanced diet that includes 1,200 to 1,500 milligrams of calcium—the equivalent of four to six 8-ounce glasses of milk. If dairy products don't agree with you, a calcium supplement such as Tums E-X may be used. A supplement of vitamin D (400 IU each day) will help your body absorb the calcium, whether from your diet or a supplement.

that the benefits of HRT far outweigh any potential risks.

About 10 percent of women receiving HRT have minor side effects, such as breast tenderness, nausea, headaches, fluid retention, or irregular vaginal bleeding. For most women, however, these side effects do not interfere with continuing the hormone therapy.

Some women should not use HRT (such as those with a history of breast cancer), but other drugs are available to help relieve menopausal symptoms. The decision to use or not to use HRT is best made jointly by each woman and her medical provider.

Whether you choose to use HRT or not, there are some nonhormonal measures you can use to help relieve menopausal symptoms.

DECISION GUIDE FOR MENOPAUSE SYMPTOMS

SYMPTOMS/SIGNS	ACTION
Irregular periods that don't return to normal within 3 months (i.e., periods less than 20 days from the start of one to the start of the next cycle; cycles more than 90 days apart; bleeding longer than 8 days)	
Bleeding between periods or bleeding heavy enough to soak a pad or tampon an hour for 2 to 3 hours in a row	
Any vaginal bleeding after no periods for 6 months or longer	
Pain or burning during urination	
Vaginal bleeding after intercourse	
Symptoms not relieved by self-care	
Hot flashes, vaginal dryness, or irregular periods	

 Call the advice nurse

 Use self-care

For more about the symbols, see p. 3.

MISSED PERIODS

For most women, the first thing to come to mind when a menstrual period is missed is pregnancy. Although pregnancy is a common cause of missed periods, there are many other factors that can cause a woman not to menstruate (**amenorrhea**). Stress, being very overweight or underweight, birth control pills, regular hard exercise, and the approach of menopause are all common causes of amenorrhea. Menstrual periods may not resume for several months after a woman gives birth or while she is breastfeeding.

Periods usually begin between the ages of 11 and 14, although some girls begin earlier and others later. But if a girl has not started to menstruate by age 16, she may have one type of amenorrhea. Hormone imbalances or problems with the ovaries, uterus, or vagina may be at fault. If menstruation hasn't begun by age 16, it is wise for the girl to see a medical provider.

Although birth control pills are sometimes prescribed to regulate irregular periods, they can also have the opposite effect, causing no periods. If your periods stop while you are taking one type of pill, switching to another birth control pill may solve the problem. If you are on the pill and your periods stop, talk with your medical provider. Going off the pill after being on it for a while may also disrupt your menstrual cycle for a few months while your body adjusts to the change in hormones.

The first thing to rule out if you miss a period is pregnancy. Home pregnancy tests on the market today are quite accurate beginning the first day after the missed period was supposed to begin.

If you are sure you are not pregnant, it's time to consider other possible causes. Call the advice nurse for information.

My periods have always been regular. I could predict almost to the day when they would start. But a few months ago I had a big scare. My husband and I had just moved to Minneapolis from Chicago. He was settling into a new job. I was still looking—without success. I took a waitressing job nights to keep cash coming in and looked during the day for a job in my profession. In the midst of all this, what should happen? My period doesn't come. I was in a panic.

I waited 2 weeks in fear and then broke down and bought a home pregnancy test kit. It was negative. But that still didn't explain why I missed my period. I'd heard that stress can sometimes cause amenorrhea. I knew I was stressed out! I'd even begun to lose weight. I decided to try taking time out to relax and find ways to ease the stress I was feeling. By the next month, my period returned—back on its usual schedule.

Linnea

SELF-CARE STEPS FOR MISSED PERIODS

• If you are in your 40s or 50s, a missed period may mean you are starting menopause. Before your periods stop entirely, they may be irregular for a time (see Menopause, p. 154).

• For some women, a good bout of the flu or stress at work or home can throw their menstrual cycles off. If you are under stress, find ways to relieve it. Take time out daily to meditate, listen to soothing music, or read a book. Regular exercise and getting enough sleep each night can also reduce stress.

• Rapid weight loss or being very overweight or underweight can also cause amenorrhea. If you are trying to lose weight, make sure you are eating at least 1,200 calories a day from a well-balanced variety of foods. If you are underweight, eat a well-balanced diet that provides about 2,000 calories a day. Whether you are overweight, underweight, or dieting, your medical provider may be able to help you set up a healthy diet and exercise plan.

• Very hard training and exercise can be another cause of amenorrhea. If you are in training and missing periods, easing up may return your periods to normal. If you are an endurance athlete, ask your medical provider if hormone therapy or calcium supplements might be right for you to help prevent osteoporosis.

DECISION GUIDE FOR MISSED PERIODS

SYMPTOMS/SIGNS	ACTION
Missed one or two periods, not pregnant, but under stress, dieting, near menopause, or exercising heavily	
Missed two or more periods, not pregnant, and no obvious cause	
Missed two or more periods, not pregnant, and on birth control pills	
Age 16 or older and have never had a period	
Missing periods and having irregular spotting or pain in lower abdomen	
Occasional missed period	

 Call the advice nurse   Use self-care

For more about the symbols, see p. 3.

URINARY TRACT INFECTIONS

They're bothersome, embarrassing, and painful. Occasionally, they're a sign of a serious health problem. Luckily, most cases of urinary tract infections can be cleared up quickly.

Some urinary tract infections have few symptoms—not even pain or fever. Recognizing urinary tract infections during pregnancy is especially important. **Symptoms of urinary tract infections may include:**

• Frequent and/or urgent urination, especially at night

• A burning feeling during urination

• Blood in the urine

• Pressure in the lower abdomen

• Urine that looks cloudy and/or smells very bad

When a urinary tract infection involves the bladder, the sac where urine is stored before it leaves the body, it's called cystitis. It's often caused by *E. coli* bacteria. This bacteria is common in the bowel and can cause a urinary tract infection if it gets into the urine or bladder or enters the urethra, the tube through which urine leaves the bladder. Urinary tract infections are more common in

PREVENTIVE STEPS FOR URINARY TRACT INFECTIONS

• Drink lots of water—at least 8 glasses a day.

• Women should urinate often, especially before and after sexual intercourse.

• Wear clean, cotton underwear or underwear with a cotton crotch.

• Women should wipe from front to back after using the toilet, to avoid spreading bacteria from the rectal area.

• Avoid bubble bath, perfumed soaps, douches, and deodorant tampons.

• Switch from the diaphragm to another type of birth control if urinary tract infections are a problem.

• Avoid caffeine and alcohol, which can irritate the bladder.

SELF-CARE STEPS FOR URINARY TRACT INFECTIONS

- Avoid caffeine, alcohol, and spicy foods, all of which can make the symptoms worse.
- Drink eight glasses of fluid per day. Water is the best.
- Take tepid or cool sitz baths to relieve the discomfort.
- Call the advice nurse.

DECISION GUIDE FOR URINARY TRACT INFECTIONS

SYMPTOMS/SIGNS	ACTION
Symptoms last longer than 48 hours	☎
Blood in urine	☎
Frequent, burning, urgent urination with temperature of a level you believe to be a fever	☎
Nausea and vomiting	☎
Shaking chills	☎
Four or more urinary tract infections in the past 12 months	☎
Pregnant women with any symptoms of urinary tract infection	☎
Person also has compromised immune system (HIV positive or taking radiation or chemotherapy treatments)	☎
Person also has kidney disease or kidney stones	☎
Suspect urinary tract infection	▣

☎ Call the advice nurse

▣ Use self-care

For more about the symbols, see p. 3.

I've always been prone to urinary tract infections. Since my medical provider explained some preventive steps I can take at home, my infections have happened less often. I quit using the diaphragm and switched to a different type of birth control. I also drink a lot of water, which has made a real difference. But when I get an infection, I call my medical provider's office right away for advice. I know my infections don't go away on their own, but it's nice to know I may not need an appointment every time.

Clare

women because the urethra is shorter and the anus and urethra are closer together than in men. Bacteria may also enter the urinary tract during sexual intercourse or when you use a diaphragm. Perfumed soaps, powders, and bubble bath products also may cause irritation that can lead to infection.

If the infection reaches the kidneys, it's called pyelonephritis. This can sometimes cause permanent kidney damage.

A urine specimen may be requested to diagnose a urinary tract infection. Check with your medical provider to see if this is needed, given your symptoms and history of infections. If a urine specimen is needed, you will be asked to first release some urine into the toilet, then collect a midstream "clean catch" in a special sterile container provided at the medical provider's office. Results of the urinalysis can often be obtained within an hour, but it may take 24 to 48 hours. Some medical guidelines suggest that if you have an uncomplicated urinary tract infection, a short (3-day) course of antibiotics will work. If your medical provider prescribes antibiotics for the infection, you may be asked for another urine specimen after you have finished the pills. A follow-up urine culture can show if the infection is completely gone.

This follow-up test may not be necessary if you have a history of uncomplicated infections.

Women who have frequent urinary infections and who have been appropriately evaluated by their medical provider often keep antibiotics at home and begin taking them at the first sign of a bladder infection. If you have frequent urinary tract infections, discuss this possibility with your medical provider.

VAGINAL DISCHARGE AND IRRITATION

Although makers of feminine hygiene sprays and douches would like you to believe otherwise, a healthy vagina cleans itself naturally. A clear or opaque vaginal discharge is part of this cleaning process.

However, several conditions can cause irritation in and around the vagina and changes in the color, smell, amount, or consistency of the vaginal discharge. These include vaginal yeast infections, nonspecific vaginitis, trichomoniasis, and sexually transmitted diseases, such as the herpes simplex virus type 2.

Vaginal yeast infections are usually marked by a thick, white discharge like cottage cheese, although sometimes it is clear. The vagina and labia (the lips of the vagina) may be red and swollen. Yeast infections also cause intense itching and burning in the genital area. An overgrowth of normal vaginal flora, *Candida albicans (Monilia)*, is the usual culprit. This type of infection is more likely during pregnancy, after taking antibiotics, when using birth control pills, or if you have diabetes. Spreading yeast infections through sex is rare, but if your partner has genital itching, an over-the-counter antifungal cream may be used topically.

One type of bacteria-caused vaginal infection is *Gardnerella*. Symptoms include a yellow or white vaginal discharge, itching, burning during urination, and pain in the vaginal area following intercourse. If you think you may have *Gardnerella*, call the advice nurse. Bacterial vaginal infection is usually treated with specific oral antibiotics.

Trichomoniasis is caused by a tiny organism. Symptoms include a yellow-green frothy discharge from the vagina, itching, and sometimes pain. The discharge may or may not have a bad odor. Because the *Trichomonas* parasite can live in the male prostate gland, your partner should also be treated to prevent reinfection. Call the advice nurse if you have symptoms.

Sexually transmitted diseases (STDs) can also cause vaginal irritation, and some cause an abnormal vaginal discharge. (For more information on STDs and their prevention, see p. 211.)

Although other vaginal infections usually require examination and treatment by a medical provider, yeast infections can usually be treated safely and well at home.

PREVENTIVE STEPS

- Clean perineal area (area between the vagina and rectum) daily with water.

- Wear cotton underwear or underwear with a cotton crotch.

- Avoid tight-fitting jeans and pantyhose.

- Avoid deodorant tampons or frequent douches.

- Avoid a high-carbohydrate diet.

- Use adequate lubrication during intercourse.

- Avoid scented or deodorant soaps, laundry detergents, or fabric softeners that cause irritation.

SELF-CARE STEPS FOR VAGINAL DISCHARGE AND IRRITATION

• Use an over-the-counter anti-fungal vaginal cream or sup-pository (such as Monistat, Gyne-Lotrimin, Mycelex). Follow the package directions and be sure to use all the medicine.

• Apply cool compresses to the perineal area (area between the vagina and rectum) or soak in an oatmeal bath product (Aveeno bath treatment).

• Avoid bubble baths, vaginal sprays, and douching (unless prescribed). Soaking in a tub of plain, lukewarm water, however, is helpful.

• Avoid sexual intercourse for a few days to prevent further irritation.

• If home treatment doesn't relieve your symptoms, or if symptoms get worse, call the advice nurse.

DECISION GUIDE FOR VAGINAL DISCHARGE AND IRRITATION

SYMPTOMS/SIGNS	ACTION
Self-care fails to relieve symptoms, or symptoms worsen	
Yellow or greenish vaginal discharge with itching, burning during urination, and/or pain during or after intercourse	
Sores in the genital area	
Lower abdominal pain	
Itching; white, cottage-cheese-like discharge; redness and swelling around vagina and labia	

 Call the advice nurse   Use self-care

For more about the symbols, see p. 3.

I'd never had a vaginal yeast infection before, but I had heard about them. And I was pretty sure all the symptoms I was having fit. The itching and discharge were driving me crazy! Because this was the first time I'd had these symptoms, I called the medical provider's office to make sure. The nurse recommended a nonprescription vaginal cream and gave me some "recipes" for cool compresses to soothe the itching. What a relief!

Sonya

INJURIES AND ACCIDENTS

Even with the best precautions, accidents can happen. The key to a quick and effective response to accidental injuries when they do happen is to learn basic first-aid techniques ahead of time and keep on hand supplies necessary to care for injuries (see Stocking Your Own First-Aid Kit, p.7). This section discusses some common accidents and injuries and how you can take care of nonurgent problems at home.

Use the Decision Guides to see if your symptoms clearly need emergency medical services, require a call to the advice nurse, or can be treated using self-care. It is important to consider your own medical history and your current health when deciding what kind of care is right for you. If you have any conditions that do not seem to be healing normally, if the Self-Care Steps provided do not seem to help, or if you are uncertain about your symptoms, call the advice nurse. The advice nurse will evaluate your symptoms and recommend the next best steps for you to take.

BITES

Human Bites

Human bites happen more often than you think and are usually done by children while playing or fighting. Another frequent source human bites is the result of a person punching someone in the mouth and then discovering that the skin over the knuckles has been broken by the intended victim's teeth.

Infection can result due to the amount and type of bacteria in the human mouth. If a human bite breaks the skin, thoroughly wash the area, then call the advice nurse. The possibility of AIDS being spread through the bite of an HIV-infected person, however, is considered extremely unlikely.

Animal Bites

More than 2 million dog bites resulting in puncture wounds or cuts are reported each year. Half of the victims are children. Millions of bites and nips from other animals are believed to go unreported.

Animal bites raise four concerns: bleeding, the possibility of viral infections like rabies, potential damage to the underlying tissue and the possibility of bacterial infections like tetanus.

Perhaps the best way to treat an animal bite is in advance, before you are bitten. Avoid wild animals, especially if they let you approach. Don't pester unfamiliar dogs or cats or attempt to pet them if they appear at all unfriendly.

SELF-CARE STEPS FOR HUMAN BITES

• Check for bleeding if you have a human bite. If the wound is bleeding, apply direct pressure and try to raise the wound above heart level. Wash it vigorously with mild soap and a wash cloth under running water for at least 5 minutes.

• Check to be sure you've received a tetanus booster within the last 10 years. A booster for tetanus may be recommended sooner if you have a wound at high risk for tetanus. Watch the wound site closely for signs of infection, and call the advice nurse if you have been bitten hard enough to penetrate the skin.

SELF-CARE STEPS FOR ANIMAL BITES

• Wash all animal bites vigorously with soap and under running water for 5 minutes, even if they have not bled. Apply an antiseptic ointment (bacitracin, Neosporin) to shallow puncture wounds, and watch for signs of infection. Deep puncture wounds, especially cat bites, can carry a greater risk of infection. If an animal bite penetrates the skin, call the advice nurse.

• The main carriers of rabies are wild animals —most often skunks, raccoons, bats, and foxes. Rabid animals act strangely, attack without provocation, and may drool or foam at the mouth. If a pet has bitten you, the animal needs to be confined and watched for 10 days if possible.

DECISION GUIDE FOR HUMAN OR ANIMAL BITES

SYMPTOMS/SIGNS	ACTION
Bite results in severed body part	
Wild animal bite	
Bite by a strange dog or cat	
Unprovoked animal bite or concern that the animal is ill	
No tetanus booster received within the last 10 years	
Signs of infection (See Decision Guide, p. 122)	
Bite that penetrates the skin, especially on face, hand, or foot	
Pain that gets worse rather than better within 3 days	
Human bite that is the result of violence or assault	
Any human bite that penetrates the skin	& 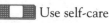
Human bite that does not penetrate the skin	

 Seek help now   Use self-care

Call the advice nurse   *For more about the symbols, see p. 3.*

BURNS

Also see Chemical Burns, p.167; and Household Electrical Shocks, p. 173.

Burns occur when the skin touches hot surfaces, liquids, steam, or flame (also see Chemical Burns, p. 167). Skin burns are graded by degree. The higher the number, the more severe the burn. **First-degree** burns are slight burns affecting the top portion of the skin. Symptoms include redness, pain, and minor swelling.

Second-degree burns affect the top layer of skin and the second layer. These burns cause redness, pain, swelling, and some blisters. Although second-degree burns are probably the most painful burns, most can be treated successfully at home if only a small amount of skin is burned.

Third-degree burns destroy all skin layers and may penetrate deep below the surface of the skin. The damaged skin may be red, white, or charred black. Because there is a lot of nerve damage, there may be no pain and little bleeding. Third degree burns, large-area burns, burns that result in a lot of blistering, or serious burns on the hand or face probably should be seen by a medical provider.

In **severe burns**, the wound will weep or ooze large amounts of plasma—the clear liquid portion of blood—from damaged blood vessels in the wound area.

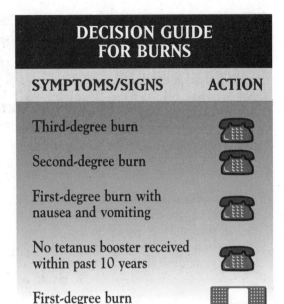

DECISION GUIDE FOR BURNS

SYMPTOMS/SIGNS	ACTION
Third-degree burn	☎
Second-degree burn	☎
First-degree burn with nausea and vomiting	☎
No tetanus booster received within past 10 years	☎
First-degree burn	🩹

☎ Call the advice nurse

🩹 Use self-care

For more about the symbols, see p. 3.

SELF-CARE STEPS FOR BURNS

- For fast pain relief, soak a small-area burn in cold water or apply cold, wet compresses. Do not use ice water or snow, unless that is the only source of cold available. The wet, cooling action stops the burning process below the skin surface by dissipating the heat that remains after the initial burn.

- Take acetaminophen (Tylenol, Tempra, or a generic) to relieve pain.

- Do not break blisters that may form over a burn since this could lead to infection.

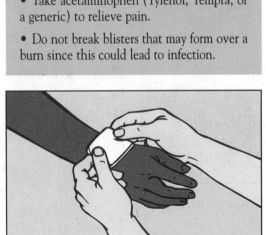

For minor burns: soak burned area in cold water, use bacitracin to prevent dehydration, apply a light gauze bandage, and tape where skin is not burned.

SELF-CARE STEPS FOR SEVERE BURNS

• If the person's clothes are on fire, smother the flames with a blanket, towel, rug, or coat. Wrap it over the flames, pressing down to keep air from reaching the fire. The person may struggle or attempt to run. Get him or her on the floor so the burning surface is uppermost and flames can rise away from the body.

• Pull away any bits of clothing that may be smoldering. Leave any material that is burnt but extinguished and sticking to the skin. Solvents stocked by hospital emergency departments can safely remove these bits.

• Cover the burn with a clean, dry dressing that covers the entire burn area. Do not apply butter, first-aid creams, or antiseptics to the wound. Do not rupture blisters that form on the burn.

• Cover the person with a blanket and raise his or her feet 8 to 12 inches. **Do not elevate the person's feet if you suspect head, neck, back, or leg injuries.**

• If conscious and showing no signs of vomiting, the person should be encouraged to drink tepid water to replace fluids and salts lost in weeping plasma.

First-Degree Burn

Minor burns injure the epidermis, or outside skin layer. The skin will be red, dry, or swollen. These burns may peel and are usually painful. Examples include mild sunburns or slight scaldings. Medical attention is not needed unless a larger area of skin is damaged. Such burns usually heal within 5 to 6 days without permanent scars.

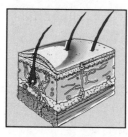

Second-Degree Partial-Thickness Burn

Some of the skin layers beneath the surface are injured by partial-thickness burns. These burns are marked by blisters, local swelling, clear fluid discharge, and mottled skin. The pain may be severe. If the burn covers an area larger than a square inch, call the advice nurse. Healing takes 3 to 4 weeks and may leave scars.

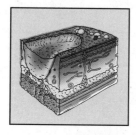

Third-Degree Full-Thickness Burn

Full-thickness burns destroy all of the skin layers and any or all of the nerves, muscles, bones, or fat underneath. These burns have a charred appearance. The tissues surrounding or beneath the burn may be white or look waxy. Full-thickness burns are either very painful or painless, depending upon nerve damage. Scars may occur, depending upon the severity of the burn.

CHEMICAL BURNS

Chemical burns are caused by being doused or splashed with a harsh acid or alkaline chemical. These chemicals can burn the skin in exactly the same way as fire. A chemical burn can be a serious medical problem.

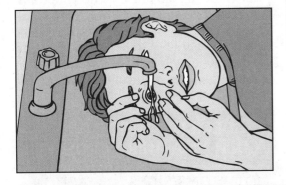

DECISION GUIDE FOR CHEMICAL BURNS	
SYMPTOMS/SIGNS	**ACTION**
Burn involves eye	☎ & 🩹
1st, 2nd, or 3rd degree chemical burn	☎ & 🩹

☎ Call the advice nurse   🩹 Use self-care

For more about the symbols, see p. 3.

Flush eye with cool, clean water for at least 20 to 30 minutes.

SELF-CARE STEPS FOR CHEMICAL BURNS

Skin Burns

• Flush the burned area with a gentle, constant spray of water for at least 10 minutes using a hose, bucket, or shower. Remove all clothing on the burned area and keep flushing until you are certain all the chemical has been washed away.

• After flushing, call the advice nurse or your medical provider for more instructions. Dry the wound site and cover with a clean cloth or dressing.

• Do not apply first-aid ointments, antiseptics, or home remedies to chemical burns. Cool, wet dressings work best to relieve pain.

Eye Burns

• Speed in removing a chemical from the eye is vital. Before calling the advice nurse, begin flushing the eye right away with a constant stream of cool, clean water for at least 20 to 30 minutes. A stream of water can't harm the eye, and thorough washing can reduce the risk of permanent eye damage. Use milk if water is unavailable. Do not bandage the eye before seeing a medical provider.

• To flush the eye, hold the person's head under a faucet or use a pitcher of water, a plastic squirt bottle, a drinking fountain, or shower spray. Hold the eyelids open for proper flushing. Make sure the water runs from the inside corner of the eye (near the nose) outward, so that the contaminated water doesn't flow into the unaffected eye.

• If both eyes are affected, let water flow over both or quickly alternate flushing each eye. Make sure water reaches all parts of the eye by lifting and separating the eyelids. Another method is to submerge the top half of the person's face in a large bowl or sink. Have the person open both eyes and move the eyelids up and down. **This technique should not be used with young children who are upset or who cannot hold their breath.**

• Advise the individual not to rub his or her eyes. After flushing the eye, call the advice nurse.

If you exercise in the cold, wear clothing that draws perspiration away from your skin—like silk, wool, or polypropylene. Otherwise, when you stop for a rest, a sweat-drenched shirt can chill you so badly that hypothermia may set in.

Susan, Cross-Country Skier

Hypothermia can occur at temperatures as high as 45° F. With cool weather and a wind, you can lose vital body heat in just a few hours. It can happen much faster in colder conditions. If you're going to be outside for a long time, always bring along foul-weather gear.

Exercise Physiologist

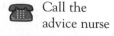

Emergency, call 911

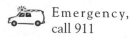

Call the advice nurse

Use self-care

For more about the symbols, see p. 3.

COLD WEATHER EXPOSURE

Many of us live in regions where winter brings the threat of exposure problems such as frostbite and hypothermia (the loss of vital body heat). Fortunately, most cold weather risks are easily managed by using good judgment and the proper clothing.

Frostbite

Frostbite occurs when the skin and tissues below freeze after exposure to very cold temperatures. Hands, feet, nose, and ears are the areas most commonly affected.

Frostbitten areas are cold, white, or grayish-yellow, and hard to the touch. The area may feel very cold and numb, or there may be pain, tingling, or stinging. As the area thaws, it becomes red and painful.

Call the advice nurse if the affected area is still numb after 45 minutes of trying to warm it.

Hypothermia

Hypothermia happens when the body's core temperature drops through exposure to cool and/or damp conditions. The symptoms of hypothermia include

SELF-CARE STEPS FOR COLD WEATHER EXPOSURE

• If you suspect that you are getting frostbite, get out of the cold immediately.

• Warm the frostbitten area by putting it in barely warm, not hot, water (100°). Do not rub the frostbitten area.

• To treat hypothermia, get out of the cold and remove any damp or wet clothing. Dress in warm dry clothes and wrap in blankets or get into a warm bath. Drink warm, nonalcoholic drinks such as coffee, tea, cocoa, or hot cider.

uncontrollable shivering; cold, pale skin; slurred speech; memory lapses; fumbling, stumbling, or staggering; and abnormally slow breathing. The person may feel tired or apathetic. The condition becomes grave when shivering stops, muscles become stiff, and skin turns bluish.

Call the advice nurse if the symptoms are only shivering and cold, pale skin. The advice nurse will be able to recommend the necessary steps to take next. If the person develops other symptoms of hypothermia, get medical help as soon as possible.

DECISION GUIDE FOR COLD WEATHER EXPOSURE

SYMPTOMS/SIGNS	ACTION
Unconsciousness	🚑
Stiff muscles and bluish skin	☎
Confusion, slurred speech	☎
Numb skin that does not improve after 45 minutes	☎
Blistered skin	☎
Headache	☎
Nausea, dizziness, vomiting, or uncontrollable shivering	☎
Pale, cold, clammy skin or cold, white, or grayish-yellow skin	☎
Rapid pulse and breathing	☎
Numb skin	▭

CUTS

Also see Puncture Wounds, p. 176.

Simple cuts can become not-so-simple infections, so it is important to know how to treat them properly.

Minor cuts damage only the skin and the fatty tissue beneath it. They usually heal without permanent damage. More serious cuts may damage muscles, tendons, blood vessels, ligaments, or nerves.

The four major concerns in treating a cut are:

- To stop the bleeding, apply direct pressure to the wound

- To avoid infection, clean the wound thoroughly

- To promote healing, bring the edges of the skin together

- Make sure tetanus immunization is up-to-date

SELF-CARE STEPS FOR CUTS

The next time you get caught on a nail, sliced by a knife, or even cut by a piece of paper, follow these steps:

Stop the Bleeding

- Cover the wound with a gauze pad or a thick, clean piece of cloth. Use your hand if nothing else is available.

- Press on the wound hard enough to stop the bleeding. Don't let up on the pressure even to change cloths. Just add a clean cloth over the original one.

- Raise the wound above heart level, unless this movement would cause pain.

- Call the advice nurse immediately if blood spurts from a wound or bleeding does not stop after applying pressure for 20 minutes, as measured by a clock.

Clean the Wound

- Wash the cut with soap and water or use hydrogen peroxide (3 percent solution). Don't use Mercurochrome, Merthiolate, or iodine. They are not necessary and can be very painful.

- Make sure no dirt, glass, or foreign material remains in the wound.

- If the cut is badly contaminated, the advice nurse can determine if a tetanus shot is necessary.

Bandage the Wound

- Bandage a cut (rather than seeing a medical provider for stitches) when its edges tend to fall together and when the cut is not very deep.

Are Stitches Needed?

- A cut will need stitches when external bandages cannot hold the edges of the wound close enough together to promote healing and reduce scarring. Cuts heal from side to side, so the length of the wound does not determine whether stitches are necessary.

- Stitches may also be called for when the wound continues to bleed for a long time.

- Even though stitches are put in under sterile conditions, the stitching material is foreign to the body and can make it easier for infections to develop.

- Most cuts do not need stitches and can be taken care of at home following basic self-care techniques. If you feel a cut might need stitches, call the advice nurse.

SELF-CARE STEPS FOR APPLYING STERI-STRIPS

Applying Steri-strips

Steri-strips, also called butterfly bandages, are adhesive bandages that do not contain any gauze. They are used to hold the edges of a wound together in the same way stitches do. Steri-strips are available at most drug stores. To apply steri-strips:

1. Gather all the materials you will need including steri-strips, cotton swabs, and tincture of benzoin. (This is used to help the steri-strips stick to the skin, and is available at most drugstores.)

2. Use the cotton swab to apply the tincture of benzoin around the edge of the cut. Do not put the liquid on the cut itself.

3. Allow the tincture of benzoin to dry for a few seconds and remove the protective backing from the first steri-strip.

4. Pull the edges of the skin together so they just meet and place the first steri-strip across the middle of the wound.

5. Place the second and third steri-strips on either side of the first bandage, halfway between the outer ends of the cut and the middle of the cut where the first strip is in place.

6. Continue to add new steri-strips between two bandages that are already in place until steri-strips extend along the length of the cut at 1/4 inch intervals.

7. Replace the steri-strips with fresh ones every 48 hours until the edges of the wound heal and bandages are no longer necessary.

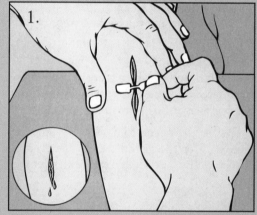

Place the first steri-strip across the middle of the cut.

Place the next steri-strip between the middle and outer ends of the cut.

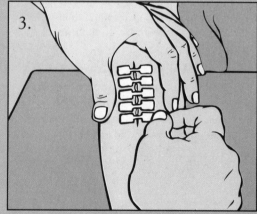

Add new steri-strips until they cover the length of the cut at 1/4 inch intervals.

DECISION GUIDE FOR CUTS

SYMPTOMS/SIGNS	ACTION
Numbness or weakness	☎
Uncontrolled bleeding after 20 minutes (by the clock) of direct pressure	☎
Unable to move fingers or toes normally	☎
Cut doesn't heal after 14 days	☎
No tetanus booster received in the past 10 years	☎
Cut badly contaminated	☎
Cut is deep or irregular or the edges of the wound cannot easily be held together with a bandage or steri-strips	☎
Signs of infection (See Decision Guide, p. 122)	☎
Cut is deep and located on the face, chest, abdomen, back, palm, finger, knee, or elbow	☎
Bleeding stops within 20 minutes (by the clock) of direct pressure	🩹
Cut is shallow	🩹

☎ Call the advice nurse

🩹 Use self-care

For more about the symbols, see p. 3.

HEAD INJURIES

Traffic or work accidents, falls, and fights can cause head injuries. Fortunately, most head injuries are minor.

A **concussion** is a brief loss of consciousness due to a blow to the head. The most common symptom is a constant headache that may get worse, sometimes accompanied by vomiting. Other symptoms can include blurred vision, sleepiness, and memory problems. Athletes who have had a head injury should not return to their sport without a medical evaluation. People taking anticoagulants (drugs to prevent blood clotting) need to take special precautions to prevent falls because they could bleed more easily from a blow to the head.

Call the advice nurse if a head injury results in loss of consciousness, breathing difficulty, or a neck injury. Every person with a head injury that isn't bleeding should be watched for 24 hours for symptoms. In the absence of nausea, vomiting, or other symptoms, careful observation is the best way to monitor a head injury.

SELF-CARE STEPS FOR HEAD INJURIES

- If the head is bleeding, apply pressure to control bleeding.
- Clean the wound and bandage it if possible. Apply an ice bag for swelling.
- Check to see if the individual's pupils are equal in size.
- Check skin color every few hours. Wake a child every 2 hours to observe breathing and to be assured of consciousness. Wake an adult every few hours to check breathing and level of consciousness.
- Question the person about name, age, and address to check his or her level of confusion.
- Limit activity for 24 hours after the injury, if possible.

In head injury cases, the eyes should be examined to see if the pupils are constricting evenly. This can be done at home by shining a flashlight in the eyes to see if both pupils become smaller, even when the light is only in one eye. Unequal pupil size can be a symptom of internal bleeding. It requires immediate medical attention.

Urgent Care Physician

ACCIDENT PREVENTION

Adults

- Wear a helmet when riding bikes, horses, or motorcycles, or when using in-line skates.
- Use seat belts in automobiles.
- Wear hard hats at industrial sites.
- Never dive into shallow water.

Children

- Childproof your home.
- Be very careful when picking up and carrying infants.
- Do not use baby walkers and never leave infants alone on beds, changing tables, or other high places.
- Supervise outside play.
- Teach safety in crossing streets.
- Have children wear a helmet when biking, riding horses, or wearing in-line skates.
- Use seat belts and car safety seats in vehicles.
- Teach children not to dive into shallow water.

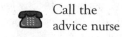 Call the advice nurse

 Use self-care

For more about the symbols, see p. 3.

DECISION GUIDE FOR HEAD INJURIES

SYMPTOMS/SIGNS	ACTION
Bleeding from the scalp lasts longer than 10 minutes with pressure	
Person appears dazed or confused or is hard to awaken	
Person loses consciousness	
Seizures occur	
Person has difficulty walking or talking normally	
Headaches increase in severity	
Vomiting persists	
Person has blurred vision or unequal pupils	
Person has severe headache or neck pain	
Breathing is difficult	
Bloody drainage occurs from the person's nostrils or ears	
Severe swelling around area of injury within 2 hours	
Person experienced a head injury but does not show obvious symptoms	

HOUSEHOLD ELECTRICAL SHOCKS

Although getting a shock from an electrical appliance or socket in your home can be a frightening experience, the majority of shocks require no treatment. If you are concerned about symptoms resulting from a shock, call the advice nurse.

SELF-CARE STEPS FOR HOUSEHOLD ELECTRICAL SHOCKS

• Check to see if the person is disoriented or confused by asking him or her the current day and month.

• If a person seems confused following a shock or falls unconscious, call **911**.

PREVENTING HOUSEHOLD ELECTRICAL SHOCKS

• Check to see that there is no exposed wiring in your home. If you discover exposed wiring, do not touch it—call a qualified electrician to fix the problem.

• If there are small children in the house, cover electrical outlets with plastic protectors. These can be purchased in most hardware stores.

• Always unplug electrical appliances before attempting to repair.

• Avoid using any electrical appliance (including hairdryers) around standing or running water.

DECISION GUIDE FOR HOUSEHOLD ELECTRICAL SHOCKS

SYMPTOMS/SIGNS	ACTION
Loss of consciousness	
Confusion or disorientation following electrical shock	
Extensive burns	
Concern about symptoms not listed above	

 Emergency, call 911

Call the advice nurse

For more about the symbols, see p. 3.

INSECT BITES/STINGS

Although most bug bites and stings are harmless, some can be very dangerous. Here's how to tell the difference between a bite or sting that's a bother and one that's a serious medical problem. The reaction to minor bites and stings is local, confined to the area around the bite itself.

Dangerous, life-threatening reactions to insect bites and stings occur throughout the body. The reaction appears on a part of the body separate from the sting site. Generalized reactions include hives or swelling all over the body, shortness of

Scratching an insect bite can lead to infection. An ice cube will help calm a painful insect bite. Calamine lotion, hydrocortisone cream, or an appropriate dose of Benadryl can help relieve an itchy bite.
Pediatrics Nurse

Wash bite in cool running water.

breath, wheezing, swelling of the throat that causes difficulty swallowing, nausea, stomach cramping, vomiting, loss of bowel and bladder control, weakness, dizziness or fainting, drop in blood pressure, shock, or unconsciousness. Refer to the Decision Guide for insect bites/stings if any of these symptoms develop.

Allergic to Bees?

People who are allergic to bee stings need to know about effective treatment methods. Anyone who has had an allergic reaction to an insect sting should follow the suggestions below:

- Carry a bee sting kit at all times. A medical provider can prescribe one. These kits contain injectable adrenaline that can be lifesaving.

- Carry a card or wear a bracelet that alerts others to the condition.

- Ask the medical provider if venom desensitization injections will help. This series of injections can reduce the reaction to bee, wasp, hornet, or yellow jacket stings for some allergic people.

To remove a stinger, scrape it gently with a credit card, fingernail, knife blade, or other rigid object. Do not squeeze with your fingers or tweezers, because this can inject more venom into the skin.

SELF-CARE STEPS FOR INSECT BITES/STINGS

Bees, mosquitoes, flies, chiggers, ticks, gnats, and other insects can all produce painful stings or bites. Here's what to do for local insect stings and bites:

- Remove the stinger when stung by a bee. Scrape over the stinger (which looks like a splinter) with a credit card, fingernail, knife blade, or other rigid object. Do not remove it with your fingers or tweezers, because you may inject more venom into the skin.

- Apply cold quickly. Cool compresses or ice packs will help relieve the pain and prevent swelling from most bug bites. The longer you wait to apply a cold treatment, the worse the local reaction will be. Apply cold packs for no more than 20 minutes at a time to avoid frostbite.

- Wash the site of the bite and the surrounding area thoroughly with soap and water.

- Don't scratch the itch. Apply calamine lotion or hydrocortisone cream. Take Benadryl (an antihistamine) if itching or more local swelling occurs. Benadryl will help reduce late-appearing symptoms but is not an effective emergency treatment.

Preventing Insect Bites

Avoid perfumes, aftershave, scented hair sprays, and scented deodorants. Wear insect repellent, light-colored clothing, long-sleeved tops, long pants, socks, and shoes. Floral patterns attract bees; so do food, beverages, and garbage cans. If a bee comes near you, avoid sudden movements. Stay still or move away slowly.

DECISION GUIDE FOR INSECT BITES/STINGS

SYMPTOMS/SIGNS	ACTION
Severe trouble breathing	
Pain that gets worse rather than better after 3 days	
Rash all over the body	
Swelling all over the body	
Signs of infection (See Decision Guide, p. 122)	
Bite by a brown house spider or black widow spider (most common in the South)	
Nausea, vomiting, loss of bowel and bladder control	
Dizziness or fainting	
Hives or swelling all over the body	
Muscle spasms or weakness	
Difficulty walking	
Difficulty keeping eyes open when awake	
Temperature of a level you believe to be a fever following a bite or sting	
Throbbing pain	
Burning, redness	

NOSEBLEEDS

Many things can bring on a nosebleed—a change in altitude, excessive nose blowing, or a bang or punch to the nose. Dry weather or certain medications can dry out the membranes inside the nose, also causing them to bleed. Nosebleeds rarely signal more serious illnesses and can almost always be handled with self-care.

SELF-CARE STEPS FOR NOSEBLEEDS

 • Get into a sitting position. Do not tilt your head back or lie down. Pinch affected nostril(s) shut by pressing just above the flares and just under the nasal cartilage on either side for 20 minutes (timed with a watch or clock) while you breathe out through your mouth.

• To prevent nasal linings from drying out, use a humidifier or vaporizer to add moisture to the air in your home. Place a small amount of petroleum jelly along the middle of each nostril one to three times daily to help moisten the membranes.

• If repeated nose blowing or sneezing is causing nosebleeds, try to blow more gently and take an antihistamine to reduce sneezing. Avoid scented tissues which can irritate your nose, causing more sniffling and sneezing.

• If you have recently moved to a high altitude location, be patient. The body takes several weeks to adjust to the change in altitude and the nosebleeds will eventually subside.

 Call the advice nurse

Use self-care

For more about the symbols, see p. 3.

DECISION GUIDE FOR NOSEBLEEDS

SYMPTOMS/SIGNS	ACTION
Nosebleeds every day for a week	
Bleeding doesn't stop after 15 minutes (by the clock) of direct pressure	
Nosebleed resulting from violence or assault	
Nosebleed resulting from an accident, change of altitude, dry air, cold, or allergy	

 Call the advice nurse

Use self-care

For more about the symbols, see p. 3.

PUNCTURE WOUNDS

Also see Cuts, p. 169; and Bites, p. 163.

A puncture wound is a small but deep hole produced by a sharp object such as a pin, nail, tack, needle, tooth, or fang. These wounds are often deep and narrow, with little bleeding. Puncture wounds can become infected because they are difficult to clean and germs are not washed out by the flow of blood.

DECISION GUIDE FOR PUNCTURE WOUNDS

SYMPTOMS/SIGNS	ACTION
Signs of infection (See Decision Guide, p. 122)	
No tetanus shot within past 10 years	
Animal or human bite (see Bites, p. 163)	
Possible foreign object in wound	
Bleeding doesn't stop after 20 minutes (timed with a watch or clock) of direct pressure	
Wound doesn't heal within 2 weeks	
Minor puncture wound	

 Call the advice nurse 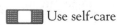 Use self-care

For more about the symbols, see p. 3.

SELF-CARE STEPS FOR PUNCTURE WOUNDS

 • Allow the wound to bleed freely unless a lot of blood has been lost or the blood is spraying out. Bleeding will cleanse the wound and help prevent infection. After several minutes, stop the bleeding by applying pressure to the wound and raising it above the level of the heart.

• Next, clean the area around the wound with soap and warm water. For the next 3 days, soak the wound in warm water for 15 minutes several times a day. This will clean the wound from the inside.

• Do not tape the wound closed or apply antibiotic ointment. Sealing off the wound can increase the risk of infection. Signs of infection usually take more than 24 hours to develop. Call the advice nurse if redness, swelling, or pus appears around the wound; if pain or a fever develops; or if the wound does not heal within 2 weeks.

SCRAPES AND ABRASIONS

Scrapes or abrasions occur when one or more layers of skin are torn or scraped off. They happen so often they may seem unimportant, but they should be treated to reduce the chance of infection or scarring.

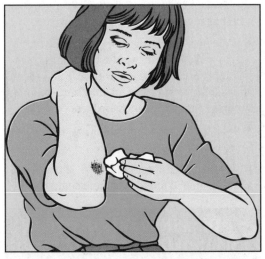

Carefully remove any dirt or particles from a scrape.

Scrapes are usually caused by falls onto the hands, knees, or elbows. This exposes millions of nerve endings, all of which carry pain impulses to the brain. Because scrapes can affect so many nerve endings, they are usually much more painful than cuts.

DECISION GUIDE FOR SCRAPES AND ABRASIONS

SYMPTOMS/SIGNS	ACTION
Signs of infection (redness, swelling, warmth and discharge)	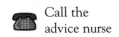
Scrape cannot be adequately cleaned or debris may remain in the wound	
Bleeding does not stop after 20 minutes (timed with a watch or clock) of direct pressure	
Minor scrape	

Call the advice nurse

Use self-care

For more about the symbols, see p. 3.

SELF-CARE STEPS FOR SCRAPES AND ABRASIONS

• It is important to carefully clean scrapes to help prevent infection. Carefully remove all dirt and debris. Use soap and warm water or hydrogen peroxide to thoroughly scrub the wound for no less than a minute or two. If you don't wash the wound for a full minute, you are not cleaning it well enough.

• Next, apply direct pressure to the wound, using gauze or a clean cloth to hold on the wound and stop the flow of blood. If the gauze or cloth becomes soaked with blood, do not remove it. Instead, place another clean layer of cloth or gauze directly on top and reapply pressure. Because blood takes a while to clot, you may have to apply pressure for 5 to 10 minutes. Raising the wound above the level of the heart will also help reduce the blood flow. If you can-

not control the bleeding, call the advice nurse.

• On the scalp or a fingertip, you may apply an ice pack wrapped in a towel to constrict the blood vessels and stop the bleeding. Apply the ice pack for no longer than 15 minutes or until the wound begins to feel numb. After a 10-minute rest, the ice pack may be reapplied. This 15 minutes on, 10 minutes off procedure can be repeated several times.

• Within 24 hours, remove the bandage and wash the area with mild soap and running water. The wound should be washed daily with plain tap water and soap. Change bandages two to three times daily. Watch for signs of infection. (see infected wound, p.122)

SMASHED FINGER OR TOE

Dropping a heavy object on your foot or smashing your finger in a car door are common injuries. When injuries like these involve only the end segment of the finger or toe and don't result in a deep or bad cut, they can often be treated successfully at home.

Blood often pools under the nail of the smashed finger or toe, causing severe throbbing pain due to the pressure under the nail. Often the nail is partly pulled off during the accident. **Do not remove the nail.** Call the advice nurse, who will help determine what you should do.

STEPS FOR REMOVING BLOOD FROM UNDER THE NAIL

If there is blood pooled under the injured nail that is causing severe pain, follow these steps to remove the blood and relieve the pressure.

• Wash hand or foot thoroughly with soap and water.

• Straighten a metal paper clip.

• Holding the paper clip with a pair of pliers, heat the tip in a flame until it is red-hot.

• Apply the hot end of the paper clip to the nail over the discolored area.

• Allow the hot paper clip to burn a hole through the nail until the blood begins to ooze out of the hole. (This won't hurt, but you may notice an odor as the paper clip burns through the nail.)

• Remove the paper clip and press on the nail with your fingers until all the pooled blood is out from under the nail.

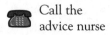 Call the advice nurse

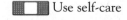 Use self-care

For more about the symbols, see p. 3.

SELF-CARE STEPS FOR SMASHED FINGER OR TOE

 • If the person can move the finger or toe easily and the injury does not involve the nail bed, apply an ice pack to reduce swelling and use acetaminophen (Tylenol, Tempra, or a generic) or a similar nonprescriptive pain reliever.

• If the finger is bleeding, apply pressure on the wound and elevate above the heart until bleeding stops. Wash the wound with soap and water, and watch for any signs of infection (redness, swelling, warmth and increased tenderness).

• Wrap the finger or toe in a thick gauze bandage to protect the injury.

• Wearing open-toed sandals or slippers will allow an injured toe to heal more comfortably.

DECISION GUIDE FOR SMASHED FINGER OR TOE

SYMPTOMS/SIGNS	ACTION
Bone fracture suspected	
Numbness in finger or toe	
Nail completely pulled off	
Pain gets worse rather than better within 12 hours	
Finger or toe swells to over 1 1/2 times its original size	
Finger or toe turns white or feels cold to the touch	
Pus develops under injured nail	
Pressure under nail not relieved with self-care	
Minor discomfort	

MISCELLANEOUS PROBLEMS

Some medical problems such as the ones covered in this chapter do not fit into standard categories. Most of the time, these are minor problems unrelated to any serious illness. Occasionally, however, these conditions can be symptoms of a larger problem. This section covers several of these conditions and suggests how to care for nonurgent problems at home.

Use the Decision Guides to see if your symptoms clearly need emergency medical services, require a call to the advice nurse, or can be treated using self-care. It is important to consider your own medical history and your current health when deciding what kind of care is right for you. If you have any conditions that do not seem to be healing normally, if the Self-Care Steps provided do not seem to help, or if you are uncertain about your symptoms, call the advice nurse. The advice nurse will evaluate your symptoms and recommend the next best steps for you to take.

ALLERGIC REACTIONS

For Hives, see p. 120; for Poison Ivy/Poison Oak/Poison Sumac, see p. 124; for Rashes, see p. 126; for Allergic Reactions (children), see p. 131.

Over 40 million Americans are allergic to pollens, molds, drugs, insect bites, animals, cosmetics, foods, dusts, and other substances. These substances are called allergens. Symptoms may be seasonal or year round.

Suspect allergies if you have a family history of allergies or frequently have these symptoms:

- Sneezing or a runny nose
- Hives or rashes
- Itchy throat and eyes
- A sore throat or a dry cough
- Wheezing

Allergic rashes *See Rashes, p. 126.*

Asthma *See Asthma, p. 241.*

Insect stings *See Insect Bites/Stings, p. 173.*

Seasonal nasal allergies, called "hay fever," are caused by molds and pollens of trees, grasses, and weeds and flowers. Sneezing, runny nose, itchy eyelids, and nasal congestion are common symptoms, which last as long as the exposure.

Allergic skin reactions include eczema (p. 118), hives (p. 120), and skin tissue swelling (edema).

SELF-CARE STEPS FOR ALLERGIC REACTIONS

- Avoid exposure to allergens.
- Wash pets regularly.
- Vacuum your home carefully twice weekly to control dust.
- Consider installing air conditioning and air cleaning devices in your home. Have heating and cooling systems professionally cleaned twice a year.
- Remove unnecessary carpeting, paper, and cloth materials from your home.
- Use nonprescription antihistamines carefully.
- Wear a medical alert bracelet warning of severe allergies (especially allergies to drugs).

DECISION GUIDE FOR ALLERGIC REACTIONS

SYMPTOMS/SIGNS	ACTION
Rash accompanies the allergy	
Runny nose, watery eyes, and sneezing lasts longer than 10 to 14 days	
Allergic reaction includes chest tightness, wheezing, and a hivelike rash	
Choking or difficulty swallowing	
Swelling of lips, tongue, or throat	
Rapid pulse, flushed face or skin, bluish color around lips	
Severe gastrointestinal symptoms, like vomiting or diarrhea	
Insect bite or sting causes a widespread rash (also see Insect Bites/Stings, p. 173)	
Severe asthma flare-up	
Severe trouble breathing	
Mild reaction that resembles a cold	

 Call the advice nurse

Use self-care

For more about the symbols, see p. 3.

FATIGUE

Frustrated. Apathetic. Tense and tired. Irritable. Grumpy. Unmotivated. Energyless and exhausted. These are feelings of fatigue, and everyone has had them at some time or another. They are a normal part of life. What most people refer to as fatigue is brought on by hard work or exertion and usually can be remedied by sleep.

Fatigue is an overwhelming sense of tiredness that makes your body feel weak. Fatigue can last 6 weeks or longer. Usually, fatigue is a sign that your body has not been getting enough sleep over a period of several days.

Fatigue can sometimes be traced back to drugs and prescriptions you may be taking. Many of these can rob you of energy. Chief among the over-the-counter culprits are pain relievers, cough and cold medicines, antihistamines and allergy remedies, sleeping pills, and motion sickness pills.

Too much stress can harm your health, but if there are not enough changes in your day, you will become unmotivated—and weary from boredom. Changing parts of your lifestyle may help you recharge your internal batteries.

SELF-CARE STEPS FOR FATIGUE

• Organize your time. Get up a few minutes earlier, so that you won't have to start your day feeling rushed and tired. Learn to delegate—and how to say "no" when you have enough responsibilities and activities in your life.

• Exercise regularly. You should exercise three to five times a week, for 20 to 30 minutes—and move around as much as possible during the day. Also, avoid late-night activities, as they can disrupt your regular sleeping habits and make you tired in the morning.

• Get the right amount of sleep. Most people need 6 to 8 hours of sleep each night. Shortchanging yourself on sleep will leave you exhausted, and getting too much sleep will make you feel groggy. Older people who tend to sleep less soundly and younger people with hectic schedules may also need naps during the day.

• Breathe deeply and slowly. Shallow, rapid breathing often leads to fatigue because the body gets less oxygen.

• Find your lunch style. Some people function best after eating a lighter lunch, while others need to eat their largest meal of the day at lunch. In either case, avoid high-fat foods. Because fats burn off slower than carbohydrates, they will slow you down.

• Lose weight. Stick to well-balanced meals and avoid crash diets. When your calorie intake is too restricted, it's very stressful for the body. One of the many symptoms of this type of stress is fatigue.

• Quit smoking. Smoking steals some of your body's oxygen supply, replacing it with useless carbon dioxide. Because nicotine is a stimulant, going through the consequent withdrawal symptoms can cause temporary tiredness.

• Drink less caffeine and alcohol. Alcohol is a depressant and will make you feel tired, not boost your energy. Likewise, caffeine will give you a temporary boost of energy, but when the effect wears off, your energy level will drop drastically.

• Take a break. Interrupt your workday with periodic breaks. And if you haven't gone on a vacation in a while, take that dreamed-of trip or unplug the phone and refresh at home.

• Watch less TV. If you depend on television to relax, you may find yourself relaxed into a state of lethargy. Try something more stimulating, such as reading or taking a walk.

• Find ways to calm yourself. Listen to music or relaxation tapes. Say a word, phrase, or prayer that gives you a sense of peace. Imagine yourself on a beach, at the mountains, or in your favorite spot.

DECISION GUIDE FOR FATIGUE

SYMPTOMS/SIGNS	ACTION
Consistent fatigue lasting longer than 6 weeks with no relief from self-care measures	☎
Suspicion that a new prescription medication is causing fatigue	☎
Fatigue related to a life event that is causing extreme anxiety or depression	☎
Fatigue from lack of sleep	[self-care]
Stress caused by short-term change in lifestyle	[self-care]

☎ Call the advice nurse   [self-care] Use self-care

For more about the symbols, see p. 3.

FEVER

From shivers and shakes to sweating and aches, your body's temperature is an important barometer of how well you are dealing with germs, stress, exertion, or extreme changes in weather. For good health, the body works best at a temperature of about 97° to 99° F.

Body temperature rises slightly during the day, but this change usually is not important. In fact, many people have a temperature that is always a little above or below the 98.6° F considered "normal."

A fever is a body temperature that is higher than normal for a particular individual. The actual definition of fever depends on the individual. What seems very high for one person may be only a slight fever for another.

By itself, a high temperature is not necessarily cause for concern—it can actually be a normal way for your body to defend itself against infection. Your body shivers to help produce the heat it needs to fight germs, and sweats to regulate the rise in temperature.

A fever can be a cause for concern in infants under 3 months of age, the elderly, and those with a history of heart and lung disease. But for most people, there is no medical reason to try to reduce a fever unless it is accompanied by *other symptoms* of illness.

If you call the advice nurse because you think you have a fever, describe how you are feeling at the time. This is usually more important than the actual temperature reading.

SELF-CARE STEPS FOR FEVER

• If the fever makes you uncomfortable, take aspirin or acetaminophen (Tylenol, Tempra, or a generic). For children, use acetaminophen, not aspirin.

• If taking aspirin or acetaminophen for fever symptoms, take the medication consistently until the fever goes away. Taking medication only when the fever is rising will create greater highs and lows and make your symptoms feel worse.

• Treat other symptoms such as cough, sore throat, or vomiting that may accompany your fever (see Colds, p.64; Vomiting, p.34).

• Drink eight glasses of fluid a day. When you have a fever, you lose bodily fluids, so it's important to prevent dehydration.

SPECIAL CONCERNS FOR CHILDREN

• Fever is not necessarily harmful, nor does it have to mean serious illness. Be more concerned with changes in eating or sleeping habits, coughing, pain, or other marked changes in a child's behavior.

• Fluids are very important for children so be sure to give plenty of soups, juice, or water.

• Do not give aspirin to children or adolescents. Use acetaminophen (Tylenol, Tempra, or a generic) to reduce fever.

• In children between 6 months and 5 years of age, seizures or "fits" sometimes result from fever. These seizures are seldom harmful. During a seizure, try to protect your child from hurting him or herself. Keep the child away from nearby objects, and make sure he or she is breathing freely.

• When a child under 3 months of age has a rectal temperature over 100.4° F, call the advice nurse.

HOW TO TAKE A CHILD'S TEMPERATURE

Since most children under 2 years of age cannot keep their mouths closed or remain still for an oral temperature, it is best to take their temperature rectally. Apply petroleum jelly to the thermometer for comfort, and insert it about an inch into the rectum (until you can no longer see the silver end) for about 3 minutes. Be certain you hold onto the thermometer while it is in the child's rectum so that the child doesn't roll over or move and puncture his or her large intestine. Also, you might consider using a type of thermometer that measures temperature through the child's ear, or the skin temperature sensors available at most drugstores.

DECISION GUIDE FOR FEVER

SYMPTOMS/SIGNS	ACTION
Fever lasts 3 days or more	
Back pain or painful urination and fever	
Fever with stiff neck or mental confusion	
Fever greater than 100.4° F in an infant younger than 3 months or an adult over age 75	
Fever that returns after being gone for 36 hours	
Fever that does not respond to self-care measures	
Fever for less than 3 days without other symptoms	
Fever with other symptoms (see Colds, p. 64; Vomiting, p. 34.)	

 Call the advice nurse   Use self-care

For more about the symbols, see p. 3.

Through endless trips to the medical provider with my kids, I've learned that fever without other symptoms is probably a viral infection that will go away within a few days. The best method of dealing with infection is rest. Put a cool cloth on the forehead, use common sense, and make sure your children save some energy to heal themselves.

Mother of eleven

Fever is only one of the many signs of childhood illness and is probably less important than the associated symptoms. Very high temperatures may be frightening to parents but are not necessarily dangerous to the child. Acetaminophen may be used for the child's complaints or symptoms, but is rarely needed for fever alone.

Pediatrician

Fever in the very young or very old is of concern and often needs medical attention. For the rest of us, plenty of fluids and a little time may be all that is needed.

Family Practitioner

HEADACHES

Headaches are one of the most common health complaints. They have many different causes including tension, infection, injury, and changes in the flow of blood within the head. Most headaches occur when the muscles of the head or neck become tense and contract.

Fortunately, most headaches that occur without other symptoms respond well to self-care. Nearly 90 percent of all headaches are caused by tension or stress and can be controlled.

Tension headaches are often caused by the tightening of muscles of the back and shoulders in reaction to emotional and physical stress. A tension headache may occur as pain all over the head, as a feeling of pressure, or as a band around the head.

Tension headaches are believed to be the most common cause of head pain. Although they may be caused by poor posture or working in awkward conditions, the most common triggers are stress, anxiety, and depression. Tension headaches that occur two or more times weekly for several months or longer are considered chronic, and you should consult your medical provider.

The symptoms of a tension headache can include:

- Steady pain that doesn't pulse
- A tightness, fullness, or pressure over the top of the head or back of the neck
- Occasional nausea or vomiting

Home treatment of tension headaches is often successful. Aspirin or acetaminophen can be used to relieve the

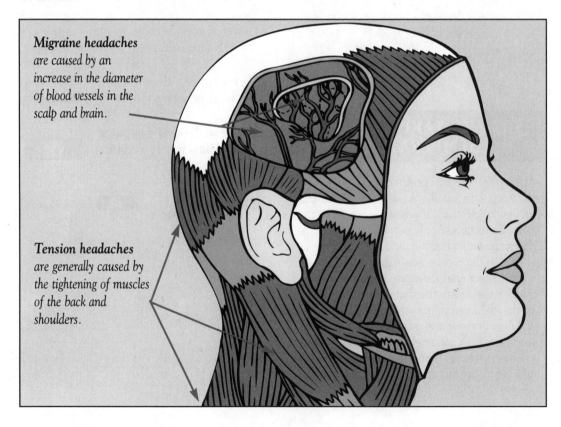

Migraine headaches are caused by an increase in the diameter of blood vessels in the scalp and brain.

Tension headaches are generally caused by the tightening of muscles of the back and shoulders.

pain. Taking a hot or cold shower, massaging the neck muscles, or lying down in a dark room may provide relief. Learning to relax using biofeedback, meditation, music, visualization, hypnosis, or taking a stress management class may also be helpful.

Migraine headaches have very specific symptoms. The pain of a migraine headache is caused by the increased dilation or widening of the blood vessels in the head. These headaches occur suddenly and often recur.

Because the person may become nauseated, migraines are sometimes called *sick headaches*. Often the affected person of a migraine will see bright spots, flashes of light, or areas of blindness just before the headache strikes. These symptoms are called an aura. Some people have great bursts of energy and activity just before a migraine starts.

A mild migraine headache may pass quickly if you go immediately to a darkened room and lie down. Place a cool, damp cloth on your forehead. Relax your entire body, focusing on the eyes, the forehead, the jaw and neck muscles, and working down to the toes.

Symptoms of migraine headache include:

- Throbbing pain

- Pain more often on one side of the head

- An aura, or preheadache phase, that can include flashes of light, bright spots, distorted vision, abdominal pain, and nausea

SELF-CARE STEPS FOR HEADACHES

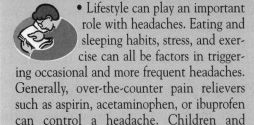

- Lifestyle can play an important role with headaches. Eating and sleeping habits, stress, and exercise can all be factors in triggering occasional and more frequent headaches. Generally, over-the-counter pain relievers such as aspirin, acetaminophen, or ibuprofen can control a headache. Children and teenagers should not use aspirin.

- For recurring headaches, a "headache calendar" may help to identify possible triggers. A headache calendar should record everything you eat, your sleep and exercise patterns, and work and home activities. Women should also record their menstrual cycles, because headaches can be triggered by hormonal changes.

- Regularly doing stretching exercises for tense neck muscles can help avoid recurring headaches (see illustration p.81).

- Have a friend massage your neck and shoulders to release tension.

- Lie down with a cool cloth over your forehead to relieve the pain of a headache.

- If your headache is due to nasal congestion, take an over-the-counter decongestant to relieve pressure in the sinuses.

- For relief from a migraine headache, try to lie down in a dark room with your eyes closed and listen to soothing music.

Possible triggers of migraine headache include hunger, fatigue, bright light, alcohol, caffeine, excitement or stress, birth control pills, and certain foods.

Most migraine headaches require professional diagnosis and treatment. See your medical provider to discuss appropriate treatment.

DECISION GUIDE FOR HEADACHES

SYMPTOMS/SIGNS	ACTION
New mental confusion	☎
Seizures	☎
Weakness, numbness, or tingling in arms or legs	☎
New vision changes	☎
Symptoms not typical of your usual headache	☎
Fever with headache	☎
Headache is still present after having slept	☎
Headache does not go away after 6 hours of self-care	☎
Occasional headaches, causing minor discomfort	🩹

☎ Call the advice nurse

🩹 Use self-care

For more about the symbols, see p. 3.

LIGHT-HEADEDNESS/ WEAKNESS/DIZZINESS

People frequently think that light-headedness, weakness, and dizziness all refer to the same thing. Actually, each term has its own meaning.

Light-headedness refers to the feeling of being about to faint or black out. Most people probably experience this feeling once in a while. Sometimes getting up quickly from a lying position can cause you to feel light-headed, especially if you have been sick in bed for a couple of days. Episodes such as these are harmless unless they lead to fainting spells. If, however, you feel light-headed when you have not changed position, call the advice nurse.

In medical terms, **weakness** is the feeling that your muscles do not have any strength. Sometimes this is a result of "overdoing it" with strenuous activity. If you muscles feel suddenly weak for no apparent reason, call the advice nurse.

Dizziness, also called vertigo, is the feeling that the room is spinning. Sometimes people who are dizzy feel that they might lose their balance and fall, or that they cannot walk in a straight line. If you feel dizzy for no apparent reason, call the advice nurse.

SELF-CARE STEPS FOR LIGHT-HEADEDNESS/ WEAKNESS/DIZZINESS

Light-headedness

• If you are prone to light-headedness, take your time getting out of bed in the morning. Also, be careful when you stand up if you have been sitting for a long time.

• Dehydration can cause you to feel light-headed. Drink plenty of fluids if you have been perspiring heavily or not eating well for a couple of days due to illness.

• Do not drive if you feel light-headed.

Weakness

• If the weakness is a result of overuse of the muscles, take aspirin, acetaminophen, or ibuprofen and let your muscles rest for a couple of days.

• For weakness that comes on suddenly or for an undetermined reason, call the advice nurse.

Dizziness

• Slowly sit or lie down if you feel dizzy to reduce the chance of falling and hurting yourself.

• Keep your eyes open and focus on an object in the room to lessen your symptoms.

• Put your head between your knees if your vision goes dark or you begin to feel faint.

• Do not drive until dizziness has passed.

DECISION GUIDE FOR LIGHT-HEADEDNESS/ WEAKNESS/DIZZINESS

SYMPTOMS/SIGNS	ACTION
Loss of consciousness	☎
Frequent or unexplained dizziness	☎
Light-headedness, weakness, or dizziness following head injury	☎
Sudden weakness for an undetermined reason	☎
Occasional light-headedness upon getting up in the morning	▭
Occasional dizziness without other symptoms	▭
Weakness from muscle overuse	▭

☎ Call the advice nurse Use self-care

For more about the symbols, see p. 3.

SECTION THREE
USEFUL MEDICAL INFORMATION

Taking good care of yourself involves more than just knowing what to do if you are sick or injured. It is also knowing how to stay well. Some of the questions medical providers hear most often involve how to prevent illness and avoid health risks. Pregnancy, birth, and child development are also popular topics of discussion with medical providers.

In this section, we have tried to present some of the information people most want to know: pregnancy and child development concerns; schedules for screening tests and immunizations; and the prevention and early detection of common health problems.

If your particular health concern is not covered here or your risk factors are not discussed, the advice nurse can provide you with more information.

CONCERNS ABOUT PREGNANCY AND NEWBORN CARE

BREASTFEEDING/ BOTTLEFEEDING

Also see Breastfeeding Problems, p. 151.

If you choose to breastfeed, you should begin nursing the baby as soon after birth as possible even though your body may not begin producing milk until the third or fourth day. Before you have milk, your breasts secrete a calorie-rich liquid called *colostrum* that contains antibodies. Do not be tempted to supplement the baby's feedings with formula during this time.

Your baby should nurse every 2 to 3 hours, day and night, during the first week. This helps the baby gain weight and stimulates your body to produce and let down milk. Infants who do not wake by themselves on this schedule, can be awakened by taking off their clothes except for the diaper, rubbing the bottoms of the feet, or placing a cold washcloth on the forehead. Once your baby is back to his or her birth weight, probably after about 2 weeks, you can feed on demand.

The baby needs to nurse at both breasts at each feeding for 10 to 15 minutes on each side. When the baby begins to suck, check to see that he or she is latched on correctly. The areola (the dark part around the nipple) as well as the nipple should be in the infant's mouth. If the baby does not latch on correctly, he or she will not feed as well and your nipples will become sore or cracked. Break the baby's suction at the end of the feeding by inserting your finger into the corner of the baby's mouth. Be sure to burp the baby well after feeding on each side.

Bottlefeeding

There are many brands of both milk- and soy-based formulas on the market. Some brands are very similar to each other while others contain certain additives. If you are considering bottlefeeding, discuss the benefits of different kinds of formulas with your baby's medical provider.

There is no set amount of formula your baby should drink at a feeding. Within the first few days after birth, babies usually take in 1 to 4 ounces at a time. You should schedule a feeding every 3 to 4 hours, day and night, until the baby is back to the original birth weight. This usually takes about 2 weeks. After that, it is no longer necessary to wake the baby for a feeding. You should burp the baby after each 2 ounces he or she drinks. The baby will not need any food other than formula for the first 4 months.

WHAT TO DO ABOUT FEEDING PROBLEMS

• **Spitting up.** Regurgitating a little bit after feeding is quite common. It is not considered vomiting unless the amount is large each time. Spitting up can be minimized by feeding your baby less at each feeding to keep his or her stomach from getting too full. Also limit the total feeding time to 20 minutes and wait at least 2 hours between feedings. Always remember to burp the baby after he or she has eaten and make sure diapers are not fastened too tightly.

• **Crying before feeding time.** Sometimes babies become fussy before it is their scheduled feeding time. Try cuddling, rocking, changing a diaper, or offering a pacifier to calm the baby. Use feeding only as a last resort.

• **Getting enough milk.** An infant's milk intake may vary from day to day, however, underfeeding is very rare, especially in bottle-fed babies. You will know if your baby is getting enough milk if he or she:

- averages a weight gain of 4 to 6 ounces a week during the first month
- produces six or more wet diapers a day and the urine is pale yellow
- is alert and active
- has a moist mouth

NURSING TIPS

• Do not supplement feedings with formula. If the baby is gaining weight, you do not have to worry about having enough milk. Your body will produce milk to meet your baby's demand. Since it is easier for the baby to get milk from a bottle than the breast, offering formula could cause the baby to lose interest in nursing. This in turn could cause your milk supply to diminish since your breasts need the stimulation of the baby's sucking to continue producing milk.

• You do not need to feed the baby for more than 20 minutes every 2 hours. The baby can get all the milk from the breast in 10 to 15 minutes of sucking. More frequent or longer feeding provides only oral stimulation and calming.

• You do not need to give the baby water unless it is a very hot day. Then tap water is fine.

• Hold your breast during nursing so that the baby can breathe more easily.

• Let your nipples air dry and clean them only with water. Change breast pads as soon as they become wet. Apply a light coat of lanolin lotion if your nipples become sore or chapped.

• If the baby is having a hard time latching on, manually express a little milk before feeding. This softens the breast and makes it easier for the baby to grasp.

• Not drinking enough fluids can interfere with your milk production. Try to drink a glass of water at each nursing in addition to your regular fluid intake.

• Try to eat a bland diet since certain foods can cause your baby to have gas. Foods to watch out for are garlic, cabbage, onions, turnips, chocolate, broccoli, rhubarb, beans, apricots, and prunes. A diet heavy in fresh fruit can also cause the baby stomach upset.

• Do not take any medication while breastfeeding without speaking to your medical provider.

• Do not try to lose weight too rapidly. Cutting back calories could affect your milk production and deprive you of the nutrients you need.

• If your breasts become hard and swollen, do not stop breastfeeding. Take warm showers or place warm, moist cloths on your breasts to relieve discomfort. Also, try to feed your baby more often to keep breasts soft and empty. You can also try changing breastfeeding position from sitting up to lying down, or from lying down on one side to the other to see if that helps the problem. Gently massaging your breasts beginning under the arm and working your way down to the nipple may help soften them. If you develop a fever, call the advice nurse.

• Relax. It may take a little practice, but most women are able to breastfeed successfully.

COLLECTING AND STORING BREAST MILK

If someone other than you is going to feed the baby or you will leave your baby in someone else's care for a length of time, you will want to pump and store your breast milk. A good manual or electric breast pump is essential. Electric pumps which can drain both breasts at once can be rented from a local hospital.

Before expressing milk, wash your hands thoroughly with soap and water. Clean your nipples with a cotton ball dipped in warm water. Milk should be expressed into a clean dry container with a tight-fitting lid such as a baby bottle. Use the milk immediately or store it in the refrigerator for up to 24 hours.

You may also freeze the milk in a plastic freezer bottle or in a disposable plastic nursing bottle closed securely with a twist tie. The amount of time milk can be frozen depends on how cold your home freezer is. You can gauge the length of time you can save your milk by how well the ice cream in your freezer keeps. If your ice cream stays hard, you can keep your milk for 3 months. If the ice cream is soft enough to be scooped easily, use your milk within 4 weeks. If your ice cream is very soft and does not freeze well at all, **it is not safe** to store your breast milk in the freezer.

CARE OF NEWBORNS

Also see "Special Complaints of Children," pp. 131-144.

When parents bring a baby home, they may find themselves wondering what to do with this new person in their household. Especially if it is a first child, parents may not be familiar with a newborn's special needs. They also may find themselves wondering if what they are observing about their baby is normal. This section outlines the special care a baby needs during the first few weeks of life. It also describes some common things that can cause new parents concern.

Routine Care for Newborns

Umbilical cord care. Wash the umbilical cord stump two or three times a day with soap and water and dry thoroughly. Swab the stump in the morning and evening with a cotton ball dipped in rubbing alcohol. Call the advice nurse if you notice any signs of infection or discharge from the cord site (see Umbilical Cord Problems, p. 144.)

Bathing and skin care. You can begin giving the newborn tub baths after the umbilical cord stub falls off at about 2 weeks old. Until then, the baby's face needs to be washed every day with warm water and mild soap. Wash the baby's hair with baby shampoo twice a week.

When giving a tub bath, use warm but not-too-hot water and mild soap. There are many baby soaps available that are less irritating to the newborn's skin than regular soap. Keep the bath short and wrap the baby promptly in warm towels to prevent shivering. It is not necessary to use any oils, powders, or creams on the baby's skin.

Circumcision care. If your baby was circumcised, use a cotton ball to wash the penis every day. Apply petroleum jelly to the penis for the first week or until it is healed to prevent the diaper from sticking to the penis.

If a plastic ring was used to circumcise the baby, no special care is needed other than keeping the area clean. The circumcision is complete when the ring falls off.

Watch for signs of infection such as increased redness or discharge from the area, with or without a fever. Call the advice nurse if you suspect an infection or if you have any other concerns.

Care of the uncircumcised penis. Wash the baby's penis using mild soap during the normal bath routine. Do not try to retract the foreskin. The child's foreskin may not retract before age 4 or older.

Common Newborn Concerns

Acne. Newborns often develop small pimples on the face, neck, chest, or back. Simply wash the areas with soap and water. Do not put lotions or creams on the pimples since these may clog the pores. The acne will usually disappear by the time the baby is 6 to 8 weeks old.

Breast swelling. High levels of female hormones in the mother's body before birth can cause babies to be born with swollen breasts. This is nothing to be concerned about and the swelling will subside. Be alert for any signs of infection in the area such as redness or increased warmth.

Gas. Gas and bloating can make an infant very uncomfortable. To decrease the baby's chance of developing gas:

- feed slowly
- burp frequently
- warm formula slightly
- make sure the hole in the nipple is not too big or too small

- make sure nipple is full of milk so the baby does not suck in air

Irregular breathing. A newborn's breathing can vary from short, quick breaths to long, deep ones. He or she may also make noises from the back of the throat which sound like snorting. All this is normal in the first few months of life.

Jaundice. The yellowing of a newborn's skin or eyes is not uncommon. Sometimes it does not appear until a few days after birth. If you notice that your baby appears jaundiced, call the advice nurse. It may be necessary to measure the level of a substance in the baby's blood called bilirubin.

Hiccups. Babies frequently get hiccups, which are not harmful. Sometimes, a few sips of water will make them go away.

Jerks and twitches. Newborn babies often twitch or jerk suddenly when they are falling asleep and wake themselves up. Wrapping the baby tightly in a light blanket can help prevent this from happening.

Sleeping. Most newborn babies sleep a lot, however, there is no set amount of time your baby should sleep. Some sleep all day, some much less. You should wake the baby every 2 to 3 hours to feed until the infant reaches his or her birth weight.

Sleeping position. Experts recommend that most infants be placed on their backs or sides to sleep until they are at least 6 months old. Babies that are premature, have upper airway diseases, or spit up a lot should not be placed on their backs. If you have questions about the best position for your baby, talk to your medical provider.

Sneezing and coughing. It is normal for newborns to sneeze and cough. This helps clear their breathing passages.

Stools. Breastfed babies have frequent yellow stools that are loose and watery. They often appear to have a curd-like or seedy consistency. Bottlefed babies have stools which vary from yellow to green in color and have the consistency of toothpaste.

Sucking/pacifiers. Infants have a strong urge to suck, especially in the first 3 to 4 months of their lives. Frequently, babies will appear restless and irritable shortly after feeding and appear to be hungry again. Offer a clean finger or pacifier to help satisfy the baby's sucking desire rather than feeding frequently.

Urine. A newborn baby should have at least five wet diapers in a 24-hour period. Urinating more often is not unusual, but if your baby has fewer than five wet diapers, call the advice nurse.

Vaginal discharge. Newborn girls often have a vaginal discharge that appears as a spot of mucus or blood on the diaper. This is a result of the high level of female hormones in the mother's body before birth. The discharge disappears shortly after birth.

MEASURING FETAL MOVEMENT

Beginning somewhere between the 18th and 26th week of pregnancy, women begin to notice the fetus moving inside the uterus. The amount of fetal movement is often determined by the activity of the mother. When a woman is active, the fetus may be calmed by the mother's body movements. When she is lying in bed and not moving as much, the fetus may become more active. Often, the fetus becomes more active when the mother eats, perhaps in reaction to an increase in blood sugar.

Between the 24th and 28th week of pregnancy, the fetus' movements are often short and erratic. After week 28, the movements become more organized and patterns begin to develop. It is important for a pregnant woman not to compare the fetal movements she feels with those of other women. Fetal movement patterns vary, and as long as there is no dramatic decrease or stopping of the movement, these variations are normal.

HOW TO MEASURE FETAL MOVEMENT AT HOME

About 30 minutes after eating a meal or drinking a sweet drink, sit in a comfortable chair with your hand on your abdomen. Feel for a kick, shift, or movement of any kind. This counts as one. Continue counting every movement you feel until you get to 10. This usually takes 40 to 45 minutes. If it takes longer than 2 hours to feel 10 movements, call the advice nurse.

MEDICATIONS IN PREGNANCY

One of the most difficult questions a woman can ask her medical provider is if a particular medication is completely safe during pregnancy. Any medication you take will have some effect on the baby, too, because it will be absorbed into your circulatory system and travel across the placenta into the baby's blood stream. There are very few medications that have been proven to cause birth defects when taken by pregnant women. That does not guarantee, however, that commonly used medications are absolutely safe.

Even though drugs are tested heavily before they are put on the market, the connection between a medication and a birth defect is sometimes hard to determine. Also, experiments using animals do not always indicate how a drug will behave when taken by humans. This is why pharmaceutical companies state that most medications have not been proven safe for pregnant women.

COMMON MEDICATIONS DURING PREGNANCY

It is important to consult your medical provider before taking any medication. Do not rely on the advice of friends and relatives to determine if a drug is safe. The following are a few conditions which may require medications.

• If a woman has a chronic disease such as diabetes or high blood pressure, taking medication is unavoidable.

• Constipation is a common problem during pregnancy and is sometimes treated with stool softeners or fiber laxatives.

• Medical providers sometimes suggest mild over-the-counter pain relievers to ease minor discomforts of pregnancy such as backaches.

• If vomiting from morning sickness in early pregnancy becomes severe, your medical provider may prescribe an anti-nausea medication.

MINIMIZING THE RISKS TO YOU AND YOUR BABY

• When considering whether or not to take a medication while pregnant, it is important to realize that leaving certain diseases untreated could also harm your baby.

• Everything you do has a potential risk, so you need to consider how great are the chances that you are putting your pregnancy in danger. For example, most pregnant women continue to drive because the risks of being injured in a traffic accident are relatively small. However, cigarette smoking greatly increases the chance of having a low birth weight baby so many women stop smoking during pregnancy. Some substances, such as crack cocaine, are so clearly linked to problems after birth that it would be irresponsible for a woman to use these drugs during pregnancy. In fact, some states consider the use of crack cocaine by pregnant women to be the crime of child endangerment.

• Your medical provider should thoroughly discuss the risks involved in taking a particular medication while pregnant. Also, you should always ask your provider to state clearly the potential harmful effects on you and your baby if you do not take the medication.

• After considering all the information, let your medical provider know what you choose to do.

PREMATURE LABOR

The typical pregnancy lasts 40 weeks. However, having the baby any time between the 38th and 42nd week is considered normal. If labor begins before the 38th week of pregnancy, it is considered premature labor. Early labor could lead to the premature birth of the baby. If the baby is delivered before the 23rd week of pregnancy it will be too young to survive outside the womb. Even if the baby is born after 23 weeks but before full term, there can be dangerous health complications.

It is often impossible to know exactly what causes a woman to go into early labor. The most important thing is to recognize the signs and act quickly. If you think labor is starting prematurely, call the advice nurse.

SIGNS OF PREMATURE LABOR

• Cramping similar to menstrual cramps sometimes accompanied by nausea, vomiting, or diarrhea

• Achy feeling in pelvic floor, thighs, or groin area

• Change in vaginal discharge—becoming watery, possibly with bloody streaks. A thick mucous plug may be discharged.

• Rupture of amniotic fluids resulting in a rush or a trickle of fluid from the vagina

• New low back pain or pressure or a change in the nature of existing back pain

WHAT TO DO IF YOU THINK PREMATURE LABOR IS STARTING

• Lie down and rest.

• Determine the frequency and length of your contractions.

• Call the advice nurse as soon as possible.

BABY AND TODDLER INFORMATION

GROWTH AND DEVELOPMENT CHARTS

The baby and toddler years are a time of rapid growth and development. Your child will go through more changes during these months than at any other time. Because each child grows and develops at a rate determined by his or her unique genetic plan, it sometimes may be difficult to tell if your child's development is "normal."

The following growth scales will help you record your child's weight and height at various milestones. By charting these points on the graph you can see if the child's growth remains on a consistent curve. The developmental chart (on p. 202) will help you track your child's progress in motor development, language, and social skills.

How to Use the Growth Charts

The four charts that follow can be used to measure a child's weight and height as compared to other children of the same age and sex. When you know your child's measurements, you can plot them on the graphs provided. The series of curved lines on each chart represent percentiles. Percentiles are determined by researching the measurements of thousands of children. They indicate how a child's growth compares with other children of the same age/sex. Each of the curves is labeled with a value at an interval between 0 and 100. Once you determine where on the percentile curve your child falls, then you can see how he or she is growing in comparison to others. For example, if your child's height measurement falls on the 60 percentile curve, then you know that out of 100 children of the same age and sex, 40 will be taller and the remaining 60 will be shorter.

To determine your child's percentile:

Choose the appropriate chart for your child's age and sex.

1. Find your child's weight or height on the left or right vertical sides of the chart. (Complete the process for either height or weight before moving on to the other measurement.)

2. Using a ruler or straight edge, follow the line that is closest to your child's measurement across the page.

3. Find your child's age along the horizontal line at the base of the chart. With a second ruler or straight edge, follow that line up the page to the point where it meets the measurement line.

4. Make a dot at the point where the two lines meet.

5. Look for where the dot falls in relation to the percentile curves.

6. The closest curve indicates your child's size in relation to other children of the same age/sex.

Growth Chart: Boys Length /Weight, Birth to 36 Months

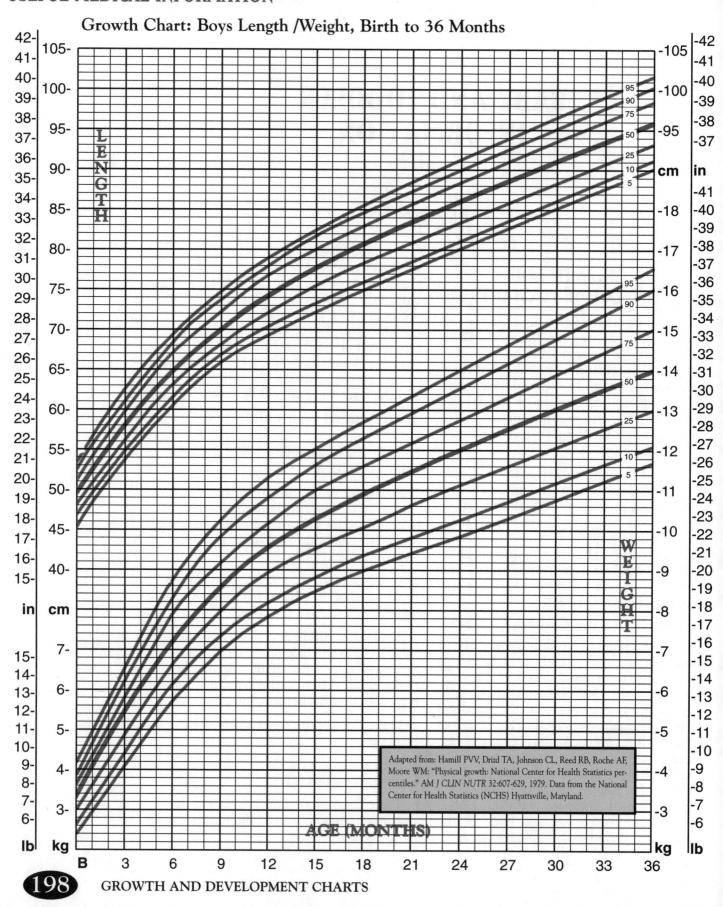

Adapted from: Hamill PVV, Drizd TA, Johnson CL, Reed RB, Roche AF, Moore WM: "Physical growth: National Center for Health Statistics percentiles." AM J CLIN NUTR 32:607-629, 1979. Data from the National Center for Health Statistics (NCHS) Hyattsville, Maryland.

AGE (MONTHS)

Growth Chart: Girls Length /Weight, Birth to 36 Months

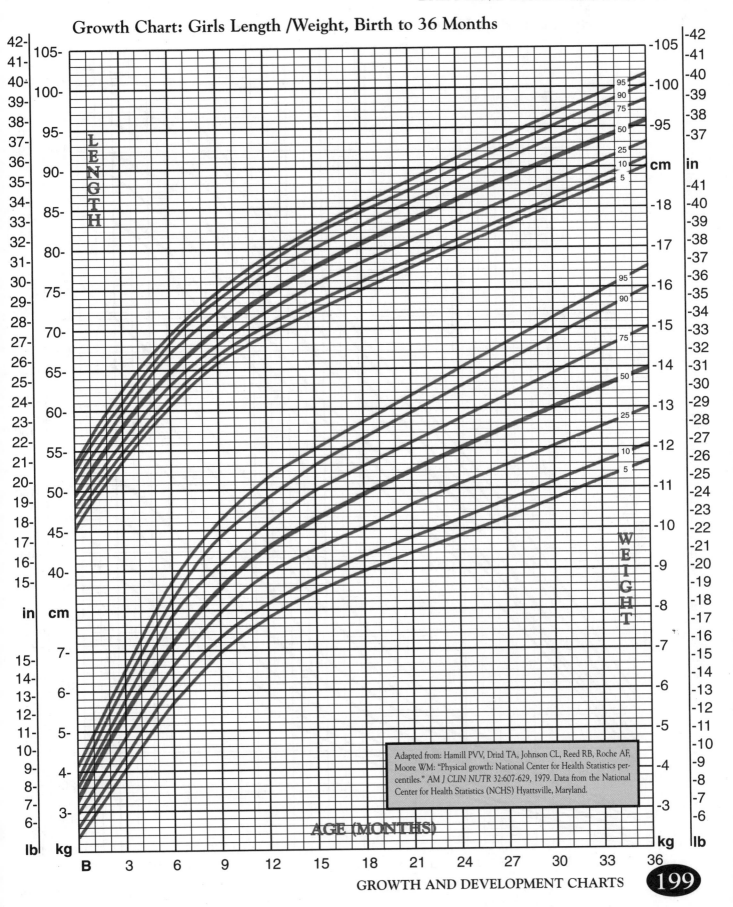

Adapted from: Hamill PVV, Drizd TA, Johnson CL, Reed RB, Roche AF, Moore WM: "Physical growth: National Center for Health Statistics percentiles." *AM J CLIN NUTR* 32:607-629, 1979. Data from the National Center for Health Statistics (NCHS) Hyattsville, Maryland.

AGE (MONTHS)

GROWTH AND DEVELOPMENT CHARTS

Growth Chart: Boys Height /Weight, Ages 2–18 years

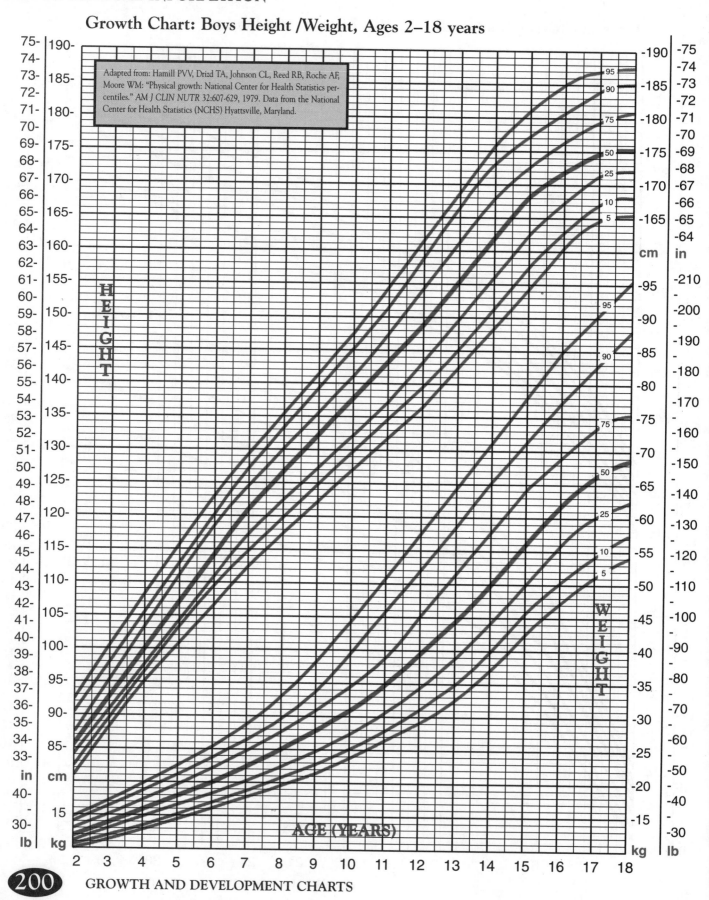

Adapted from: Hamill PVV, Drizd TA, Johnson CL, Reed RB, Roche AF, Moore WM: "Physical growth: National Center for Health Statistics percentiles." *AM J CLIN NUTR* 32:607-629, 1979. Data from the National Center for Health Statistics (NCHS) Hyattsville, Maryland.

Growth Chart: Girls Height /Weight, Ages 2–18 years

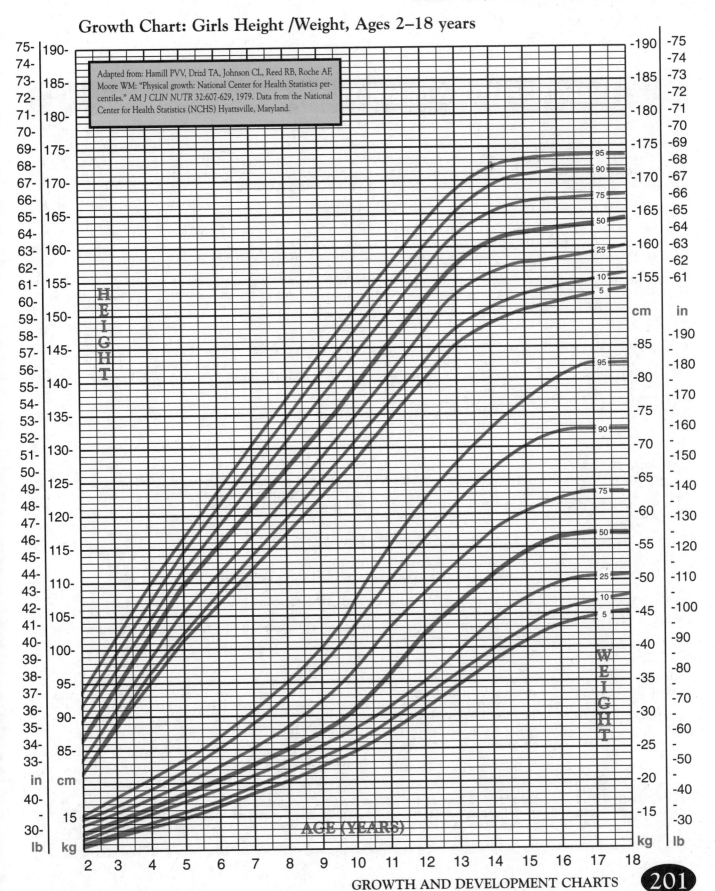

Adapted from: Hamill PVV, Drizd TA, Johnson CL, Reed RB, Roche AF, Moore WM: "Physical growth: National Center for Health Statistics percentiles." *AM J CLIN NUTR* 32:607-629, 1979. Data from the National Center for Health Statistics (NCHS) Hyattsville, Maryland.

HEIGHT

WEIGHT

AGE (YEARS)

EMERGING PATTERNS OF BEHAVIOR FOR 1 TO 5 YEARS OF AGE

15 Months

Motor: Walks alone; crawls up stairs
Adaptive: Makes tower of 3 cubes; makes a line with crayon; inserts pellet in bottle
Language: Jargon; follows simple commands; may name a familiar object (ball)
Social: Indicates some desires or needs by pouting; hugs parents

18 Months

Motor: Runs stiffly; sits on a small chair; walks up stairs with one hand held; explores drawers and waste baskets
Adaptive: Makes tower of 4 cubes; imitates scribbling; imitates vertical stroke; dumps pellet from bottle
Language: 10 words (average); names pictures; identifies one or more parts of body
Social: Feeds self; seeks help when in trouble; may complain when wet or soiled; kisses parent with pucker

24 Months

Motor: Runs well; walks up and down stairs one step at a time; opens doors; climbs on furniture; jumps
Adaptive: Tower of 7 cubes (6 at 21 months); circular scribbling; imitates horizontal stroke; folds paper once imitatively
Language: Puts 3 words together (subject verb object)
Social: Handles spoon well; often tells immediate experiences; helps to undress; listens to stories with pictures

30 Months

Motor: Goes up stairs alternating feet
Adaptive: Tower of 9 cubes; makes vertical and horizontal strokes but generally will not join them to make a cross; imitates circular stroke forming closed figure
Language: Refers to self by pronoun "I"; knows full name
Social: Helps put things away; pretends in play

36 Months

Motor: Rides tricycle; stands momentarily on one foot
Adaptive: Tower of 10 cubes; imitates construction of "bridge" of 3 cubes; copies a circle; imitates a cross
Language: Knows age and sex; counts 3 objects correctly; repeats 3 numbers or a sentence of 6 syllables
Social: Plays simple games (in "parallel" with other children); helps in dressing (unbuttons clothing and puts on shoes); washes hands

48 Months

Motor: Hops on one foot; throws ball overhand; uses scissors to cut out pictures; climbs well
Adaptive: Copies bridge from model; imitates construction of "gate" of 5 cubes; copies cross and square; draws a man with 2 to 4 parts besides head; names longer of two lines
Language: Counts 4 pennies accurately; tells a story
Social: Plays with several children with beginning social interactions and role-playing; goes to toilet alone

60 Months

Motor: Skips
Adaptive: Draws triangle from copy; names heavier of 2 weights
Language: Names 4 colors; repeats sentence of 10 syllables; counts 10 pennies correctly
Social: Dresses and undresses; asks questions about meaning of words; domestic role-playing

Reprinted with permission from *Nelson Behrman Textbook of Pediatrics*, Fourteenth Edition. Copyright © 1992, W.B. Saunders Company

IMMUNIZATION SCHEDULE

Also see Preventive Services Recommendations, p. 232.

Among the greatest achievements in modern medicine, vaccines protect children from serious diseases including mumps, measles, diphtheria, and polio. Some immunizations work by giving a very weak dose of the disease—strong enough to prompt the body's immune system to develop antibodies against the disease but not strong enough to cause it. Others offer immunity but do not cause the disease itself. The following section describes each of the major vaccines and how they are used.

Diphtheria/Pertussis/Tetanus (DPT)

The DPT shot combines all three vaccines to protect against these life-threatening diseases. Children should have five DPT shots before they enter kindergarten. Babies should have three shots by the time they reach 6 months of age—at 2, 4, and 6 months—plus one at 12 to 18 months of age and one more before entering kindergarten.

Oral Polio Vaccine (OPV)

Since becoming available in the 1950s, this vaccine has nearly wiped out polio. Experts warn, however, that without continued vaccination, the risk of contracting this crippling, potentially fatal disease could return. Children should receive four doses of oral polio vaccine by age 6. This, in most cases, provides protection for life.

Haemophilus Influenzae Type B (HIB)

HIB is a dangerous bacterium that can cause meningitis, pneumonia, and infections of other body systems. The HIB vaccine protects almost all children who receive the full four doses. It is given by injection three times before a child is 7 months old, followed by a booster at 12 to 15 months.

Measles/Mumps/Rubella (MMR)

The MMR vaccine is given by injection once at 12 to 15 months of age and again before entering kindergarten to guard against these common childhood infections. In most people, these two doses provide protection for life.

Hepatitis B Vaccine

Hepatitis B is an inflammation of the liver that can cause a range of problems—from simple flulike symptoms to severe reactions requiring hospitalization. Hepatitis B is considered the most serious form of hepatitis. The hepatitis B vaccine is given three times before age 18 months.

Chicken Pox (Varicella) Vaccine

The American Academy of Pediatrics recommends chicken pox (varicella) vaccine for children over 12 months of age who have not had chicken pox (see Chicken Pox, p. 135). A single dose should be given between 12 and 18 months of age. Older children can be immunized at the earliest convenient opportunity, also with a single dose. Healthy adolescents past their 13th birthday who have not been immunized previously and have not had chicken pox should be immunized with two doses of vaccine 4 to 8 weeks apart.

The Preventive Services Recommendations (pp. 232–233) summarize the immunization schedules for children and teenagers. They are mainly for children without symptoms of health problems and who do not have special health risks. If you have a family history of certain illnesses, your medical provider should recommend a schedule of preventive visits that is more appropriate to your child's needs.

Your child should begin receiving immunizations at birth and continue to get doses of some vaccines throughout childhood. Your child's medical provider should give you a booklet in which to record the dates when various immunizations are received. Be sure to bring this booklet with you each time you take your child for a checkup.

INTRODUCING SOLID FOODS

For the first several months of life, your baby does not need any food other than breast milk or formula. In fact, introducing solid food too early can lead to health problems. Also, there is no evidence that adding solids to the baby's diet can promote sleeping through the night at a younger age. You may start to give your baby solid foods at 4 or 5 months of age if you are bottlefeeding and between 4 and 6 months if you are breastfeeding.

When you introduce new foods to your baby, it is best to do it one at a time. Then, wait a week before trying another food. This will allow your child to become familiar with the new taste and texture and you can observe if a food allergy develops. Start with a small amount of food at a time— about 1 or 2 tablespoons. If the baby is not interested in the food, do not force eating. Simply put the food away and try again at another meal. Mealtimes should be pleasant for both you and your baby.

You can choose from many brands of commercially prepared baby food on the market. You can also make your own baby food by pureeing soft-cooked foods in a blender or food processor.

WHICH FOODS FIRST?

Introduce solid foods in the following order:
rice cereal
apple juice (dilute all juices with equal amount of water until the child is 1 year old)
applesauce
bananas
oatmeal, barley, and other cereals except wheat products
orange and yellow vegetables (squash, carrots, sweet potatoes)
other juices except for citrus
green vegetables
peaches, pears, apricots
wheat cereals
meats

A few foods should not be introduced until the child reaches the appropriate age.

6 months	yogurt
6–9 months	teething biscuits, Zwieback, Cheerios
9 months	egg yolk, cottage cheese
12 months	milk (use whole milk until age 2, then switch to low-fat), egg white, citrus fruits and juices, strawberries, chocolate, honey

TRAVELING BY AIRPLANE

Whether for a family vacation or a visit to Grandma, many parents will find themselves in the position of taking their young child on an airplane. However daunting this may seem, a little preparation can make the trip more comfortable.

Car Seats

Airlines do not require the purchase of a separate ticket for children under age 2. This means that in most cases, a parent will hold the child throughout the plane flight. Studies have not proven that a child is any less safe being held in a lap than riding in a car seat strapped to an airplane seat. Therefore, the airlines have not changed their regulations to require the use of a car seat and the purchase of an extra ticket. Parents will want to bring along a car seat as part of their checked luggage or make arrangement for one at their destination if they plan to be using a car at the other end of their flight.

Motion Sickness

Motion sickness on airplanes is not as common as it is in car, train, or boat travel. However, if your child is prone to motion sickness, you can minimize the risk by requesting an aisle seat as close to the wings as possible. Airplane turbulence is felt the least in these seats.

Ear Stuffiness

Sometimes called "airplane ears," that uncomfortable "plugged up" feeling in the ears is caused by a rapid change in air pressure, usually as the plane descends. Children can do a number of things to clear their ears and avoid the pain associated with ear stuffiness. If the child is old enough, you can offer chewing gum 15 minutes before the plane begins its landing. Younger toddlers can chew crackers and other snacks. If this doesn't work, children can try nose blowing or puffing out their cheeks while keeping the mouth and nostrils closed. For babies, sucking a pacifier or a bottle will make them swallow and help relieve the pressure in their ears.

If you know the child has had ear pain during past airplane flights, try a long-acting nasal decongestant spray an hour before traveling. If possible, don't let the child sleep during the plane's descent because swallowing, which helps clear the ears, is less frequent during sleep.

Eating

Sometimes babies and toddlers are more comfortable eating lighter meals while traveling by air. They may tolerate the flight better if their stomachs are less full, and if they do suffer from motion sickness, there is less to vomit. Also, some mothers prefer using pre-made bottles to breastfeeding while on airplanes.

Jet Lag

Just like their parents, babies and toddlers can suffer from jet lag when flying east or west across several time zones. (No matter how long the flight, jet lag does not occur when traveling north or south within the same time zone.)

Symptoms of jet lag include: fatigue, drowsiness, difficulty sleeping, mental fuzziness, irritability, and minor coordination problems. The following tips will help you and your child combat the effects of jet lag.

- Try to schedule your trip so that you arrive at close to what would be your usual bedtime based on the clocks at your destination.

- Increase the amount of sleep you and your child get before the trip.

- Eat lightly during the trip and take in plenty of liquids but avoid caffeine.

- Stay away from fatty foods and try eating fruits instead.

- Remember that it will take a few days for an infant's feeding schedule to adjust to the new time zone. He or she will still be hungry at what would be the regular feeding time at home.

BEHAVIORAL AND EMOTIONAL PROBLEMS

Whether or not you are aware of it, the everyday problems of elbowing through crowds, juggling kids and career, and confronting conflicts at home and work can take a toll on your physical and emotional health. Many times, behavioral and emotional problems stem from the stress in your environment. Other times, they have a physical or genetic root.

Many common behavioral and emotional problems are discussed in this chapter. However, this is not a complete list. If you are concerned about a problem you or someone close to you is having, call the advice nurse, who can help you determine what steps to take.

ANXIETY

Anxiety is a combination of physical and emotional symptoms marked by feelings of uneasiness, agitation, uncertainty, nervousness, and fear. Sometimes a strong sense of threat or danger accompanies anxiety. Feelings of anxiety are sometimes prompted by a life event such as the death of someone close, a change in family life, the loss of a job, or the onset of an illness or financial problems.

The most common forms of anxiety do not last very long and improve steadily over time. If you have questions or concerns about anxiety, call the advice nurse.

PHYSICAL SYMPTOMS OF ANXIETY

- Tense muscles
- Heart palpitations
- Feeling of tightness in the chest
- "Butterflies" in the stomach
- Sweating
- Headaches
- Diarrhea
- "Lump" in the throat

EMOTIONAL SYMPTOMS OF ANXIETY

- Restlessness
- Nervousness
- Feeling of impending doom
- Quickly changing emotions with dramatic highs and lows (e.g., laughing then crying)
- Fearfulness

DEPRESSION

Depression is a consistent mood of hopelessness and helplessness. It is generally a more encompassing feeling than the occasional sadness or grief most people experience from time to time. Most periods of depression usually last for a minimum of 2 weeks and can go on much longer. Mild depression might interfere only slightly with normal functioning, while more severe depression can make it nearly impossible for a person to participate in normal daily activities. Specific life events, such as the death of a loved one, can bring on a period of depression. In some cases, the cause of the depression is less specific and can be hard to identify.

Someone suffering from depression may show all or only some of the signs listed below. If you are concerned that you or someone close to you may be experiencing depression, call the advice nurse.

SIGNS OF DEPRESSION

- Lessened interest or pleasure in most daily activities
- Withdrawal from friends and family
- Feelings of worthlessness or guilt
- Anxious or negative feelings
- Significant gain or loss of weight
- Changes in sleep patterns
- Decreased sexual drive
- Fatigue
- Decreased rate and amount of speech
- Abnormal menstruation patterns
- Decreased ability to concentrate and trouble completing tasks
- Ongoing thoughts of death or suicide

EATING DISORDERS

While many people experience brief eating problems of various types, eating disorders are severe disturbances in eating behavior. One type of eating disorder is the refusal to maintain a minimum body weight—such as refusing to eat at all. Another is "binge" eating followed by deliberate attempts to expel the food by vomiting or using laxatives. Eating disorders can occur in just about anyone but are most often seen in women during the teen and young adult years.

Eating disorders are often linked to problems of self esteem and are associated with an unusual concern about body image. People suffering from eating disorders may also be depressed or anxious and have problems with the use of substances

SIGNS OF EATING DISORDERS

- Continual checking of weight using a scale or repeated checking image in mirror

- Excessive fear of gaining weight or appearing fat

- Indulging in food binges followed by periods of fasting

- Inducing vomiting after eating

- Using laxatives or diuretics without a medical reason

- Exercising compulsively

- Developing secretive or ritualistic eating habits

- Stashing food in secret places

- Stealing food

- Cessation of menstruating without other medical reason

- Maintaining self-image of being overweight that does not match reality

FEELINGS ASSOCIATED WITH EATING DISORDERS

- Anxiety
- Depression
- Guilt
- Shame
- Self disgust

such as alcohol and stimulants. For these people, eating behavior and food in general become a major focus of daily living.

An eating disorder can be a very serious condition, even to the point of being life-threatening. There is also a higher than normal rate of suicide attempts among people with this problem. If you suspect that you or a family member has an eating disorder, call the advice nurse. The nurse can help evaluate the situation and offer you advice about what to do next.

FEARS

Fear is a very common response to threatening situations. Almost everyone experiences realistic fears at some time or another. Some people, however, develop intense fears that are not typical or that seem unreasonable. These might include fear of going outside or fear of social situations. These fears can sometimes become so intense that they affect the person's normal living patterns. The person can no longer do what he or she would normally, such as keep a job or go to the movies. Or, the person may develop unusual or ritual-like behaviors that may seem "crazy" or bizarre to others.

A common type of fear is phobias. These are intense, unrealistic fears of specific things or situations that are not likely to be very dangerous in reality. Fear of insects and fear of public speaking are two examples of common phobias. These phobias can also severely affect some people, making them unable to live as they would normally.

Experiencing any of these types of fears can be very difficult for the individual. However, the problem can be treated. If you or a family member has a problem with fears, call the advice nurse. The nurse can help evaluate the situation and offer you advice about what to do next.

FEATURES OF ABNORMAL FEARS

- The fears are at times consuming and interfere with the person's daily routine.
- The person dreads the fears and will often try to resist the urge to think or behave in the way they dictate.
- The person finds the fears irresistible even though they are often absurd or irrational.
- The person often keeps the fears a secret from other people.
- The person often feels compelled to perform certain behaviors to ease the anxiety associated with the fears.
- Fears often accompany feelings of depression.

SUBSTANCE ABUSE

Substance abuse is defined as use of drugs or alcohol in a way that negatively affects a person's well being. It is a chronic problem that can cause serious physical, emotional, social, and economic problems. Substance abuse is sometimes a response to the pain a person feels from underlying emotional problems such as stress, fear, or anxiety.

Millions of people have a substance abuse problem, and millions more are affected by the substance abuse of some-

one close to them. Substance abuse takes different forms depending upon the individual. Some people drink alcohol or use drugs daily, some only on weekends, and others go on extended binges. For more information, see the Health Information Resource Guide, p. 257.

SIGNS OF A SUBSTANCE ABUSE PROBLEM

- User is unable to cut down on or stop taking the substance.
- Person has a physical craving for the substance.
- User cannot remember events that took place while he or she was under the influence of the drug or alcohol.
- Use of the substance causes physical or psychological problems or complicates existing ones.
- Substance use causes family, job, social, or legal conflicts.
- Repeated attempts to stop using the substance fail.

BEHAVIORAL CHANGES ASSOCIATED WITH SUBSTANCE ABUSE

- Agitation
- Impaired judgment
- Inappropriate social interactions
- Poor job performance
- Fear
- Anxiety
- Aggressiveness
- Lowered inhibitions
- Inflated sense of one's own importance

PROBLEMS OF SEXUALITY

Not only can health problems related to sexuality have a devastating effect on you as an individual, such problems almost always affect others as well.

This section describes how to recognize and treat common sexual problems. Because sexually transmitted diseases are becoming more common, and the consequences of getting a sexually transmitted disease (STD) can be serious, this section offers specific advice on how to protect yourself and others through safer sex.

AIDS AND OTHER SEXUALLY TRANSMITTED DISEASES

Millions of Americans are affected by sexually transmitted diseases (STDs) of all kinds. Yet, since we first began hearing about the AIDS epidemic in the early 1980s, many people seem to have forgotten that other STDs are still a cause for concern. Although AIDS is the most deadly STD, other diseases such as syphilis, gonorrhea, genital herpes, hepatitis B, and chlamydia also pose serious health risks.

Acquired Immune Deficiency Syndrome (AIDS)

An estimated 1 million to 1.5 million Americans have been infected with the **human immunodeficiency virus (HIV)**— the virus that leads to AIDS. The virus is spread through some types of sexual contact, shared intravenous (IV) needles, and introduction of infected blood or semen into the body. Once a person becomes infected with HIV, it can take years before AIDS actually develops. Although drugs like zidovudine (AZT) can slow progression of the disease, at this point there is no cure. HIV also damages the immune system, allowing a person to get other infections.

Even if an infected person is otherwise healthy and has not yet developed AIDS, *any time* after he or she becomes infected with HIV this person can spread it to other people. This can occur through unprotected sexual contact (intercourse without a condom) or shared IV drug needles.

Chlamydia

About 3 million to 4 million people in the United States have this bacterial infection. Those at high risk for chlamydia infections include sexually active young adults (under age 25, especially teenagers), those who have several sexual partners or a new sexual partner within the last two months, and those whose sexual partner has chlamydia. In women, chlamydia can cause inflammation of the cervix and pelvic inflammatory disease (PID)—a leading cause of ectopic pregnancies (when the fetus attaches and grows in the fallopian tubes instead of in the uterus) and infertility in American women. In men, it can cause inflammation of the urethra, the organ through which urine passes, and the epididymis, where sperm are stored. Fortunately, chlamydia is easily cured by taking antibiotics for a week.

Genital Herpes (Herpes Simplex Virus Type 2)

An estimated 20 million people in the United States have genital herpes. Herpes simplex virus type 2 causes painful sores and blisters on the genitals and around the mouth. Even after the initial outbreak of sores heals, an infected person may carry the virus for years, with new sores erupting from time to time. The herpes virus can be spread to other people through sexual contact whether sores are present or not. Although there is no cure for herpes, there are drugs that can reduce the length and pain of herpes outbreaks.

Gonorrhea

About 2 million Americans get gonorrhea each year. In men, the infection can cause inflammation of the genitals and rectum. In women, it can cause painful PID and complications during pregnancy. People who have several partners are at high risk for gonorrhea, but anyone can get infected. Fortunately, gonorrhea can be treated with antibiotics.

Hepatitis B Virus (HBV)

HBV is a disease that causes inflammation of the liver and can lead to cirrhosis and cancer of the liver. It can be transmitted sexually. High-risk factors for getting HBV include IV drug abuse, having several sexual partners, or having a partner who is currently infected or a chronic carrier. If you think you have recently been exposed to HBV, your doctor may be able to give you hepatitis B immune globulin to prevent hepatitis from developing.

Syphilis

In early stages, this infection causes ulcers on the genitals, rectum, and throat which are often painless. If left untreated, it can produce warts in the genital area, contagious sores on other parts of the body, disease of the lymph nodes, and later problems with the nervous system and heart and mental illness. Unfortunately, the number of syphilis cases in America is now at its highest point since 1950. Syphilis, however, can be treated with antibiotics.

Special Risks during Pregnancy

Sexually transmitted diseases pose special risks during pregnancy. All the STDs discussed above can be passed from mother to child during pregnancy, at birth, or shortly after. Often, STDs can lead to serious health problems for newborns. Women who have syphilis, gonorrhea, or chlamydia can be treated with antibiotics during pregnancy to prevent complications for themselves and their babies. Women with active genital herpes sores may need to deliver by caesarean section to keep their babies from getting the virus. Women who are HIV positive should take the drug zidovudine (AZT) during pregnancy to reduce the risk of passing the virus to the baby.

For more information on AIDS and other sexually transmitted diseases, see the Health Information Resource Guide, p. 257.

PREVENTIVE STEPS

The two best ways to prevent sexually transmitted diseases are to abstain from sex or to have a mutually monogamous sexual relationship with someone who is uninfected. If neither option works for you, here are some other things you can do to reduce your risk:

• Always use a latex condom and spermicidal gel. Choose latex condoms with receptacle tips rather than natural-membrane condoms, which may be more likely to break or to allow viruses and bacteria to pass through. The spermicide nonoxynol 9 has also been shown to provide added protection against HIV, HBV, and herpes simplex virus. It also reduces the risk of chlamydia and gonorrhea in women.

• Limit the number of sexual partners you have. Remember that when it comes to STDs, having sex outside of a mutually monogamous relationship puts you at the same risk as if you had sex with all your partner's partners. Thus, the more sexual partners you have, the greater your risk for STDs.

If you think you may have an STD, see your medical provider. He or she can advise you on whether you should be tested, and treat you properly if you test positive.

Keep in mind that neither condoms nor spermicides offer foolproof protection. In fact, condoms fail at a rate of 10 to 15 percent as a result of flaws or improper use.

SEXUAL PROBLEMS

The "right way" to make love and the "right" frequency for sex are simply what work best and are most satisfying for each couple. Unfortunately, however, anxiety and physical, emotional, or relationship issues can sometimes interfere with a person's or couple's ability to enjoy or participate fully in sex.

Simply growing older, too, brings changes in sexual function for both men and women. Most people don't have the same intensity of sexual desire at age 55 that they had when they were 20. Intensity of sexual desire declines slowly with age, though interest in sex seldom disappears totally. Similarly, as people grow older, they may need more time and more direct genital stimulation before reaching orgasm.

In older men, erections are usually not as firm as they once were and more time (days, as opposed to hours) may be needed after ejaculation before they are able to have another. In postmenopausal women, vaginal dryness may cause discomfort during intercourse. Water-soluble lubricants, however, are available to help this problem (see Menopause, p. 154).

Unfortunately, without knowing that such changes are a normal part of aging, many people worry that something is wrong with them sexually or with their relationships.

Common sexual problems that can occur at any age include differing or decrease in sexual desire, erection problems, rapid ejaculation, and problems with orgasm. Often these problems are caused by a combination of physical and psychological or relationship issues.

The first of these issues, differing sexual desire, is problematic only if a couple cannot find a mutually satisfying compromise. Sexual desire naturally varies from person to person. Some may want sex three times a day; others, three times a year. There is no "right" or "normal" level of desire.

Diminished desire is common in both men and women in times of stress, when ill or recovering from an illness, or when tension exists in their relationship. Alcohol and certain drugs can also cause a loss of desire. These same factors can cause temporary erection problems (impotence) and inhibit orgasm in both men and women.

At some time in life, most men will have temporary erection problems, during which they are unable to achieve or keep enough of an erection for intercourse. About 30 million American men, however, have a long-term problem that could benefit from medical treatment, counseling, or both. Of all long-term sexual problems, 50 to 75 percent have a physical cause, such as diabetes, vascular problems, or drug side effects.

Early ejaculation (when semen is released before you or your partner have time to achieve climax) and delayed ejaculation often can be relieved by making adjustments in lovemaking.

For both men and women, there's more to sex than intercourse. Touching, kissing, caresses, massage, even holding hands and talking are all as important to intimacy and sexual pleasure as intercourse. In women, orgasm is achieved by stimulating the clitoris. A very high percentage of women do not have orgasms during intercourse. Orgasm from oral or manual stimulation of the clitoris, however, is just as satisfying as vaginal orgasm. In men, stimulating the head of the penis brings orgasm. As men age, they often need more direct stimulation of the penis to achieve an erection or orgasm. But foreplay that focuses only on the genitals doesn't always give either partner time to become mentally and emotionally aroused for sex—an important step to orgasm. Whole-body massage and caresses can help arouse and prepare a man or woman for more direct genital stimulation.

Couples and individuals can often fix sexual problems on their own, but sometimes need medical help or counseling. Your medical provider can recommend a qualified counselor or a doctor specializing in sexual health. Call the advice nurse if you have questions or concerns about sexual problems.

PREVENTION AND SCREENING OF COMMON HEALTH PROBLEMS

No one likes unpleasant surprises, especially when they concern one's health. The sooner you learn about your health risks, the better. Preventing health problems can help increase your chances of living a longer, healthier life.

Many people assume that an "annual physical" is the best way to prevent problems, however, most medical providers agree that an annual physical is a worn-out tradition. There is simply no scientific evidence that a yearly pilgrimage to your medical provider will prevent health problems. The U.S. Preventive Services Task Force has stated that the emphasis of preventive exams should be on health counseling and health behavior.

Experts question the value of many routine tests such as blood tests and urinalysis and are increasingly recommending tests based on personal health risks. This section offers information about common preventive exams. You may be surprised to learn that many tests are not needed as often as were previously recommended (see Preventive Services Recommendations, p. 231).

Your medical provider can help you weigh the pros and cons of having certain exams. If it is unclear to you whether a screening test would help you, ask yourself these questions: Is it likely that many other tests and exams will be done if the results of a screening test are inconclusive? What are the odds of detecting a disease through this test? Could any harm come from having this test? Given my age and health history, how effective is the treatment for the disease that may be detected through this test? If you ask these questions and pay careful attention to the answers, you can be a partner with your medical provider in deciding whether the test is appropriate for you.

You can do more to protect your health than all the medical providers, hospitals, new medical equipment, and medical scientists put together. That's because the decisions you make, especially about exercise, diet, and substance use, are clearly the best predictors of your long-term health.

Cancer Prevention: Risk Factors You Can Control

Avoid Smoking and Secondhand Smoke

Smoking causes two-thirds of all lung cancer deaths and also increases the risk of cancers of the mouth, pharynx, larynx, esophagus, pancreas, uterus, cervix, kidney, and bladder. Research also shows that the smoke blown your way from others' cigarettes may even be worse than smoke directly inhaled, because its tar content has not been reduced by going through the cigarette's filter. When you quit smoking, your lungs begin healing themselves, and some smoking-induced precancerous changes can be totally reversed.

Avoid Excessive Alcohol Use

Heavy drinkers may have a twofold to sixfold risk of developing throat or mouth cancer. The chances of developing cancer of the pancreas, liver, breast, stomach, and rectum also are greater if you drink alcohol. The news is even worse for drinkers who smoke. The risks of throat and mouth cancers escalate 15-fold, and the risks of esophageal cancer may increase by as much as 25-fold. Heavy drinking may keep the liver from detoxifying potentially cancer-causing substances from smoking. It also may irritate and make tissues of the mouth, throat, and esophagus more prone to cancer.

Eat Less Fat

Scientists are finding that a high-fat diet can increase the risk of breast and colon cancer. It also is a suspect in prostate and ovarian cancer. Fat may cause the body to make some bile acids that promote cancer, and definitely increases production of hormones. This tends to trigger the growth of some tumors in overweight people. Several suspected cancer-causing chemicals are first stored in animal fat and then in the body fat of humans who eat the animals.

Eat More Fiber

Research from the National Cancer Institute shows that if most people had 20 to 30 grams of fiber daily, their risk of getting colon cancer would be cut in half. The insoluble fiber found in wheat bran, whole-grain cereals and breads, vegetables and fruits, and the soluble fiber in such foods as oat bran and beans flushes possible cancer-promoting waste through the intestines and colon. It also may flush out fats and bile acids.

Protect Your Skin from the Sun

Most skin cancers are caused by too much exposure to the sun's ultraviolet rays and the high-energy bulbs in tanning parlors. It's easy to protect yourself from this threat: try to avoid direct sunlight between 10:00 a.m. and 2:00 p.m., wear protective clothing when you are out in the sun, and use sunscreen with a sun protection factor of at least 15.

Maintain a Healthy Weight

Overweight women have higher death rates from cancer of the uterus, gallbladder, cervix, ovaries, and breast. More overweight men die from colon, rectal, and prostate cancers. Eating healthy foods in moderation and exercising regularly will help you tone up and lose weight. Researchers are trying to find out exactly how exercise protects the body. Not only does 30 minutes of exercise at least three times each week combat obesity, it also helps reduce stress and regulate bowel movements.

Avoid Environmental Hazards

Workplaces are now regulated so that hazardous materials are not routinely released into the air, but if you work around chemicals or dust, let your medical provider know this during your next physical examination. Whenever you use paint, varnish, or any other chemical indoors, leave windows open. Have your house checked for radon leakage. Use pesticides and herbicides carefully, and wash fruits and vegetables before eating them.

Cancer Management

If cancer is detected and confirmed, several treatment options or combined options may be available. Surgery, radiation, and chemotherapy are the most common treatments. Antihormone therapy, immunotherapy, and regional perfusion are less common.

Surgery

The oldest form of cancer treatment, surgery involves removing a tumor or cancerous growth.

Radiation Therapy

Radiation works by killing the cancer cells by exposing them to high doses of X-rays.

Chemotherapy

Drugs that kill cancer cells by interfering with how they reproduce are taken orally or injected into the body.

Antihormone Therapy

These drugs have been successful in treating breast and prostate cancers. The antihormone medication most commonly used to treat breast cancer, tamoxifen, has some side effects, including hot flashes.

Immunotherapy

Drugs are used to boost the body's own ability to fight cancer in the same way it wards off infections. The best known of these, interferon, has been successful in treating a rare form of leukemia but less successful against other cancers.

Regional Perfusion

Drugs are introduced to only the part of the body that has cancerous tissue. Damage to healthy tissue is minimal, the drugs may be more effective, and there are fewer side effects.

Support Is Available

Discovering you have cancer and looking ahead to an uncertain future can be frightening. Many cancer patients and their families find it helpful and reassuring to talk with others who also are dealing with cancer. Emotional support is available for those who wish to join a cancer support group. For more information on how to locate a support group, ask your medical provider or contact the American Cancer Society (see the Health Information Resource Guide, p. 257).

BREAST CANCER

Breast cancer is the most common type of cancer in American women. Each year in the United States, more than 182,000 women learn they have this disease. Although breast cancer may not be prevented, it often can be survived. Early detection increases the breast cancer survival rate. Women with small, localized breast cancers (where the cancer has not spread beyond the breast) have a 90 percent chance of living more than 10 years after cancer treatment.

Understanding the Risk

The average woman has a one-in-eight chance of having breast cancer during her lifetime. Several factors, however, can increase your risk:

Family history. Your risk doubles if your natural mother or sister has had breast cancer. It is even higher if they developed breast cancer before menopause.

Premalignant cells on biopsy. Women who have had a previous breast biopsy that was benign but showed certain suspicious cells are at increased risk.

Age. Two-thirds of all breast cancers occur in women over 50. As you grow older, your risk increases.

Childbirth and menstruation. Never having children, or giving birth to your first child after age 30, increases your risk of breast cancer. Having your period begin before the age of 12 or starting menopause after the age of 50 may also add to your risk.

Other factors. Other factors linked to breast cancer include obesity and a history of ovarian or endometrial cancer. Even so, the most important risk factors are growing older and a personal or family history of breast cancer. You'll want to be very careful if you are at a higher risk.

Breast Cancer Screening Tests

There are three key parts to breast cancer screening: mammography, breast self-exams, and clinical breast exams performed by a medical provider. When to begin mammography and clinical breast exam and how often these tests should be performed is a subject of ongoing debate in the medical community. However, most medical professionals agree that regular clinical breast exams and mammography should begin at age 50 and be repeated at least every 2 years. For women between the ages of 40 and 49 who do not have special risk factors, the evidence regarding the benefit of mammography with or without clinical breast exams is conflicting. Since opinions vary widely among medical providers on this issue, it is best for women in this age group to discuss their particular risks with their own medical providers.

Mammograms. The most effective early detection method available today is mammography—a low-dose X-ray of the breast. Mammograms can detect breast cancers while they are very small, sometimes 2 years earlier than they can be felt by a woman or her medical provider.

In the past 25 years, mammograms have improved considerably. The X-rays are much more sensitive, and far less radiation is used. Today we use 1/40 the amount of radiation required just 20 years ago. The risk of 10 mammograms causing breast cancer is one in 25,000—much less than many of the normal risks of daily life.

Mammography, however, is not perfect. In some cases, a lump that you can feel during a breast exam may not appear on a mammogram. The lump would still need to be checked, even if the mammogram is normal. Mammography, like most other tests, can also show abnormal results where there is no cancer. This occurs in about one out of every 100 mammograms.

There is ongoing debate in the medical community over how often a woman should have a mammogram and when to begin having them. The Institute for Clinical Systems Integration recommends a baseline mammogram between ages 35 and 40 only for women with any high-risk factors (p. 218). Between the ages of 40 and 49, all women should have a mammogram at least once every 2 years. A yearly mammogram is recommended for women over the age of 50. Experts also suggest that women who have not had breast cancer detected may stop mammography screening at age 75.

The American Cancer Society recommends that women start having mammograms every 1 to 2 years at age 40. After age 50, the ACS recommends women have a mammogram once each year.

After looking at research from around the world on the potential benefits and harms of mammography for women younger than age 50, the National Cancer Institute concluded that there is no clear overall benefit and also no clear overall harm to using this screening test for women under the age of 50.

However, many people in the medical community still disagree on this issue. Now that you know more about these issues, you may want to discuss your options with your medical provider at your next scheduled visit. Whether or not you decide to have a mammogram at this time, it's important to remember that regular breast self-exams and clinical breast exams by your medical provider are wise practices to follow for early detection of breast cancer.

Clinical breast exam. Many medical providers do routine breast exams for women of all ages during general physicals or pelvic exams. The provider will check each breast using fingertips to feel for lumps, and look for other suspicious changes—such as dimpled, scaling, or puckered skin or fluid leaking from the nipple. When combined with a mammogram, a breast exam by a medical provider is the best way to detect cancer in its early stages.

Breast self-exam. Many women are afraid to examine their breasts because of what they might find. Most breast lumps are not cancerous. Even if a breast lump is cancerous, your best defense is early detection. Breast self-examination (BSE), described on the next page, is easy and takes only about 5 minutes a month. Among women with breast cancer, 34 percent said they first discovered their breast cancer through BSE. BSE is a way to discover any change from what is "normal" for you. Your medical provider can review this technique with you.

Performing a Breast Self-Exam

Many health professionals strongly recommend that women perform monthly breast self-examinations to increase their chances for early detection if they develop breast cancer. In fact, the American Cancer Society recommends monthly BSE for all women age 19 and older. The procedure is actually quite simple and takes only about 5 minutes a month.

The best time to do BSE is 1 week after the start of your period. If you have already passed through menopause, do BSE on the first day of each month. If you've had a hysterectomy, ask your medical provider to advise you on the best time for you to perform BSE.

What to Look For

It's normal for women's breasts to feel lumpy, to swell, or to become tender, especially around the time of menstruation. By performing BSE each month, you will become familiar with the feel, shape, and size of your breasts, making it easier for you to notice changes should they occur. **Here are some things to look for while examining your breasts:**

- New lumps or changes in the size or shape of existing lumps
- Change in the shape or contour of your breasts or unusual swelling
- Changes in skin color or texture
- Dimpling, puckering, crusting, or rash in the skin, especially around the nipple
- Any fluid leaking from the nipple

HOW TO DO A BREAST SELF-EXAM

1. While in the shower, raise your right arm, placing your hand on the back of your head. Starting at the outer edge of the right breast, use the pads of the fingertips of your left hand.

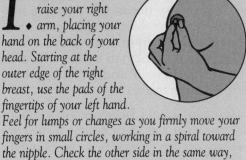

Feel for lumps or changes as you firmly move your fingers in small circles, working in a spiral toward the nipple. Check the other side in the same way, then gently squeeze each nipple to check for any discharge.

Pads of fingertips   Small circles about the size of a dime.

2. After your shower, clasp your hands together and raise your arms above your head with elbows bent. In a mirror, look for changes in shape or contour, as well as any skin changes, such as dimpling or rashes.

3. Still standing before the mirror, lower your arms. Place your hands on your hips, pull your shoulders and elbows forward, and lean slightly toward the mirror. Look again for any changes in shape or contour, and for skin changes.

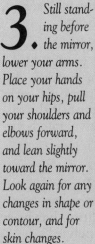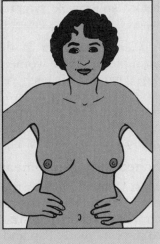

4. Finally, lying down, place a rolled towel or pillow under one shoulder and place the hand on that same side over your head. Examine your breast again as you did in the shower, this time checking your armpit as well. Repeat this on the other breast.

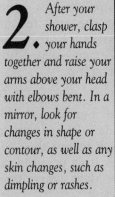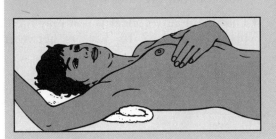

5. Call your the advice nurse if you find anything that concerns you. See Preventive Services Recommendations, p. 231, for information on when to schedule mammograms.

I hadn't been in to see my medical provider for a Pap smear in years. But my daughter kept reminding me about the importance of having this screening test, so I started going for a Pap test again.

Betty, age 62

CERVICAL CANCER

The most effective early cervical cancer detection method available today is the Pap test, or Pap smear. It is a simple procedure that involves swabbing a small sample of cells from a woman's cervix and transferring them to a slide. The cells are then examined and evaluated by a certified laboratory.

Women should begin having regular Pap smears at age 18 or earlier if they are sexually active. There is some disagreement about when women should stop having Pap smears. Some say there is no upper age limit; others suggest having your last Pap smear at age 65 if there is no history of problems. Talk with your medical provider about your situation.

Done regularly, Pap smears make it possible for medical providers to find early evidence of cervical cancer. This can be done before any visible symptoms are present, when the disease is easier to cure.

Cervical cancer is diagnosed in an estimated 13,500 women yearly. About 4,400 women die each year from the disease. For those women diagnosed early, the survival rate is 89 percent. If the disease hasn't spread, the survival rate is virtually 100 percent.

Scheduling Pap Smears

Most women consider the Pap smear and pelvic exam to be the major part of an annual checkup. The tradition has been to have a "yearly Pap and pelvic."

However, a panel of experts analyzed the most recent scientific and medical research about Pap smears and concluded:

While it is extremely important to have Pap smears on a regular basis, it is no longer considered necessary for most women to have a Pap smear every year.

Because most cervical cancers grow very slowly, a Pap smear done every 2 to 3 years will provide the same early detection benefit as an annual Pap smear.

You may be able to extend the interval between Pap smears to 2 to 3 years if you have had annual normal Pap smears for at least 3 years in a row (documented in your medical records).

More frequent Pap smears are still recommended for women with a history of abnormal cell changes that may lead to cancer in the next 5 years and for women who are HIV positive (or otherwise immunosuppressed).

You and your medical provider can decide together on a Pap smear schedule that is most appropriate for you. Remember that he or she may recommend more frequent visits for other reasons—such as a breast exam—depending on your age and health status.

For Best Results

Try to schedule your periodic health exam (that may include a Pap smear) to take place about 1 week before the start of your period. If this isn't possible, at least try to avoid the days when your menstrual flow is heaviest.

Don't use a vaginal douche or any type of vaginal medication or lubricant for 24 hours before having a Pap smear.

Help your medical provider determine the Pap smear schedule best for you by:

- Telling him or her the approximate dates of your previous Pap smears.

- Discussing any concerns you may have about waiting 2 to 3 years between Pap smears.

COLON CANCER

Colon cancer is a common cancer that can be detected and prevented in many people if simple steps are followed. The rate of colon cancer among men and women is about the same, with 6 percent of women and 5 percent of men getting this disease during their lifetime.

Colon cancer ranks second only to lung cancer, with more than 152,000 new cases reported each year. The earlier the cancer—or any changes in the colon that might lead to cancer—is found, the better the chance for cure. Indeed, early detection increases the cure rate to 91 percent.

Understanding Your Risk

No one knows for sure what causes colon cancer, but we do know some of the risk factors. Your chances of developing colon cancer are higher if you have a history of ulcerative colitis, severe dysplasia (precancerous changes), or Crohn's disease or if your mother, father, sister, or brother has had colon cancer.

Age plays a role, too. Most cases occur in people over age 65. Fewer than 2 percent of cases occur in those under age 40.

Screening Tests

The three tests most commonly used for colon cancer screening are the digital (finger) rectal exam, testing the stool for blood, and sigmoidoscopy. Screening exams can be mildly uncomfortable, but generally these tests are easy and safe to do. Experts still disagree about how often the colon should be examined and how effectively tests detect cancer in people who have no symptoms. Your medical provider can help you decide if you need any of these tests:

Sigmoidoscopy

A slender lighted tube called a flexible sigmoidoscope is inserted into your rectum after you have had an enema. With this device, the physician can see about 27 inches into your colon. About 80 percent of cancers and polyps (growths) that might become cancer can be found this way, because they tend to build up at the lower end of your bowel.

Stool Test for Blood

Because polyps and cancers produce small unnoticeable amounts of blood, which are carried away in the stools, tests such as "Hemoccult" or "guaiac" are used to detect bleeding. By carefully following the directions for the test, you will make the results more reliable. Some medical guidelines suggest this test is unnecessary for average risk patients.

Digital Rectal Exam

Using his or her finger, the medical provider feels for lumps (polyps) in your rectum that could be cancer. The effectiveness of this screening method is limited because less than 13 percent of colon cancers are within a finger's reach.

If the results of any of these tests are abnormal, your medical provider will probably order more studies. Sometimes these tests are not accurate, creating either a false promise of good health or a false alarm about the frightening possibility of cancer.

The recommendations for colon exams vary. The Institute for Clinical Systems Integration recommends annual digital rectal exams beginning at age 50, and sigmoidoscopy every 5 years between ages 50 and 80. The American Cancer Society and national medical societies recommend annual digital rectal exams for adults over 40, annual stool blood testing starting at age 50, and sigmoidoscopy every 3 to 5 years beginning at age 50.

Given the cost, inconvenience, and uncertainty about the effectiveness of colon cancer screening, you and your medical provider may decide it is unnecessary for you. On the other hand, if you are at high risk for colon cancer—particularly if you have a close family member who has had the disease—your provider may recommend more extensive testing.

Those with a history of cancer are clearly candidates for regular screening. Remember, these are only screening tests, and if you have symptoms that persist you should see your medical provider no matter what your last screening test showed.

SELF-CARE STEPS FOR COLON CANCER

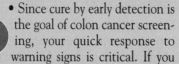 • Since cure by early detection is the goal of colon cancer screening, your quick response to warning signs is critical. If you have a change in your bowel habits (black stools, thin stools, blood in your stools, or intermittent or persistent diarrhea or constipation) an exam of your colon to find the cause may be done, regardless of your age. Cancer, however, is just one of the many possible causes of these symptoms.

• Several dietary factors are thought to play a role in colorectal cancer. Obesity, total calorie intake, and high-fat diets have been implicated in causing cancer in both animal and human research. A diet high in fiber may be helpful in preventing colon cancer. Foods high in fiber include whole-grain cereals and breads, beans, potatoes, brown rice, fruits and vegetables.

GLAUCOMA

Glaucoma refers to a group of eye diseases where pressure inside the eyeball increases, damaging the optic nerve. If the disease goes untreated, it can result in blindness. Loss of sight due to glaucoma cannot be reversed, however, detecting and treating the disease can halt its progression. Glaucoma is one of the leading preventable causes of blindness in the United States.

Glaucoma Screening

Your medical provider can perform a simple test to measure the pressure inside your eyeball. He or she uses a special device that blows a jet of air against the eye. The procedure is painless and can be done as part of a regular vision screening. Studies suggest that you first should be tested for glaucoma when you are 40 years of age. Your medical provider will recommend how often you should repeat the test.

PREVENTIVE STEPS

Studies have not conclusively linked glaucoma to any particular risk factors. The key to preventing blindness from glaucoma is early detection and treatment. Have eye exams on the schedule recommended by your medical provider. If you have changes in your vision or concerns about your sight, call the advice nurse.

HIGH BLOOD CHOLESTEROL

High blood cholesterol is one of the biggest risk factors for heart attack, which is the leading cause of death in America. Cholesterol is a waxy substance your body produces to help it function properly. A diet containing too much fat, cholesterol, and calories contributes to high blood cholesterol. Neither fat nor cholesterol dissolves in the bloodstream. Instead, both are carried through the body in packages called *lipoproteins*.

Cholesterol found in low-density lipoproteins (LDL cholesterol) is considered most responsible for plaque formation that clogs the arteries, leading to stroke and heart attack. High-density lipoproteins (HDLs)—known as "good cholesterol"—are thought to be responsible for removing extra cholesterol from the blood and thereby cutting down the risk for coronary heart disease.

Measuring Your Cholesterol

Your medical provider will take a small sample of your blood either by pricking your finger or drawing blood from a vein. The blood is then analyzed, usually at a lab, for the amount of total cholesterol it carries. Sometimes the proportions of LDL and HDL are also measured. If you have specific questions about the test, discuss them with your medical provider.

Classifying Your Cholesterol

Total blood cholesterol measurements below 200 mg/dl are classified as "desirable," those 200 to 239 mg/dl as "borderline high," and those 240 mg/dl and above as "high." Because cholesterol levels can fluctuate from day to day, an average of two or more measurements should be used for classification. The benefit of "knowing your number" comes from your ability to take action and control your cholesterol—and that means making a long-term commitment to change.

Reducing Your Risk

Your chance of developing heart disease depends on more than just the amount of cholesterol in your blood. To get a better idea of what your cholesterol number means and what action you should take, start by identifying and adding up your other **risk factors for heart disease**. Such factors include:

- Male (45 years and older)
- Female (55 years and older or early menopause without hormone replacement therapy)
- Family history of early heart disease (before the age of 55)
- Cigarette smoking
- High blood pressure (140/90 mmHg or higher)
- Low levels of HDL-cholesterol (less than 35 mg/dl)
- Diabetes or impaired glucose tolerance

Just as these factors combine to increase your risk of heart disease, healthy habits—such as eating a low-fat diet, regular exercise, and not smoking—can reduce your risk. Many people can lower their blood cholesterol simply by increasing their level of physical activity, and changing the way they eat—avoiding foods high in fat, especially saturated fat and cholesterol. The higher your cholesterol level is, the greater the benefits will be if you lower it.

Screening Recommendations

Regular cholesterol testing should begin at age 35 for men and age 45 for women. The test should be repeated every 5 years until age 75. (See also Preventive Services Recommendations, p. 231.)

HIGH BLOOD PRESSURE

High blood pressure, or hypertension, affects one in every four adults. It is a main risk factor for two of the top three leading causes of death in America—heart disease and stroke.

Although hypertension cannot be cured, it can usually be controlled. Advances over the last 30 years in detecting and treating it have contributed to a 50 percent reduction in deaths from heart disease, and a 57 percent reduction in deaths from stroke since 1972.

The risks for developing high blood pressure are greater for certain groups of people. **People at particular risk include:**

- African Americans

- People whose parents have high blood pressure

- People with high-normal blood pressure

What Is Blood Pressure?

Each time the heart beats, blood is pumped to all parts of the body. For blood to circulate, it needs a certain amount of force or pressure. Blood pressure is the force the flow of blood exerts on your arteries.

Two numbers are used to measure your blood pressure:

132 (systolic)/ 84 (diastolic)

The higher number, the **systolic pressure**, refers to the pressure inside the artery when the heart squeezes to pump blood through the body. The lower number, the **diastolic pressure**, refers to the pressure inside the artery when the heart is relaxed and filling with blood. The numbers are recorded as "mmHg" (millimeters of mercury).

You are considered to have high blood pressure when your readings are consistently 140 mmHg or greater systolic and/or 90 mmHg or greater diastolic.

The term **borderline** is sometimes used to describe hypertension in which the blood pressure only occasionally rises above 140/90 mmHg.

Standardized Measurement
The Importance of Standardized Measurement

Measuring blood pressure is not as quick and easy as it may seem. In addition to the normal minute-by-minute fluctuations in blood pressure, several biological factors, such as anxiety, eating, and pain, can also influence a blood pressure reading. If the people taking the readings don't use the same technique to measure blood pressure, the results may vary as well. Since blood pressure readings are an important test for diagnosing and treating high blood pressure, a standardized measurement technique is recommended to reduce as many of these variables as possible.

You should expect your medical provider to follow the American Heart Association standards when measuring your blood pressure:

- Measure your arm for proper blood pressure cuff size

- Support your arm at the level of your heart

- Get an estimate of your systolic blood pressure by feeling the pulse at your wrist and inflating the cuff

- Inflate the cuff quickly and deflate it slowly

- Tell you your blood pressure numbers

To guard against incorrectly diagnosing high blood pressure on one elevated reading, readings from two or more separate visits should be used. In a study of patients being screened for high blood pressure, 275 patients with high blood pressure on one reading were referred for three more blood pressure screening visits. Normal blood pressure was recorded for 215 (78 percent) of these patients after these visits.

Your Contribution to Accuracy

Worry, poor eating habits, tobacco, air temperature changes, exertion, and pain can create results that are not your usual blood pressure. **To maximize the accuracy of your blood pressure measurement:**

- Do not eat, smoke, drink caffeine, or exercise for at least 30 minutes before you have your blood pressure measured.

- Wear short sleeves or loose sleeves that can be easily pushed up when you have your blood pressure taken. For consistency, use the same arm for each reading.

- Sit quietly with your legs uncrossed for a period before having your blood pressure measured.

- Bring along your blood pressure records and a list of any drugs you are currently taking.

- If using home blood pressure equipment, follow the standard measurement technique and bring equipment in yearly for comparison.

Scheduling Readings

Blood pressure can vary widely from time to time, so several readings need to be averaged from two or more visits before you can be classified as having high blood pressure. The Joint National Committee on High Blood Pressure (JNC) has developed new classifications that now identify different stages of hypertension. These stages need to be considered, in addition to your health history and risk factors for heart disease, to decide how to manage hypertension. The JNC recommends routine blood pressure checks at least once every 2 years for people with normal blood pressure (below 130/85 mmHg).

Many medical providers routinely check blood pressure every time a patient is seen at the office. The following blood pressure classification table has more guidelines on how often you should have your blood pressure checked. (See also Preventive Services Recommendations, p. 231.)

*If you are not taking antihypertensive drugs and are not acutely ill.

†When systolic and diastolic pressures fall into different categories, the higher category should be used to classify your blood pressure status.

CLASSIFICATION OF BLOOD PRESSURE FOR ADULTS AGE 18 YEARS AND OLDER*

Category	Systolic† (top number)	Diastolic† (bottom number)	What to do
Normal	Lower than 130	Lower than 85	Recheck in 2 years
High-normal	130–139	85–89	Recheck in 1 year
Hypertension			
Stage 1	140–159	90–99	Confirm within 2 months
Stage 2	160–179	100–109	See provider within 1 month
Stage 3	180–209	110–119	See provider within 1 week
Stage 4	210 or higher	120 or higher	See provider immediately

Source: 1993 Joint Committee on Detection, Evaluation, and Treatment of High Blood Pressure

SELF-CARE STEPS FOR HIGH BLOOD PRESSURE

You may be able to reduce your blood pressure by taking the following steps:

• **Lose weight.** Being overweight increases your risk of developing high blood pressure. Weight loss in even modest amounts can lower and help control blood pressure.

• **Exercise regularly.** Regular, aerobic exercise—such as walking, running, bicycling, or swimming laps—can prevent and reduce high blood pressure. More activity can also help reduce weight and stress. Many experts recommend 30 to 45 minutes of aerobic exercise three to five times a week.

• **Control salt in your diet.** Not everyone is sensitive to the blood pressure-raising effects of too much sodium, but there is no simple way to find out such sensitivity. Since the amount of salt in the average American diet raises blood pressure for about half of those with high blood pressure and interferes with some blood pressure-lowering drugs, cutting down on salt is recommended for anyone with high blood pressure. Limit salt to less than 2,300 milligrams per day by not adding it to your food and by limiting processed, convenience, and fast foods, which are traditionally high in sodium.

• **Limit alcohol.** Drinking too much alcohol can raise blood pressure, add weight, and make high blood pressure control harder. Avoid alcohol or do not have more than two drinks a day. A drink is defined as 12 ounces of beer, 4 ounces of wine, or 1.5 ounces of 80-proof liquor.

• **Quit smoking.** Smoking cigarettes does not cause high blood pressure, but smoking is a major risk factor for cardiovascular disease. That is why everyone, especially people with high blood pressure, needs to quit smoking—better yet, never start.

• **Eat less fat.** Some evidence shows that a low-fat diet may reduce blood pressure and lower blood cholesterol. Eating less fat will also aid in weight loss.

PROSTATE CANCER

The prostate is an organ that surrounds the bladder opening and urethra of males. Enlargement of the prostate is a common disorder among men over 60 years of age. Cancer of the prostate is as common as lung cancer among males. However, fewer than 1 percent of men under age 50 have detectable prostate cancer. Past the age of 80, more than 50 percent of males have been shown to have some stage of prostate cancer. Although prostate cancer is serious, only a small percentage of men who get the disease die of it.

If you have a relative (father or brother) who has had prostate cancer, you may be at higher risk for getting this cancer.

Symptoms

You should consider any block to your normal flow of urine a warning sign, even though such symptoms rarely mean you have cancer.

Screening

There is no clear evidence that screenings are of value.

Prostate cancers are being diagnosed more often in younger and middle-aged men. The most commonly used method for early detection of prostate cancer is a digital rectal exam in which the medical provider uses his or her finger to feel through the wall of the rectum for abnormal growth in the prostate (see illustration). However, because only part of the prostate can be felt, many prostate cancers are likely to be missed by such an exam. Studies also show that as often as 60 percent of the time an abnormal finding proves to be a false alarm after further tests.

Your medical provider may also consider some of the new approaches for detecting prostate cancer, including tran-

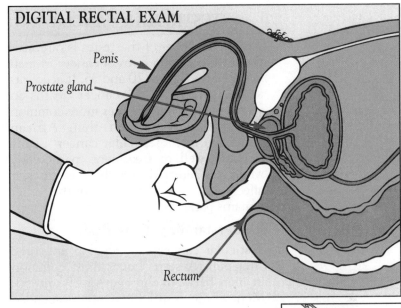

DIGITAL RECTAL EXAM

Penis

Prostate gland

Rectum

srectal ultrasound or a prostate-specific antigen blood test—especially if you are at high risk or if your rectal exam was abnormal. These tests, however, haven't been proven effective when used alone for screening. But when a digital rectal exam is abnormal, these screening studies greatly increase the rate of cancer detection.

Prostate Screening Recommendations

The National Cancer Institute and the American Cancer Society recommend a digital rectal exam every year for men over age 40. Recently, the U.S. Preventive Services Task Force recommendations differed. The task force concluded that for men without symptoms or special risk factors there is not enough evidence to recommend either for or against routine digital rectal exams. Other, more extensive prostate screening methods—such as transrectal ultrasound or prostate specific antigen testing—are not recommended for routine screening. Men should discuss their particular risk with their own medical provider.

The digital (finger) rectal exam is the most commonly used method for early detection of prostate cancer. The medical provider uses his or her finger to feel through the wall of the rectum for abnormal growth in the prostate.

TESTICULAR CANCER

Although cancer of the testes is rare, it is the most common form of cancer in men between the ages of 20 and 35. It accounts for 12 percent of all cancer deaths in young men. It is four times more common among Caucasian men than African American men. Testicular cancer usually responds well to treatment, particularly when it is detected early. In most cases, it affects just one testicle, and the other remains perfectly healthy.

Understanding Your Risk

Testicular cancer can develop any time after puberty starts but is most common in men between the ages of 29 and 35. Men whose testes have not descended into the scrotum or did not descend until after age 6 are at a much higher risk for this type of cancer.

Screening Recommendations

Not all experts agree on how effectively testicular self-examination detects cancer. Nor do they agree on the need for men who have no special risk factors to have routine testicular examinations by a professional. If you have a history of undescended testes, however, you should be examined periodically by your medical provider. If symptoms such as pain, swelling, or heaviness in your testicles last as long as 2 weeks, you should see your medical provider as soon as possible.

SELF-CARE STEPS FOR TESTICULAR CANCER

While there is no way to prevent testicular cancer, organizations such as the National Cancer Institute and the American Cancer Society recommend that men do a monthly self-exam to check for possible lumps or nodules in the testes.

Testicular self-examination is easy and takes only a few minutes. Testing is best done after a warm shower or bath, when the scrotal skin is relaxed. **You should call the advice nurse if you notice any of these symptoms:**

• Pain, swelling, or a feeling of heaviness in your scrotum or testicles

• A dull ache in your lower abdomen or groin

• A lump or a change in the way a testicle feels when examined

How to do a testicular self-exam—Begin by standing in front of a mirror. Look for signs of swelling in the scrotum. Next, examine each testicle with both hands. With your index and middle fingers underneath and your thumbs on top, gently roll each testicle, feeling for lumps.

PREVENTIVE SERVICES RECOMMENDATIONS

Some preventive health services—like immunizations—can help you avoid certain health problems. Also, medical providers use screening tests to detect diseases before symptoms actually appear. Such early detection can help stop the disease or keep it from getting worse. Despite this, many health experts question the effectiveness of screening tests in detecting disease soon enough to prevent health problems. Even for those tests that experts agree are effective, there is still debate on how often the tests should be done. This disagreement means you need to play an active role in your health care.

How can you help prevent future health problems? By learning more about health care prevention, and finding out what screening tests can and cannot do for you. With your medical provider you can discuss your personal health habits and set goals for behavioral change—the primary focus of any prevention discussion.

The guidelines in this section are for exams that are recommended by the U.S. Preventive Services Task Force as of January 1996. Read these guidelines; better yet, *study* them. Then, together with your medical provider, plan a preventive exam schedule appropriate for you. (See also Prevention and Screening of Common Health Problems, p. 215.)

These recommendations apply to most children. For a description of who is at high risk and needs more frequent screenings or immunizations, refer to the explanation of the numbered footnotes in the Risk Factors for Children box at bottom right.

PREVENTIVE SERVICES RECOMMENDATIONS

PREVENTION STEP	RECOMMENDATIONS
Birth to Age 23 Months	
Lab Tests	
Cholesterol	Not recommended for healthy children[3]
Hemoglobin or hematocrit	At the clinical discretion of the medical provider
Lead screening	Recommended for children at high risk[4]
Tuberculin skin test	Recommended for children at high risk[1]
Urinalysis	Not recommended for healthy children
Immunizations	
Chicken pox (varicella)	12 to 18 months unless the child has already contracted chicken pox
Diphtheria/pertussis/tetanus (DPT)	2, 4, 6, and 12 to 18 months
Hepatitis B	Birth, 1 to 2 months, and 6 to 18 months
HIB	2, 4, 6, and 12 to 15 months
Measles/mumps/rubella (MMR)	12 to 15 months
Oral polio vaccine (OPV)	2, 4, and 6 to 18 months
Exams	
Hearing exams	Special hearing tests may be recommended at the clinical discretion of the medical provider[2]
Ages 2 to 6	
Lab Tests	
Cholesterol	Not recommended for healthy children[3]
Lead screening	Recommended for children at high risk[4]
Tuberculin skin test	Recommended for children at high risk[1]
Urinalysis	Not recommended for healthy children
Immunizations	
Chicken pox (varicella)	1 dose if child is younger than age 13 and has never been immunized or never had the chicken pox
Diphtheria/pertussis/tetanus (DPT)	4 to 6 years old
Measles/mumps/rubella (MMR)	4 to 6 years old
Oral polio vaccine (OPV)	4 to 6 years old
Exams	
Blood pressure	At every medical visit
Eye exam	Before entering school
Hearing exam	Once by age 3

PREVENTIVE SERVICES RECOMMENDATIONS

PREVENTION STEP	RECOMMENDATIONS
Ages 7 to 12	
Lab Tests	
Cholesterol	Not recommended for healthy children[3]
Tuberculin skin test	Recommended for children at high risk[1]
Urinalysis	Not recommended for healthy children
Immunizations	
Chicken pox (varicella)	1 dose needed if not received in infancy and child has never had chicken pox
Hepatitis B	3 doses needed if not received in infancy
Measles/mumps/rubella (MMR)	12 years old (only if second dose not received in childhood)
Exams	
Blood pressure	At every medical visit
Scoliosis screening	Not recommended for healthy children; may be recommended at the clinical discretion of the medical provider
Vision and hearing exams	May be recommended at the clinical discretion of the medical provider
Ages 13 to 18	
Lab Tests	
Cholesterol	Not recommended for healthy adolescents[3]
Urinalysis	Not recommended for healthy adolescents
Immunizations	
Chicken pox (varicella)	2 doses 4 to 8 weeks apart if child has never had chicken pox and never been immunized
Tetanus/diphtheria	14 to 16 years old
History/Counseling	
Sexual practices	Weigh risks and provide appropriate information/advice
Tobacco/alcohol/drug use	Weigh risks and provide appropriate information/advice
Exams	
Blood pressure	At all visits
Pap smear (women)	At age 18 or after first sexual activity

These recommendations apply to most children. For a description of who is at high risk and needs more frequent screenings or immunizations, refer to the explanation of the numbered footnotes in the Risk Factors for Children box below.

Risk Factors for Children

(1) Children suspected of having tuberculosis, children who live in households with cases of tuberculosis, or children who are new immigrants from areas known to have tuberculosis should be tested.

(2) Vision and hearing tests given at school do not need to be repeated by the medical provider. Special hearing tests should be given to children with infections at birth, family history of hearing problems, low birth weight, low Apgar scores, or malformation of the head or neck.

(3) Children and adolescents at high risk are those who have a family history of very high cholesterol in an immediate family member before age 50 for men or age 60 for women.

(4) Children at high risk include those who live in—or often visit—housing built before 1950 that is run down or undergoing renovation; who come into close contact with other children who have high lead exposure; whose parents work in lead-related occupations; or who live near hazardous waste sites, busy highways, or lead processing plants.

PREVENTIVE SERVICES RECOMMENDATIONS

PREVENTION STEP	RECOMMENDATIONS
Ages 19 to 39	
Lab Tests/Exams	
Blood pressure	Every 2 years (test more often if risk factors are present[3] or if blood pressure is higher than 130/85 mmHg)
Chest X-ray	Not recommended for healthy adults
Cholesterol and HDL	*For men:* Every 5 years beginning at age 35 (test more often if total cholesterol is higher than 240)
Urinalysis	Not recommended for healthy adults
Immunizations	
Chicken pox (varicella)	Two doses 4 to 8 weeks apart if adult has never had chicken pox and never been immunized
Diphtheria/tetanus	Every 10 years
Hepatitis B	Three doses if at risk[4] and never previously immunized. One dose at first medical visit, a second dose 1 month later and a third dose 6 months after the second.
Influenza	Yearly if at risk[1]
Pneumonia vaccination	At least once if at risk[2]
Rubella titer/immunization	Women lacking evidence of immunity
For Women	
Breast cancer screening	
Clinical breast exam	At the recommendation of the medical provider
Mammography	At the recommendation of the medical provider
Self-exam	Monthly
Pelvic exam/Pap smear	Every 3 years (more often if risk factors are present[6])

These recommendations apply to most adults. For a description of who is at high risk and needs more frequent screenings or immunizations, refer to the explanation of the numbered footnotes in the Risk Factors for Adults box on p. 236.

PREVENTIVE SERVICES RECOMMENDATIONS

PREVENTION STEP	RECOMMENDATIONS
Ages 40 to 64	
Lab Tests	
Cholesterol and HDL	*For men:* Every 5 years; *For women:* Every 5 years beginning at age 45; (test more often if total cholesterol is higher than 240)
Hemoccult test (for "hidden" blood in stool)	Beginning at age 50 or at the recommendation of the medical provider
Urinalysis	Not recommended for healthy adults
Immunizations	
Diphtheria/tetanus	Every 10 years
Hepatitis B	Three doses if at risk[4] and never previously immunized. One dose at first medical visit, a second dose 1 month later and a third dose 6 months after the second.
Influenza	Yearly if at risk[1]
Pneumonia vaccination	At least once if at risk[2]
Rubella titer/immunization	Women lacking evidence of immunity
Exams	
Blood pressure	Every 2 years (test more often if risk factors are present[3] or if blood pressure is higher than 140/85 mmHg)
Chest X-ray	Not recommended for healthy adults
Sigmoidoscopy	Every 5 years beginning at age 50; yearly thereafter or at the recommendation of the medical provider
For Men	
Prostate specific antigen	Not recommended for healthy men
For Women	
Breast cancer screening	
Clinical breast exam	At least every 2 years beginning at age 50; age 40 to 49 discuss with medical provider
Mammography	At least every 2 years beginning at age 50; age 40 to 49 discuss with medical provider
Self-exam	Monthly
Pelvic exam/Pap smear	Every 3 years; more often if risk factors present[5]

These recommendations apply to most adults. For a description of who is at high risk and needs more frequent screenings or immunizations, refer to the explanation of the numbered footnotes in the Risk Factors for Adults box on p. 236.

PREVENTIVE SERVICES RECOMMENDATIONS

PREVENTION STEP	RECOMMENDATIONS
Age 65 and Older	
Lab Tests	
Cholesterol	Every 5 years until age 75 (test more often if total cholesterol is higher than 240)
Hemoccult test (for "hidden blood" in stool)	At the recommendation of the medical provider
Urinalysis	Not recommended for healthy adults
Immunizations	
Diphtheria/tetanus	Every 10 years
Influenza	Yearly
Pneumonia vaccination	Once at age 65 or at the recommendation of the medical provider
Exams	
Blood pressure	Every 2 years (test more often if risk factors are present[3] or if blood pressure is higher than 140/85 mmHg)
Chest X-ray	Not recommended for healthy adults
Sigmoidoscopy	Every 5 years
Vision/hearing exams	Starting at age 65 or at the recommendation of the medical provider
For Women	
Breast cancer screening	
Clinical breast exam	At least every 2 years before age 70; age 70 and older discuss with medical provider
Mammography	At least every 2 years before age 70; age 70 and older discuss with medical provider
Self-exam	Monthly
Pelvic exam/Pap smear	Every 3 years (optional if low risk[6])

These recommendations apply to most adults. For a description of who is at high risk and needs more frequent screenings or immunizations, refer to the explanation of the numbered footnotes in the Risk Factors for Adults box below.

Risk Factors for Adults

(1) Residents of chronic care facilities such as nursing homes, people with diabetes or chronic lung or kidney disease, health care workers with patients at high risk.

(2) Chronic heart, kidney, or lung disease; diabetes; alcoholism; cirrhosis; sickle cell disease.

(3) Smoking, high blood pressure, family history of heart disease, diabetes, high blood cholesterol, obesity, sedentary lifestyle.

(4) Men who have sex with other men; history of sexual activity with multiple partners; recently acquired another sexually transmitted disease; intravenous drug users; individuals in health-related jobs who are frequently exposed to blood products; recipients of certain blood products including hemodialysis patients; international travelers to countries where the disease is prevalent.

(5) History of sexually transmitted disease, first intercourse before age 18, had several sexual partners.

(6) Women may consider discontinuing Pap smears after age 65 if they have had consistently normal results in the past.

CHRONIC DISEASE INFORMATION

When it comes to living with chronic health problems—those that can last a long time—it is important to know what type of person has the disease. That's because a person's responses can play such a vital role in how the disease progresses or doesn't progress and what effect the disease has on lifestyle. If you have a chronic health problem, you know the kind of demands, both physical and emotional, that having a long-term disease can create. You may not realize that the decisions you make about your lifestyle and the amount of effort you bring to your own therapy can have a very big impact on the long-term effects of your illness.

Experts who treat particular chronic conditions know that there is an important body of knowledge that is unique to each disease. For example, someone with arthritis will benefit from learning a great deal about his or her particular form of the disease, how it can be treated, and how to prevent complications. This information will be very different from the information needed by someone with hypertension. Your medical provider is your best resource for helping you understand how to manage your condition. If necessary, he or she can refer you to other medical professionals who specialize in treating your condition.

Although each chronic disease requires special knowledge and behaviors from the patient and the medical provider, there are many health practices that will help any chronic condition.

Living with a chronic health problem can take its toll emotionally. Learning skills to deal with stress is beneficial, no matter what disease you have. If you are part of a family, coping with a disease can disrupt former routines and can require special skills in resolving unexpected problems. You may benefit from family counseling or other approaches to good communication and conflict resolution.

When you are diagnosed with a chronic condition, you will benefit from becoming a central member of your health care team. Expressing your personal needs and interests will make you the central figure in the decisions that will affect your health.

ARTHRITIS

One in seven Americans has arthritis, making it the leading chronic illness for those over age 45.

Joint pain, also called rheumatic pain, is a common medical problem, ranking among the most frequent reasons that people visit their medical providers. When pain occurs, most people's first reaction is to think "arthritis." Although this is a natural response, often joint or muscle pain is due to something other than arthritis. Other structures that surround the joint—such as the tendon, bursa, or muscle—are often the source of the pain.

What Is Arthritis?

Arthritis is an inflammation of a joint. Over time, this inflammation can lead to the breakdown of the protective surface surrounding a joint. This deterioration can lead to chronic pain and cause a loss of function.

When Is Joint Pain Serious?

If joint pain occurs with fever and sudden, significant swelling in many joints, or if you feel severe pain, you should call the advice nurse. If you feel pain without swelling or fever, it is generally safe to wait and see what happens.

Arthritis is the inflammation of a joint. The illustration on the right is typical of osteoarthritis, where the protective cartilage cushion on the bone breaks down, and the bones of the joint rub against one another.

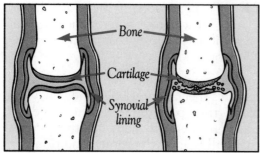

Bone

Cartilage

Synovial lining

Normal Joint   Arthritic Joint

STEPS FOR EASING ARTHRITIS PAIN

OVER-THE-COUNTER MEDICINES

Frequently, over-the-counter medicines are the first treatment choice for arthritic pain. Two main types of medicines are used to treat arthritis: simple pain relievers and anti-inflammatory medicines, which relieve pain and decrease inflammation. Neither type is perfect for all situations. When used correctly, however, both can be very beneficial.

Pain Relievers

Pain relievers such as acetaminophen (Tylenol, Tempra, or a generic) very effectively control pain. Acetaminophen, like any medicine, must be taken over time to determine its effectiveness. Therapeutic doses can be as high as two extra-strength tablets three to four times daily. This dose may need to be used for several days before determining whether it will be effective for long-term treatment.

Acetaminophen's advantage is that most people can tolerate it. It is known for being gentle to the stomach. Acetaminophen does not cause gastrointestinal problems.

Anti-Inflammatory Medications

Medicines that relieve pain and decrease inflammation are called anti-inflammatory drugs. These include aspirin, ibuprofen (Advil, Motrin, or a generic), and naproxen sodium (Naprosyn), all of which are available over the counter. Anti-inflammatories are effective pain relievers and have the added advantage of decreasing modest levels of inflammation, which usually helps decrease pain.

Anti-inflammatory medications have more side effects than simple pain relievers. The biggest concern is ulcers or bleeding from the stomach. These problems occur more frequently in patients with a history of ulcers, elderly patients, those with other underlying illnesses, or those who are also taking other medicines. Some anti-inflammatories may also cause stomach upset. However, these side effects are relatively uncommon.

OTHER HELPFUL PRODUCTS

Other products useful in treating arthritis are available in most drugstores. Products such as aspirin in cream form have achieved limited success. Products that create heat where you apply them may give short-term pain relief.

Devices

Some assistive devices support painful areas or improve function in affected joints. The range of options is very broad. Wrist splints cut down wrist movement, which often relieves pain caused by arthritis, tendinitis, or carpal tunnel syndrome. Tennis elbow straps often decrease pain by altering the mechanical stresses of the injured tendon, and padded arch supports and heel pads decrease various kinds of foot pain. Examples of other devices include doorknob extenders, enlarged handle grips for silverware, adjustable canes, and special pillows to support the neck while sleeping.

Nutrition

Many people are interested in using diet to control disease. A well-balanced diet like those supported by the American Heart Association, the American Diabetes Association, and the American Cancer Society is the cornerstone of any dietary program. Following these guidelines makes it less likely that other illnesses will create problems that could complicate your arthritis.

Maintaining your ideal body weight is also a key to better health and can be very useful to treat arthritis. Carrying extra pounds increases the wear and strain on painful arthritic joints.

Continued on next page

STEPS FOR EASING ARTHRITIS PAIN

Also, some foods may affect arthritis symptoms. Fish oils can cut down on inflammation that often comes with rheumatoid arthritis. Studies suggest that fairly high doses are needed to achieve this effect, and inflammation is only modestly reduced; however, the effects are real. As a practical matter, substituting fish for meat is sensible. Fish oil pills also are available. If you choose to supplement your diet with fish oil pills, it's best to discuss this with your medical provider.

Other approaches

Exercise is important to maintain good health, especially for the patient with arthritis. Exercise helps preserve joint health and function, even for damaged joints. By improving the function of structures that surround the joint—such as the tendons and the muscles—exercise decreases the joint's workload.

There is no preferred exercise for arthritis. The best advice is to choose an exercise that you like and begin adding it to your regular activities. Exercise duration should be short at first, and gradually increased. Aerobic exercises are ideal and low-impact activities such as walking, biking, and water exercises are usually most comfortable to do. As long as the activity does not increase pain or swelling, it is probably not causing any more joint damage. If pain and/or swelling occurs and lasts for more than 30 minutes after the activity, it is probably the wrong type of exercise or it was done too intensely.

Schedule changes

Sometimes, schedule changes make a big difference to the way joint pain affects your life. People with arthritis are often less mobile and suffer more pain in the morning. Shifting activities until later in the day may help you take advantage of your greatest mobility and make it easier to deal with the pain. This strategy is particularly helpful for patients with inflammatory arthritis.

Reducing stress

Stress—personal, social, and emotional—also takes its toll. Finding better ways to deal with stress may help decrease pain from arthritis and other joint conditions. Some stress reduction options include meditation, biofeedback, and professional counseling. Exercise is also an excellent stress reliever.

Community resources

Most communities have organizations and programs to serve people with arthritis or other disabilities. The Arthritis Foundation has chapters in every state. The organization provides educational materials and co-sponsors support groups, self-help programs, educational seminars, and exercise classes. It also supports research of the causes and cures of arthritis. For more information, see the Health Information Resource Guide, p. 257.

Transportation services—for people unable to drive or travel by public transportation—are usually available within larger communities. Social service agencies also may offer help in finding child care services, homemaking help, and meals-on-wheels programs. Additional assistance may be available to help explore financial and health care options. Many health care organizations offer specific programs designed to help people cope with arthritis.

ASTHMA

If you have asthma, you have plenty of company. About 13 million Americans cope with this lung disease, including over 4 million children. Asthma causes more days missed from work and school than any other chronic illness.

Asthma tends to run in families. It happens more often to people whose family members have asthma, hay fever, or eczema, but anyone can develop asthma at any age. About half of all people with asthma get the disease before age 10. Another third or so develop it before age 40.

There is no cure for asthma, but by working with their medical providers, patients can learn to control the symptoms of the disease. With proper treatment, most asthma patients can lead normal, active lives.

Asthma can cause shortness of breath, wheezing, coughing, and chest tightness. Symptoms range from mild to life threatening.

Asthma is a common disease affecting about 5 percent of the U.S. population. That's why it is so important for people with asthma to understand the disease and their own symptoms and triggers.

Asthma symptoms fall into two categories: acute and chronic. Symptoms may last just a few minutes, several days, or even weeks. Asthma symptoms come on gradually in some patients, very quickly in others.

What Causes the Problem?

No one knows exactly what causes asthma, but medical providers do know that the lining of the bronchial tubes—the air passages in the lungs—is extremely sensitive in people with asthma.

When something triggers an asthma episode, the bronchial tube lining gets inflamed and swollen, and more mucus is produced, leaving less room for air to pass through. Meanwhile, the bands of muscle around the outside of the bronchial tubes tighten, further blocking the flow of air and causing coughing, wheezing, and shortness of breath.

Asthma Triggers

Allergies to pollen (from trees, grasses, and weeds), dust mites, mold spores, and animals can cause episodes of asthma.

Infections and irritants are nonallergic triggers for asthma. These can include viral infections (such as colds and the flu), cigarette smoke, chemical fumes, smog, poor air quality, aspirin and other anti-inflammatory drugs, cold air, and changes in the weather.

Asthma may also be related to exposure to certain materials at work such as grain dust, flour (commonly known as baker's asthma), or chemicals.

Certain types of exertion or exercises may also trigger asthma episodes.

Note: Intense emotions such as fear and worry can trigger an asthma episode, but they don't cause the condition. Experts believe that emotional problems can result from asthma, but should not be considered a cause of the disease.

Treatment

The goal of asthma treatment is to have complete control, so that a person can do the activities of his or her choosing.

Treatment for an asthma episode involves identifying the specific triggers and eliminating patients' exposure to them. Acute attacks can be treated with medicine.

There is nothing more frightening than watching your child struggle for breath and not knowing how to help. Since Andre was diagnosed with asthma, I've learned to watch for the warning signs of an attack, and learned what to do when they occur. Andre still has difficulty breathing sometimes, but we both stay a lot calmer and just follow our action plan. It's made a world of difference to both of us.

Rachelle

Daily Record and Peak Flow Meters

Medical providers work together with asthma patients first to control acute asthma and then to manage the symptoms by finding out what triggers the episodes. Patients may be asked to keep a daily record of symptoms, possible triggers, and medicine taken. They also may be asked to monitor their lung function with an instrument called a **peak flow meter,** which tells how well the patient is breathing. This information will help the medical provider decide when to add the next level of medicine needed to keep the patient's symptoms under control. Through this treatment program, patients learn how triggers affect their asthma and how their lungs respond to medicine.

Action Plan

The patient and medical provider or primary asthma care provider develop a written asthma action plan so that patients will be able to recognize warning signs of an asthma episode early and take the right steps to treat it. Each patient should also have a plan to follow if an episode should become severe.

Medicines

There are many different types of asthma drugs. Many people need daily doses of prescription drugs to keep their symptoms under control. Medicines are most often taken through an inhaler or nebulizer (a compressed air device for administering medication to the lungs). But medicine can also come in liquid, capsule, or tablet form. Every medicine has its own set of possible side effects. Be sure to discuss possible side effects and what to do about them with your medical provider.

There are two general kinds of asthma drugs. The first ones are called **bronchodilators**. These drugs relax the muscles around the airways, so they can open up and let air in more easily. Bronchodilators come in many different forms.

The second type of medicine prescribed for asthma is called **anti-inflammatory agents.** They reduce the swelling and mucus that lead to congestion. Anti-inflammatory agents are commonly used to effectively treat people with moderate to severe asthma. The person is able to get the benefit of the medicine without the side effects, because when the medicine is inhaled it goes only to the lungs, not to the rest of the body.

Oral corticosteroids (such as prednisone, prednisolone, and methylprednisolone) are stronger types of anti-inflammatory medicine. Although these drugs can have side effects, they are usually safe when taken according to instructions and are primarily used for short-term control.

Another type of anti-inflammatory drug is cromolyn or nedocromil. These medicines can be given with an inhaler or nebulizer. They don't help during an asthma episode, but do work to prevent asthma episodes. Both cromolyn and nedocromil have few side effects. Although it doesn't work for everyone and can require as much as a month of usage before any benefit is seen, cromolyn can be especially useful for children with allergies. Both drugs are most effective when taken on a regular, preventive basis.

Patients usually have questions and concerns about these drugs, and should discuss these issues with their medical provider.

Asthma is a serious medical condition. It's not something you can treat by yourself. In partnership with your medical provider, however, you can use self-care techniques to manage your asthma, reduce the severity and frequency of your symptoms, and cut down on your trips to the clinic and hospital. Call the advice nurse if you have questions about asthma or you or someone close to you is having difficulty managing asthma symptoms.

CARING FOR YOUR ASTHMA

• Become an asthma expert. Find out as much as you can about the disease. Attend patient information sessions and asthma support groups. Read books about asthma. Some good ones are *One Minute Asthma: What You Need to Know*, Thomas F. Plaut, M.D.; *Children with Asthma: A Manual for Parents*, Thomas F. Plaut, M.D.; and *Asthma: The Complete Guide to Self-Management of Asthma and Allergies for Patients and Their Families*, Allan M. Weinstein, M.D. For more information, see the Health Information Resource Guide, p. 257.

• Follow the asthma action plan established by you and your medical provider. Know the warning signs of an asthma episode. Make sure you have written instructions for what to do in an asthma emergency. Keep a record of your episodes, drugs, peak flow readings, and responses to drugs.

• Manage your medicines. Know the kinds of drugs you should take, how much, and how often. Know the possible side effects and what you can do to minimize them. Make sure you know which drugs should be taken first, and follow the instructions carefully. Don't run out of your medicines. Ask your medical provider or pharmacist to check all new drugs for possible interactions with the asthma drugs you are taking.

• Monitor your condition. Learn how to use a peak flow meter. It can help detect an impending episode early, because lung capacity can drop as much as 24 hours before any symptoms appear. If you keep daily records of your symptoms and peak flow readings, you will be able to begin treatment soon enough to reduce the number and severity of asthma episodes.

• Identify and avoid triggers. Your record keeping will help you determine what triggers your asthma episodes. If inhalants such as dust and animal dander are high on your list, take steps to keep your living areas free of these triggers. Steer clear of irritants, wood smoke, and automobile exhaust fumes.

• Don't smoke and stay away from areas where others are smoking.

• When an episode occurs, follow your asthma action plan: stay calm, stop your activity, take a few relaxed breaths, drink extra fluids, and then use your inhaler. Treat symptoms within minutes of their onset. It takes less medicine to stop an episode in its early phase.

• Stay physically fit. You should be able to control your asthma so you can exercise.

• Keep good records of your drugs and dosages. Make sure someone else in your family knows where to find this information in an emergency.

• See your medical provider for regular follow-up exams.

When we found out that my cat, Whiskers, made my asthma worse, the doctor said we needed to give him away. Whiskers lives with my grandma now. I've also learned more about my asthma. When I use my nebulizer, I don't cough and wheeze as much.

Emily, age 6

SPECIAL CONCERNS FOR CHILDREN

Asthma causes more hospital and emergency department visits than any other chronic childhood disease. Children with well-controlled asthma, however, should be able to do any activity or sport they choose.

Many children "outgrow" their asthma symptoms, although the underlying condition, that extra-sensitive bronchial tube lining, remains throughout life. About half of children with asthma outgrow it by age 15. Asthma can recur in the adult years. Smoking may trigger the return of the problem.

Education of both parent and child is key to treating asthma in children. Understanding the disease and the child's specific triggers and warning signs can help parents follow through with timely, effective treatment.

Children too young to use an inhaler are often treated with a machine called a **nebulizer**.

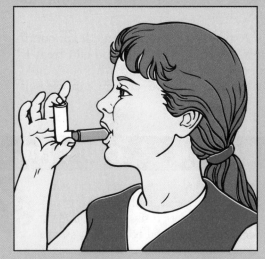

This device uses compressed air to turn a solution of liquid medication into a fine mist that the child breathes in through a mask or mouthpiece.

HOW TO USE AN INHALER

1. Assume a standing position. Shake the container well before using. Remove the cap and hold the container upright.

2. Place a spacer (usually a cardboard or plastic tube) on the end of the inhaler. There are a variety of spacers available. A spacer is a holding chamber that allows you to use inhaled medications more effectively. If no spacer is available, hold the inhaler 1 to 2 inches from your mouth. Without a spacer, too much medication may end up in your mouth rather than in your lungs.

3. Breathe out normally, then position the spacer in your mouth. Place it on top of your tongue and close your lips around it.

4. As you start to breathe in slowly through your mouth, press down on the top of the inhaler container. It will administer a puff of medicine.

5. Continue breathing in slowly for 3 to 5 seconds, until your lungs are full.

6. Hold your breath for 10 seconds to allow the medicine to be deposited in your lungs.

7. In some cases, depending upon the drugs used, you will need to wait 1 to 3 minutes before taking another puff on your inhaler. This allows your lungs to open up, and the second treatment works even better. Check with your medical provider for proper instructions.

CHRONIC OBSTRUCTIVE LUNG DISEASE

Chronic obstructive lung disease is the fifth leading cause of death in the United States. Although many people think first of emphysema when they hear chronic obstructive lung disease, chronic bronchitis is actually more common and equally serious because it can lead to emphysema, and eventually cause death if it is not controlled.

Cigarette smoking is the number one cause of chronic obstructive lung disease, accounting for 82 percent of cases. Other causes include repeated exposure to lots of dust (such as in coal mines, granaries, or metal molding shops), chemical vapors, and possibly air pollution. A small percentage of emphysema cases are inherited.

Like acute bronchitis, **chronic bronchitis** is an inflammation of the lining of the bronchial tubes, which lead to the lungs. This causes the bronchial tubes to produce excess amounts of mucus. As chronic bronchitis progresses, the cilia or tiny hairs that sweep away irritants from the air passages may stop working or die off. Unlike the occasional 1- to 2-week bout with acute bronchitis after a cold or flu in otherwise healthy people, those with chronic bronchitis have inflammation and subsequent coughing, with mucus, for at least 3 months each year.

Emphysema occurs when the tiny air sacs (alveoli) in the lungs become larger and lose their elasticity. When this happens, the lungs become less able to get oxygen into the blood. This leads to shortness of breath, eventually making even the most basic tasks, such as eating or getting dressed, difficult and tiring.

Although neither chronic bronchitis nor emphysema can be cured, with medical treatment the damage they cause to the lungs and heart can be slowed and their symptoms can be eased. Neither disease appears overnight. Chronic bronchitis often begins as repeated cases of acute bronchitis following colds. With chronic bronchitis, however, coughing and mucus production occur more frequently and last longer after each cold,

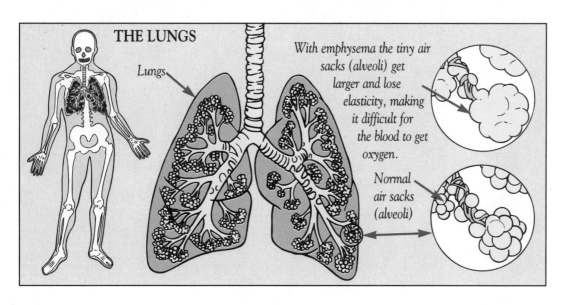

THE LUNGS

Lungs

With emphysema the tiny air sacs (alveoli) get larger and lose elasticity, making it difficult for the blood to get oxygen.

Normal air sacs (alveoli)

until the bronchitis is finally there whether you've had a cold or not. Likewise, emphysema comes on gradually, often beginning as shortness of breath with exercise or activity.

Because of this gradual onset, you should call the advice nurse at the first signs of shortness of breath or "smoker's cough." (See Health Information Resource Guide, p. 257.)

DECREASING SYMPTOMS OF CHRONIC OBSTRUCTIVE LUNG DISEASE

• *Quit Smoking!* Talk to your medical provider about the different methods available for quitting smoking. Continuing to smoke will only hasten the progression of emphysema.

• Drink plenty of fluids. Six to eight glasses of clear fluids a day, such as juice or water, will help keep air passages clear of mucus, making it easier to breathe.

• Eat a well-balanced diet. If you have emphysema, spread your meals out. By eating five or six small meals a day, you avoid having a full stomach, which will interfere with your breathing.

• Strengthen your heart with aerobic exercise and build your upper-body strength. Strengthening the muscles in your upper body will make breathing easier. Moderate aerobic exercise, such as 15 minutes of daily walking, will make your heart less susceptible to complications of chronic obstructive lung disease. Exercise and a healthy diet will also build your resistance to illness and infection.

• Do breathing exercises. If you have emphysema, ask your medical provider about exercises to help you breathe better.

• Get a flu shot each fall and a pneumococcal pneumonia vaccination at least once.

DIABETES

Diabetes occurs when the body can't properly use or produce insulin, a hormone made in the pancreas that breaks down carbohydrates in food. Insulin brings glucose from the blood into the cells, where it is used for energy.

When insulin isn't available or the body doesn't use it properly, blood glucose levels rise. Uncontrolled, high blood glucose levels can cause serious health problems, including heart disease, kidney disease, blindness, or nerve damage. Keeping your blood glucose level as close as possible to normal (70 to 115 mg/dl before a meal) is the key to having a more healthy, energetic life.

Although there are different types of diabetes, the cause—the body's inability to use food properly—is the same. The major types of diabetes are Type I (insulin-dependent), Type II (non-insulin-dependent), and gestational diabetes.

Type I (Insulin-Dependent)

This type of diabetes may develop at any age, but most often occurs in children, teenagers, or young adults. Symptoms include being very thirsty, hungry, and tired, and needing to urinate often. Children with Type I diabetes rarely have these symptoms for longer than a few weeks before it is diagnosed.

With Type I diabetes, the pancreas stops producing enough insulin. To make up for this lack of insulin, people with Type I diabetes inject themselves with insulin.

Type II (Non-Insulin-Dependent)

The most common form of diabetes, Type II diabetes usually develops gradually with few, if any, symptoms. The pancreas keeps making insulin; however, the body is not using it effectively. This leads to a buildup of glucose in the blood. Often Type II diabetes is diagnosed by tracking a gradual increase in blood glucose levels.

Gestational Diabetes

This type of diabetes is discovered through a routine blood test for glucose during the course of a woman's pregnancy. Closely monitoring blood glucose levels helps women have safe pregnancies and healthy babies. Gestational diabetes usually disappears at the end of the pregnancy, but mothers may be at increased risk for developing diabetes in the future.

Risk Factors for Developing Diabetes

- Obesity
- Over age 40
- A family history of diabetes
- Race (diabetes is more common among American Indians, Hispanics, and African Americans)
- History of impaired glucose tolerance (IGT)
- High blood pressure or high levels of blood fats (cholesterol, triglycerides)
- Women who have had gestational diabetes
- Women who have had babies that weighed more than 9 pounds

Once you have diabetes, you have it for life. There is no cure. The disease can be successfully managed by controlling blood sugar through proper nutrition and exercise. A healthy lifestyle also can reduce your risk for developing diabetes. For more information about diabetes, see the Health Information Resource Guide, p. 257.

WARNING SIGNS OF DIABETES

Call the advice nurse if you have any of these symptoms:

- Extreme thirst
- Unusual tiredness
- Excessive appetite
- Frequent urination
- Tingling or numbness in legs or feet
- Cuts or bruises that are slow to heal
- Blurred vision or any change in vision

HEART DISEASE

There are many forms of heart disease. The most common is known as **atherosclerosis**, or hardening of the arteries. Cholesterol joins with calcium and scar tissue and builds up in the arteries. When cholesterol levels are too high, the circulatory system becomes choked—and the result is a dam of plaque that narrows the channels the blood flows through. American Heart Association research shows that hardening of the arteries is responsible for more than 90 percent of all heart attacks.

You suffer a **heart attack** when blood can't bring enough oxygen to the heart muscle. This is usually caused by narrowing of the arteries leading to the heart muscle. You may get a warning sign that the heart muscle is not getting enough oxygen in the form of chest pain that moves to the left arm, jaw, or shoulder blade. This is known as **angina**. It usually occurs with exertion but can happen when at rest, as well. Don't ignore it.

Another form of heart disease is **congestive heart failure**. The heart muscle is weakened by high blood pressure, previous heart attack, atherosclerosis, a congenital heart defect, or a muscle disease known as cardiomyopathy. Just as a hand with weak muscles can't squeeze all the water out of a dishcloth, a weak heart muscle can't pump effectively, allowing fluid to collect in the body and lungs.

Risk Factors You Can Control
High Cholesterol

The body tries to flush the excess cholesterol away by "packaging" the cholesterol with a substance known as high-density lipoprotein, or HDL. Low-density lipoprotein, or LDL, on the other hand, carries this cholesterol straight to the artery walls.

Total blood cholesterol is probably the number with which you are most familiar. Guidelines suggest a total cholesterol level of less than 200 is best. (See also High Blood Cholesterol, p. 225.)

High Blood Pressure

The second leading risk factor for heart attacks and the major cause of stroke is high blood pressure, or hypertension.

Blood pressure that is below 140 (systolic) and 90 (diastolic) is considered normal—120 over 80 is considered an ideal reading. Stress, caffeine, exercise, infection, and other factors may temporarily affect blood pressure readings. (See also High Blood Pressure, p. 226.)

Smoking and Secondhand Smoke

Smoking increases your risk of heart attack by damaging your lungs, lowering your HDL ("good cholesterol") level, and raising your blood pressure. According to Dr. W. Virgil Brown, a former president of the American Heart Association and director of the Division of Arteriosclerosis and Lipid Metabolism at Emory University School of Medicine, the HDL cholesterol level of a two-pack-a-day smoker may increase by eight points when that person stops smoking.

In addition, smoke contains a glycoprotein that makes your blood clot more easily and weakens the blood vessel walls. The oxygen in the blood is replaced with inhaled carbon dioxide. This damages the heart muscle and makes the blood vessel walls even more susceptible to atherosclerosis.

Lack of Exercise

American Heart Association research shows that regular aerobic exercise actually strengthens the heart muscle, boosts HDL levels, lowers blood pressure, slows the progression of diabetes, and helps ward off obesity. About 30 to 40 minutes of moderate exercise, 4 or more days a

CLOGGED ARTERIES

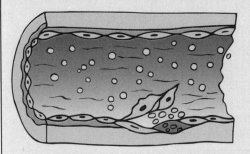

Atherosclerosis begins with a damaged spot in the artery. Cholesterol and other fats from the bloodstream build plaque on artery walls.

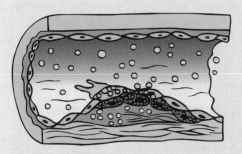

Two types of blood cells contribute to the buildup of plaque: macrophages (large white cells) and platelets (small blood cells that coagulate blood). The macrophages fill up with cholesterol and cholesterol packs in between.

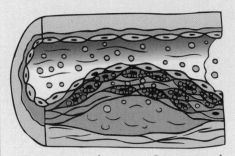

Plaque narrows the arteries. Sometimes a clot can form in an artery narrowed by plaque, causing angina or a heart attack. Blockage in an artery leading to the brain causes a stroke.

week, is recommended. It is not necessary to do all of your exercise at once. However, the exercise should increase your heart rate and keep it elevated for at least 20 minutes.

Obesity

Research shows that obesity should be considered a major risk factor for heart disease, rather than one that just contributes to other risk factors—such as diabetes and hypertension.

Diabetes

People with diabetes are very susceptible to heart disease. People with poorly controlled diabetes often have several health problems, including high cholesterol and other circulatory disorders that lead to atherosclerosis, hemorrhages of the tiny blood vessels in the eyes, and poor circulation to the feet and hands. Smoking makes these problems worse.

Uncontrollable Risk Factors

Age

Heart disease is more common among older people because it reflects the wear-and-tear on the body; however, it doesn't have to be part of aging. For example, atherosclerosis may take 20 to 30 years to get to the point where the arteries are blocked enough to cause trouble—and may be halted in its course if diagnosed in time for the person to make the needed changes.

Gender

Middle-aged men have more heart attacks than women of the same age. This changes after menopause. After the age of 60 the rates are almost equal.

Heredity

Unfortunately, heart attacks, high blood pressure, and high cholesterol levels run in families. However, don't use your genes as an excuse not to take the necessary steps to offset this risk. Control those risk factors you can control.

Getting More Help

Your family and friends can provide great support and encouragement as you tackle each of your risk factors. Bring one of these people to your next appointment with the medical provider to help you take notes and ask questions—and to offer emotional support if needed. For more information on heart disease, see the Health Information Resource Guide, p. 257.

LOW BACK PAIN

Also see Acute Back Pain, p. 76.

Pain in the lower back is very common. It can be caused by inflammation of structures in the back—such as the joints, muscles, or discs. Most often it is made worse by certain activities. It can also be affected by physical or psychological stresses.

Uncommonly, back pain can be caused by serious problems like infection or other conditions that your medical provider can distinguish from the more common types of back pain described here.

Fortunately, over 90 percent of people with low back pain completely recover within 4 to 6 weeks. When pain or weakness last longer than 6 weeks, however, more specialized treatments may be needed. For this reason, it is important to keep your medical provider informed of your progress.

Persistent Back Pain and Sciatica

If your back pain and sciatica (also known as "radiating leg pain") persist longer than 6 weeks, you may need other evaluation. Some type of back education class or instruction should be considered if you have chronic back pain and sciatica to help you learn to handle your back problems.

If there has been no significant improvement, you may need to consult with experts in the problems that can cause chronic back pain. Most often, these are medical providers who work in departments of rehabilitation medicine, orthopedics, and neurosurgery. In certain cases, other medical specialists in neurology, occupational medicine, and rheumatology, among others, may be consulted.

Because each patient is a special case, your medical provider may order certain procedures to determine the best course of care. Either way, it is important to understand how back problems get better and what to expect if they don't. If you have questions about low back pain or concern about symptoms you may be having, call the advice nurse.

EXERCISES TO KEEP YOUR BACK FIT

It is important to keep your back flexible and strong. Back exercises can help prevent back problems and improve posture. Aerobic exercise also is very effective for patients with lower back pain. You should plan regular, daily walks as soon as you can, along with other exercise as tolerated. Swimming or biking are also good activities for the lower back.

The back exercises shown below should be started at home or with the help of a physical therapist, and should be started as soon as the pain improves. Do not do any exercises that make the pain or stiffness much worse.

The Pelvic Tilt

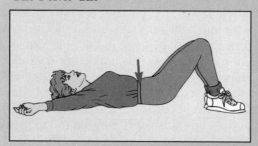

Lie flat on your back (or stand with your back to a wall), knees bent, feet flat on floor, body relaxed. Tighten abdominal muscles and tilt pelvis so that the curve of the small of the back is flat on the floor (or wall). Tighten the buttocks muscles. Hold 10 seconds and then relax.

Knee Raise

Lie flat on your back, knees bent, feet flat on floor. Do a pelvic tilt (see left) and raise your knees slowly to your chest one at a time as shown. Hug knee gently, let go, then lower your bent leg slowly. Do not straighten your knees.

Partial Press-up

First, lie face down on a soft, firm surface. Rest for a few minutes, relaxing completely. Second, staying in the same basic position, raise your upper body enough to lean on your elbows. Let your lower back and your legs relax as much as you can. Hold this position for 30 seconds at first. Slowly work up to 2 minutes.

OBESITY

Despite many claims, there is no "perfect or ideal" weight. Good health comes in a variety of sizes and shapes. A combination of many factors adds up to a healthy weight, including how much weight is fat, where the fat is stored, and any medical problems that would benefit from more or less weight. Obesity or having extra body fat increases the risk of developing non-insulin-dependent diabetes, high blood pressure, high blood cholesterol, and some cancers, as well as other health problems. Consider the following questions and chart to help determine your healthy weight range.

- Are you within the suggested weight range? The higher weights in the ranges generally apply to men, who tend to have more muscle and bone. The lower weights more often apply to women.

- Where is your fat stored? Extra fat stored below the waist seems especially difficult to shed. However, on the plus side, it's also less likely to pose a health risk. Studies show that fat stored above the waist, in the upper abdominal area, is linked with an increased risk of diabetes and heart disease. One easy way to identify the level of health risk your weight is causing is to find your waist/hip ratio. This ratio is a quick, easy way to determine your risk. Here's the formula: Waist measurement divided by hip measurement equals risk ratio. A ratio of more than 1.0 for men and more than 0.8 for women may mean a higher health risk.

Example:

Waist (38 inches) / Hip (42 inches) = Risk ratio (0.9)

- Do you have a weight-related medical problem or a family history of one? If you—or a relative—have had elevated blood pressure, cholesterol, or blood sugar levels, a weight in the lower end of the range could be best for your health.

SUGGESTED WEIGHTS FOR ADULTS

Height*	Weight in Pounds†	
	19–34 yrs	35+ yrs
5' 0"	97–128	108–138
5' 1"	101–132	111–143
5' 2"	104–137	115–148
5' 3"	107–141	119–152
5' 4"	111–146	122–157
5' 5"	114–150	126–162
5' 6"	118–155	130–167
5' 7"	121–160	134–172
5' 8"	125–164	138–178
5' 9"	129–169	142–183
5' 10"	132–174	146–188
5' 11"	136–179	151–194
6' 0"	140–184	155–199
6' 1"	144–189	159–205
6' 2"	148–195	164–210
6' 3"	152–200	168–216
6' 4"	156–205	173–222
6' 5"	160–211	177–228
6' 6"	164–216	183–234

Higher weights generally apply to men and lower weights to women in each height category.

* Without shoes   † Without clothes

Source: National Research Council, 1989.

Causes of Obesity

There are many complex risk factors for obesity, including environment, genetics, physical inactivity, and eating too many calories and fats. Just as there are no simple explanations for how weight problems start, there are no simple solutions. Weight loss requires a combination of fewer calories taken in, more calories used up, and behavior changes.

Dangers of Fad Diets

If there were a simple solution to take off extra pounds, no one would have a weight problem. And although most people recognize that fad diets aren't the answer, the short-term reward of rapid weight loss is hard to resist. These quick weight-loss plans cost consumers up to $5 billion annually.

Most people, however, don't know how risky these diets may be. Very low-calorie diets or diets that restrict certain foods can be dangerous and should never be used without medical supervision.

There is growing concern that long-term use of very low-calorie diets may actually make lasting success more difficult to maintain. When the body is threatened by a drastic reduction in calories, it responds by conserving energy output—slowing down the rate at which calories are burned. Increasing calories back to a normal level results in a rapid weight gain. A repeated pattern of quick loss followed by rapid gain (often called "yo-yo dieting") may even sabotage future weight loss attempts by actually altering body composition. The loss usually reflects a loss of "metabolically active" muscle tissue which is then replaced by "metabolically inactive" fat when normal eating is resumed.

Changes in body composition after cycles of losses/gains can be dramatic enough that, even when a stable weight is achieved, the body is "fatter" and has a lower metabolic rate. Instead of enduring a "diet" you can hardly wait to go off, focus on developing better eating and exercise habits.

Your Calorie Needs

Remember that eating and exercise aren't the only factors that affect your weight, but they are the ones you can control. Metabolism and body composition help determine the number of calories your body burns at rest, and these tendencies are often inherited.

The number of calories you need depends on how many calories your body burns up. People burn calories at different rates, depending on many factors, including activity, body size, genetics, age, health, and gender. Calories also describe how much energy a food supplies. People need over 50 nutrients from foods, including those that supply calories—such as carbohydrates, proteins, and fat—and those that help with other body functions, such as vitamins, minerals, and water. Quality calorie choices meet nutrient needs without adding extra, unneeded, calories.

YOUR CALORIE NEEDS

Typical Calorie Needs for Maintaining Weight

	Calories/Day
Women	1,800–2,100
Men	2,100–2,400

Recommended Calorie Ranges for Losing Weight

	Calories/Day
Women	1,200–1,500
Men	1,500–1,800

CALCULATING YOUR FAT LIMITS

To limit your fat calories to less than 30 percent:

If your planned daily calorie intake is:	Your daily fat intake should be less than:
1,200 calories	40 grams
1,500 calories	50 grams
1,800 calories	60 grams

Or use the following formula:

(Calorie intake x 0.3) / 9 = your maximum grams of fat per day

Example:

1,800 calories x 0.3 = 540 / 9 = 60 grams of fat per day

Controlling Portions

As important as it is to choose quality calories over empty ones, it's also important to eat a reasonable amount. Even the most nutritious and low-calorie foods can add to a weight problem if eaten in large enough quantities. Practicing portion control can help ensure that you're not getting too much of a good thing.

Calculating Your Fat Limits

Since fat is the most concentrated source of calories in a diet, it is a good target for extra calorie-cutting. It is encouraging to note that a lower-fat diet, combined with exercise, has shown effective results in studies with calorie reductions of only 150 to 200 calories per day.

Losing at a Healthy Rate

To lose weight you need to burn an extra 3,500 calories for each pound you would like to lose, since this is the approximate number of calories in 1 pound of body fat. To lose 1 pound per week, you need 500 fewer calories per day than the calories required to maintain your weight. It's best to get the 500 fewer calories from cutting your usual calories and increasing your activity level. Try eating 250 calories less per day and adding 250 calories in activity to lose that pound of fat.

Eating habits are developed throughout life in response to family and social patterns. That's why it's important to remember that the habits of a lifetime are not changed overnight. Fortunately, changes in these eating habits don't need to be dramatic to work. A good starting point is to identify and include healthy foods you enjoy.

HEALTH INFORMATION RESOURCE GUIDE

The following is a list of toll-free numbers* of organizations that can provide you with more information on health issues or resources in your area.

Acquired Immune Deficiency Syndrome (AIDS)

American Foundation for AIDS Research
800-362-6327

National Teen AIDS Hotline
800-234-8336

Alcohol and Drug Abuse (Substance Abuse)

Al-Anon Family Group Headquarters
800-356-9996

Alcohol Abuse and Drug 24 Hour Helpline
800-252-6465

National Alcohol Action Help Line and Treatment
800-234-1253
800-374-2800

National Clearinghouse for Drug and Alcohol Information
800-729-6686

Alzheimer's Disease

Alzheimer's Disease Association National Headquarters
800-272-3900

Arthritis

Arthritis Foundation Information Line
800-283-7800

Asthma and Allergies

Asthma and Allergy Network/ Mothers of Asthmatics
800-878-4403

Attention Deficit Disorder

Attention Deficit Disorder Warehouse
800-233-9273

Children and Adults with Attention Deficit Disorder (CAADD)
800-233-4050

Cancer

American Cancer Society
800-227-2345

Cancer Information Service
800-422-6237

*Numbers in service as of May 1996

Cerebral Palsy

United Cerebral Palsy Association
800-872-5827

Cystic Fibrosis

Cystic Fibrosis Foundation
800-682-6858

Diabetes

American Association of Diabetes
Educators
800-338-3633

American Diabetes Association
800-232-3472

Juvenile Diabetes Foundation
International/Diabetes Research
Foundation
800-533-2873

Down Syndrome

National Down Syndrome Society
800-221-4602

Endometriosis

Endometriosis Association
800-992-ENDO

Epilepsy

Epilepsy Foundation of America
800-332-1000

Family Planning/Pregnancy

International Childbirth Education
Association
800-230-PLAN

Planned Parenthood Federation of
America
800-662-5669

Gastrointestinal Disorders

Crohn's and Colitis Foundation of
America
800-932-2423

United Ostomy Association
800-826-0826

Headache

National Headache Foundation
800-843-2256

Head Injury

Brain Injury Association's Family
Helpline
800-444-6443

Hearing and Speech Disabilities

American Speech and Hearing
Association Helpline
800-638-8255

American Society for Deaf
Children
800-942-2732

Hearing Aid Helpline
800-521-5247

National Center for Stuttering
800-221-2483

Heart Disease

American Heart Association
800-242-8721

Liver Disease

American Liver Foundation
800-223-0179

Lupus

American Lupus Society
Information Line
800-331-1802

Lyme Disease

Lyme Disease Information
800-886-5963

Menopause

Menopause Access
800-222-4767

Mental Health

National Mental Health Consumer
Self-help Clearinghouse
800-553-4539

Neuromuscular Diseases

Multiple Sclerosis Association
of America
800-833-4672

National Muscular Dystrophy
Association
800-572-1717

Parkinson's Disease

National Parkinson's Foundation
800-327-4545

Premenstrual Syndrome

PMS Access
800-222-4767

Rare Disorders

National Organization for Rare
Disorders (NORD)
800-999-6673

Respiratory/Lung

American Lung Association
800-586-4872

National Jewish Center for
Immunology and Respiratory
Medicine Lung Line
800-222-5864

Reye's Syndrome

National Reye's Syndrome
Foundation
800-233-7393

Scleroderma

United Scleroderma Foundation
800-722-4673

Sexually Transmitted Diseases

Center for Disease Control Hotline
800-227-8922

Sickle Cell Anemia

Sickle Cell Disease Association of America
800-421-8453

Spinal Disease/Injury

National Spinal Cord Injury Association
800-962-9629

Spina Bifida Association
800-621-3141

Stroke

National Institute of Neurological Disorders and Stroke
800-352-9424

National Stroke Association
800-787-6537

Urologic and Kidney Diseases

American Foundation for Urologic Disease
800-242-2383

American Kidney Fund, Inc.
800-638-8299

Vision and Blindness

American Council of the Blind
800-424-8666

American Foundation for the Blind, Inc.
800-232-5463

National Center for the Blind
800-638-7518

National Society to Prevent Blindness
800-221-3004

INDEX

Note: *Bold faced page numbers refer to color plates.*

B

F

I

COLOR PLATES

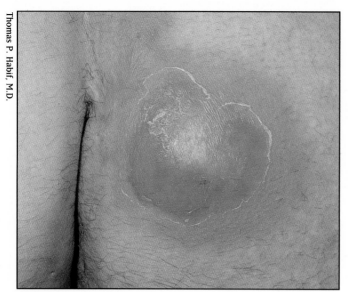

Thomas P. Habif, M.D.

Boil—see text p. 116

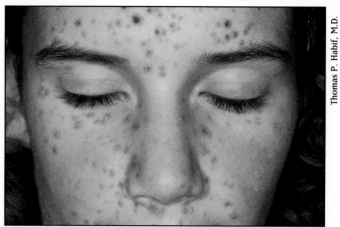

Thomas P. Habif, M.D.

Chicken pox rash—see text p. 135

Three stages of chicken pox rash—see text p. 135

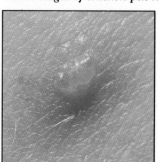

Stage one

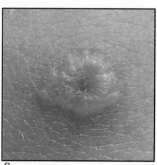

Stage two

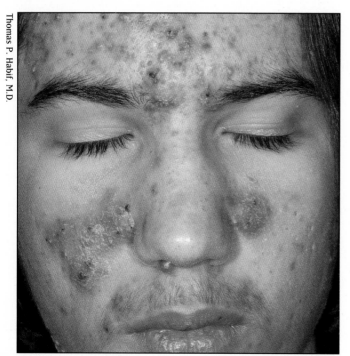

Thomas P. Habif, M.D.

Acne—see text p. 111

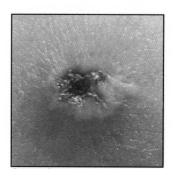

Stage three

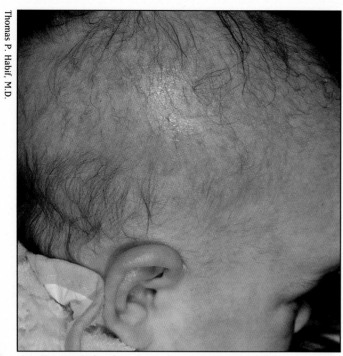

Cradle cap (*seborrheic dermatitis*)—*see text p. 137*

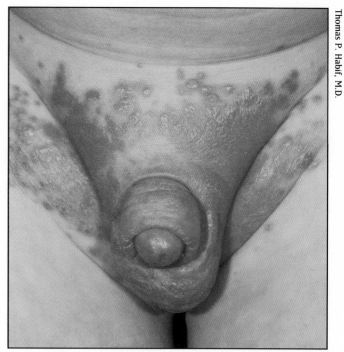

Diaper rash—*see text p. 140*

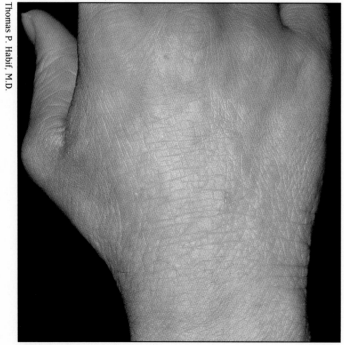

Atopic dermatitis—*see text p. 118*

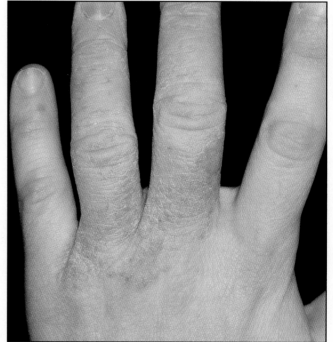

Contact dermatitis—*see text p. 118*

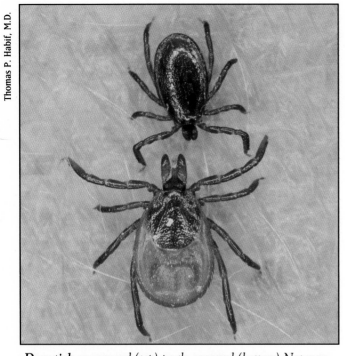

Thomas P. Habif, M.D.

Deer tick *unengorged (top) partly engorged (bottom) Not mentioned in text. For reference when talking to the advice nurse.*

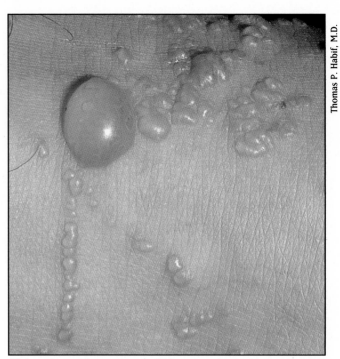

Thomas P. Habif, M.D.

Poison ivy rash—*see text p. 124*

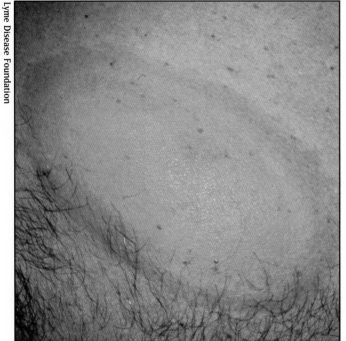

Lyme Disease Foundation

Lyme disease rash—*Not mentioned in text. For reference when talking to the advice nurse.*

Thomas P. Habif, M.D.

Head lice egg *stuck to hair shaft—see text p. 142*

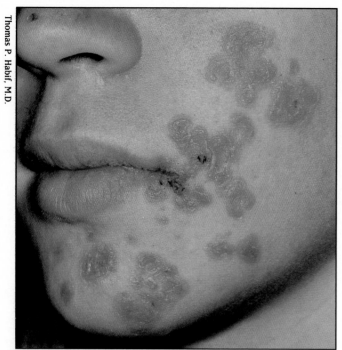

Thomas P. Habif, M.D.

Impetigo—see text p. 141

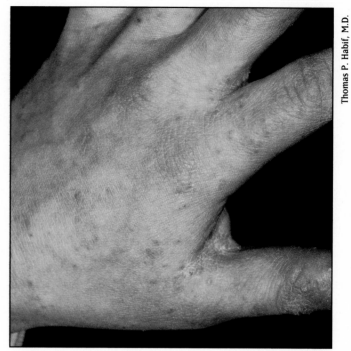

Thomas P. Habif, M.D.

Scabies—see text p. 128

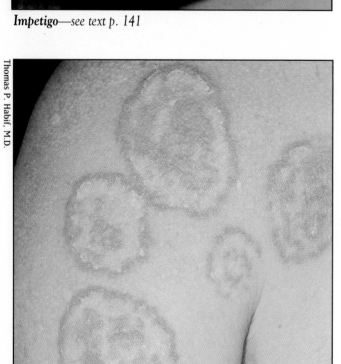

Thomas P. Habif, M.D.

Ringworm fungal skin infection—see text p. 127

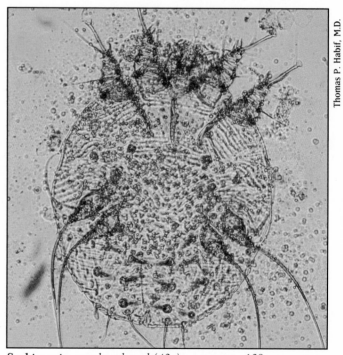

Thomas P. Habif, M.D.

Scabies mite greatly enlarged (40x)—see text p. 128

Stork bite—*see text p. 134*

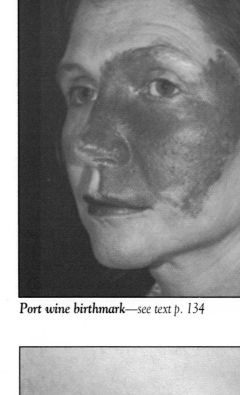

Port wine birthmark—*see text p. 134*

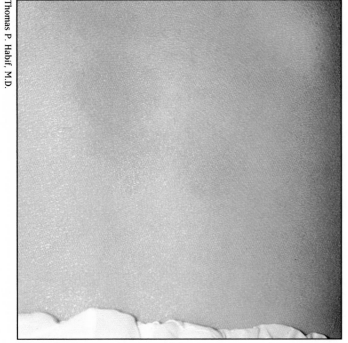

Mongolian spot—*see text p. 134*

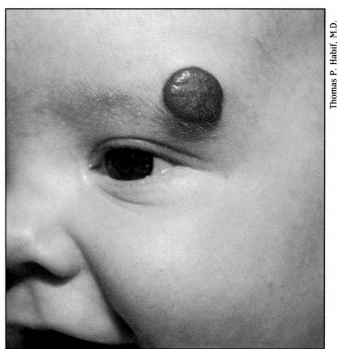

Strawberry hemangioma—*see text p. 134*

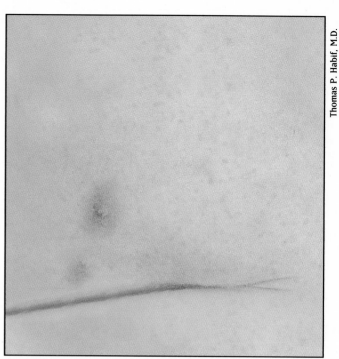

Thomas P. Habif, M.D.

Fifth disease (erythema infectiosum)—*Not mentioned in text. For reference when talking to the advice nurse.*

Thomas P. Habif, M.D.

Rubella (German measles) rash—*Not mentioned in text. For reference when talking to the advice nurse.*

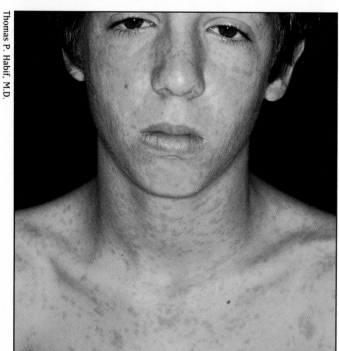

Thomas P. Habif, M.D.

Rubeola (measles) rash—*Not mentioned in text. For reference when talking to the advice nurse.*

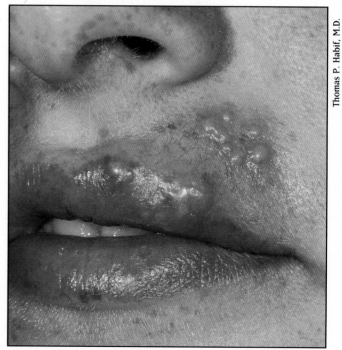

Thomas P. Habif, M.D.

Herpes simplex rash—*Not mentioned in text. For reference when talking to the advice nurse.*

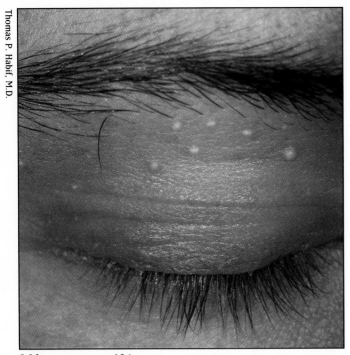

Thomas P. Habif, M.D.

Milia—see text p. 134

Thomas P. Habif, M.D.

Infected sebacious cyst—Not mentioned in text. For reference when talking to the advice nurse.

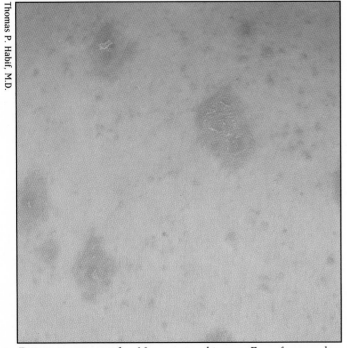

Thomas P. Habif, M.D.

Pityriasis rosea rash—Not mentioned in text. For reference when talking to the advice nurse.

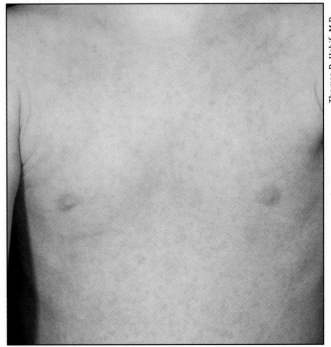

Thomas P. Habif, M.D.

Roseola rash—Not mentioned in text. For reference when talking to the advice nurse.

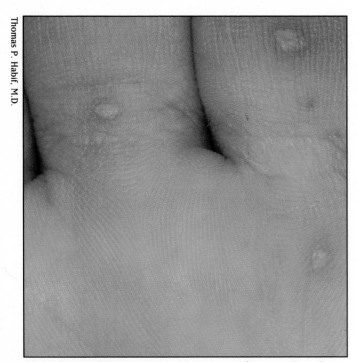

Thomas P. Habif, M.D.

Hand-foot-and-mouth rash—*Not mentioned in text. For reference when talking to the advice nurse.*

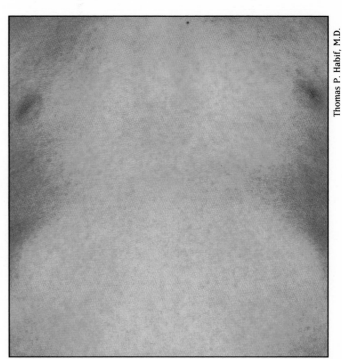

Thomas P. Habif, M.D.

Scarlet fever rash—*Not mentioned in text. For reference when talking to the advice nurse.*

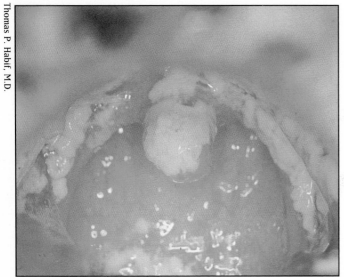

Thomas P. Habif, M.D.

Monilia rash—*Not mentioned in text. For reference when talking to the advice nurse.*

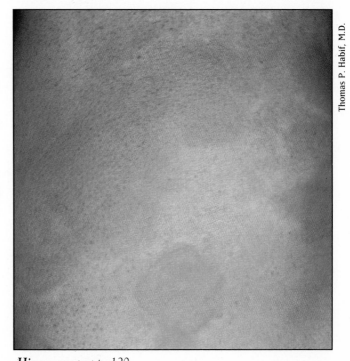

Thomas P. Habif, M.D.

Hives—*see text p. 120*